Practical
Data
Mining

Practical
Data
Mining

Monte F. Hancock, Jr.
Chief Scientist, Celestech, Inc.

CRC Press
Taylor & Francis Group
Boca Raton London New York

CRC Press is an imprint of the
Taylor & Francis Group, an **Informa** business
AN AUERBACH BOOK

CRC Press
Taylor & Francis Group
6000 Broken Sound Parkway NW, Suite 300
Boca Raton, FL 33487-2742

Version Date: 20111031

International Standard Book Number: 978-1-4398-6836-2 (Hardback)

Library of Congress Cataloging-in-Publication Data

Hancock, Monte.
   Practical data mining / Monte F. Hancock, Jr.
      p. cm.
   Includes bibliographical references and index.
   ISBN 978-1-4398-6836-2 (hardcover : alk. paper)
   1. Data mining. I. Title.

   QA76.9.D343H37 2012
   006.3'12--dc23   2011040834

Visit the Taylor & Francis Web site at
http://www.taylorandfrancis.com

and the CRC Press Web site at
http://www.crcpress.com

Dedication

This book is dedicated to my beloved wife, Sandy, and to my dear little sister, Dr. Angela Lobreto. You make life a joy.

Also, to my professional mentors George Milligan, Dr. Craig Price, and Tell Gates, three of the finest men I have ever known, or ever hope to know: May God bless you richly, gentlemen; He has blessed me richly through you.

Contents

Preface

How to Use This Book

Data mining is much more than just trying stuff and hoping something good happens! Rather, data mining is the detection, characterization, and exploitation of actionable patterns in data.

This book is a wide-ranging treatment of the practical aspects of data mining in the real-world. It presents in a systematic way the analytic principles acquired by the author during his 30+ years as a practicing engineer, data miner, information scientist, and Adjunct Professor of Computer Science.

This book is not intended to be read and then put on the shelf. Rather, it is a working field manual, designed to serve as an on-the-job guidebook. It has been written specifically for IT consultants, professional data analysts, and sophisticated data owners who want to establish data mining projects; but are not themselves data mining experts.

Most chapters contain one or more cases studies. These are synopses of data mining projects led by the author, and include project descriptions, the data mining methods used, challenges encountered, and the results obtained. When possible, numerical details are provided, grounding the presentation in specifics.

Also included are checklists that guide the reader through the practical considerations associated with each phase of the data mining process. These are *working checklists*: material the reader will want to carry into meetings with customers, planning discussions with management, technical planning meetings with senior scientists, etc. The checklists lay out the questions to ask, the points to make, explain the what's and why's—the lessons learned that are known to all seasoned experts, but rarely written down.

While the treatment here is systematic, it is not formal: the reader will not encounter eclectic theorems, tables of equations, or detailed descriptions of algorithms. The "bit-level" mechanics of data mining techniques are addressed pretty well in online literature, and freeware is available for many of them. A brief list of vendors and supported applications is provided below. The goal of this book is to help the non-expert address practical questions like:

- What is data mining, and what problems does it address?
- How is a quantitative business case for a data mining project developed and assessed?
- What process model should be used to plan and execute a data mining project?
- What skill sets are needed for different types/phases of data mining projects?
- What data mining techniques exist, and what do they do? How do I decide which are needed/best for my problem?
- What are the common mistakes made during data mining projects, and how can they be avoided?
- How are data mining projects tracked and evaluated?

How This Book Is Organized

The content of the book is divided into two parts: Chapters 1–8 and Chapters 9–11.

The first eight chapters constitute the bulk of the book, and serve to ground the reader in the practice of data mining in the modern enterprise. These chapters focus on the what, when, why, and how of data mining practice. Technical complexities are introduced only when they are essential to the treatment. This part of the book should be read by everyone; later chapters assume that the reader is familiar with the concepts and terms presented in these chapters.

Chapter 1 (What is Data Mining and What Can it Do?) is a data mining manifesto: it describes the mindset that characterizes the successful data mining practitioner. It delves into some philosophical issues underlying the practice (e.g., Why is it essential that the data miner understand the difference between *data* and *information*?).

Chapter 2 (The Data Mining Process) provides a summary treatment of data mining as a six-step spiral process.

Chapters 3–8 are devoted to each of the steps of the data mining process. Checklists, case studies, tables, and figures abound.

- Step 1—Problem Definition
- Step 2—Data Evaluation
- Step 3—Feature Extraction and Enhancement
- Step 4—Prototype Planning and Modeling
- Step 5—Model Evaluation
- Step 6—Implementation

The last three chapters, 9–11, are devoted to specific categories of data mining practice, referred to here as genres. The data mining genres addressed are Chapter 9: Detecting and Characterizing Known Patterns (Supervised Learning), Chapter 10: Detecting, Characterizing, and Exploiting Hidden Patterns (Forensic Analysis), and Chapter 11: Knowledge: Its Acquisition, Representation, and Use.

It is hoped the reader will benefit from this rendition of the author's extensive experience in data mining/modeling, pattern processing, and automated decision support. He started this journey in 1979, and learned most of this material the hard way. By repeating his successes and avoiding his mistakes, you make his struggle worthwhile!

A Short History of Data Technology: Where Are We, and How Did We Get Here?

What follows is a brief account of the history of data technology along the classical lines. We posit the existence of brief eras of five or ten year's duration through which the technology passed during its development. This background will help the reader understand the forces that have driven the development of current data mining techniques. The dates provided are approximate.

Era 1: Computing-Only Phase (1945–1955):

As originally conceived, computers were just that: machines for performing computation. Volumes of data might be input, but the *answer* tended to consist of just a few numbers. Early computers had nothing that we would call online storage.

Reliable, inexpensive mass storage devices did not exist. Data was not stored in the computer at all: it was input, transformed, and output. Computing was done to obtain answers, not to manage data

Era 2: Offline Batch Storage (1955–1965):

Data was saved outside of the computer, on paper tape and cards, and read back in when needed. The use of online mass storage was not widespread, because it was expensive, slow, and unstable.

Era 3: Online Batch Storage (1965–1970):

With the invention of stable, cost-effective mass storage devices, everything changed. Over time, the computer began to be viewed less as a machine for crunching numbers, and more as a device for storing them. Initially, the operating system's file management system was used to hold data in flat files: un-indexed lists or tables of data. As the need to search, sort, and process data grew, it became necessary to provide applications for organizing data into various types of business-specific hierarchies. These early databases organized data into tiered structures, allowing for rapid searching of records in the hierarchy.

Data was stored on high-density media such as magnetic tape, and magnetic drum. Platter disc technology began to become more generally used, but was still slow and had low capacity.

Era 4: Online Databases (1970–1985):

Reliable, cost-effective online mass storage became widely available. Data was organized into domain specific vertical structures, typically for a single part of an organization. This allowed the development of *stovepipe* systems for focused applications. The use of Online Transaction Processing (OLTP) systems became widespread, supporting inventory, purchasing, sales, planning, etc. The focus of computing began to shift from raw computation to data processing: the ingestion, transformation, storage, and retrieval of bulk data.

However, there was an obvious shortcoming. The databases of functional organizations within an enterprise were developed to suit the needs of particular business units. They were not interoperable, making the preparation of an enterprise-wide data view very difficult. The difficulty of horizontal integration caused many to question whether the development of enterprise-wide databases was feasible.

Era 5: Enterprise Databases (1985–1995):

As the utility of automatic data storage became clear, organizations within businesses began to construct their own hierarchical databases. Soon, the repositories of corporate information on all aspects of a business grew to be large.

Increased processing power, widespread availability of reliable communication networks, and development of database technology allowed the horizontal integration of multiple vertical data stores into an enterprise-wide database. For the first time, a global view of an entire organization's data repository was accessible through a single portal.

Era 6: Data Warehouses and Data Marts (since 1995):

This brings us to the present. Mass storage and raw compute power has reached the point today where virtually every data item generated by an enterprise can be saved. And often, enterprise databases have become extremely large, architecturally complex, and volatile. Ultra-sophisticated data modeling tools have become available at the precise moment that competition for market share in many industries begins to peak. An appropriate environment for application of these tools to a cleansed, stable, offline repository was needed and data warehouses were born. And, as data warehouses have grown large, the need to create architecturally compatible functional subsets, or data marts, has been recognized.

The immediate future is moving everything toward cloud computing. This will include the elimination of many local storage disks as data is pushed to a vast array of external servers accessible over the internet. Data mining in the cloud will continue to grow in importance as network connectivity and data accessibility become virtually infinite.

Data Mining Information Sources

Some feeling for the current interest in data mining can be gained by reviewing the following list of data mining companies, groups, publications, and products.

Data Mining Publications

- Two Crows Corporation
  Predictive and descriptive data mining models, courses and presentations.
  http://www.twocrows.com
- *"Information Management."* A newsletter web site on data mining papers, books and product reviews.
  http://www.information-management.com
- *"Searching for the Right Data Modeling Tool"* by Terry Moriarty
  http://www.information-management.com/issues/19980601/383-1.html
- *"Data Mining FAQs"* by Jesus Mena
  http://www.information-management.com/issues/19980101/792-1.html
- *"Data Mining & Pattern Discovery,"* Elder Research, Inc.
  http://www.datamininglab.com/
- *"An Evaluation of High-end Data Mining Tools for Fraud Detection"* by Dean W. Abbot, I.P. Matkovsky, and John F. Elder
  http://www.datamininglab.com/TOOLCOMPARISON/tabid/58/Default.aspx
- KDnuggets.com is a web site providing companies with data mining related products.
  http://www.kdnuggets.com/companies/products.html

Data Mining Technology/Product Providers

- SPSS Web Site:
  http://www.spss.com
- SPSS Products:
  http://www.spss.com/products/products/categories/data_mining/

General Data Mining Tools

The data mining tools in the following list are used for general types of data:

- Data-Miner Software Kit—A comprehensive collection of programs for efficiently mining big data. It uses the techniques presented in *Predictive Data Mining: A Practical Guide* by Morgan Kaufmann.
  http://www.data-miner.com
- RuleQuest.com—System is rule based with subsystems to assist in data cleansing (GritBot) and constructing classifiers (See5) in the form of decision trees and rulesets.
  http://www.rulequest.com/products.html
- SAS
  http://www.sas.com
- Weka 3 from the University of Waikato—A collection of machine learning algorithms for solving real-world data mining problems.
  http://www.cs.waikato.ac.nz/ml/weka/

Tools for the Development of Bayesian Belief Networks

- Netica—BBN software that is easy to use, and implements BBN learning from data. It has a nice user interface.
  http://www.norsys.com
- Hugin—Implements reasoning with continuous variables and has a nice user interface.
  http://www.hugin.dk

About the Author

Monte F. Hancock, Jr., BA, MS, is Chief Scientist for Celestech, Inc., which has offices in Falls Church, Virginia, and Phoenix, Arizona. He was also a Technical Fellow at Northrop Grumman; Chief Cognitive Research Scientist for CSI, Inc., and was a software architect and engineer at Harris corporation, and HRB Singer, Inc. He has over 30 years of industry experience in software engineering and data mining technology development.

He is also Adjunct Full Professor of Computer Science for the Webster University Space Coast Region, where he serves as Program Mentor for the Master of Science Degree in Computer Science. Monte has served for 26 years on the adjunct faculty in the Mathematics and Computer Science Department of the Hamilton Holt School of Rollins College, Winter Park, Florida, and served 3 semesters as adjunct Instructor in Computer Science at Pennsylvania State University.

Monte teaches secondary Mathematics, AP Physics, Chemistry, Logic, Western Philosophy, and Church History at New Covenant School, and New Testament Greek at Heritage Christian Academy, both in Melbourne, Florida. He was a mathematics curriculum developer for the Department of Continuing Education of the University of Florida in Gainesville, and serves on the Industry Advisory Panels in Computer Science for both the Florida Institute of Technology, and Brevard Community College in Melbourne, Florida. Monte has twice served on panels for the National Science Foundation.

Monte has served on many program committees for international data mining conferences, was a Session Chair for KDD. He has presented 15 conference papers, edited several book chapters, and co-authored the book *Data Mining Explained* with Rhonda Delmater, Digital Press, 2001.

Monte is cited in (among others):

- "Who's Who in the World" (2009–2012)
- "Who's Who in America" (2009–2012)
- "Who's Who in Science and Engineering" (2006–2012)
- "Who's Who in the Media and Communication" (1st ed.)

- "Who's Who in the South and Southwest" (23rd–25th ed.)
- "Who's Who Among America's Teachers" (2006, 2007)
- "Who's Who in Science and Theology" (2nd ed.)

Acknowledgments

It is always a pleasure to recognize those who have provided selfless support in the completion of a significant work.

Special thanks is due to Rhonda Delmater, with whom I co-authored my first book, *Data Mining Explained* (Digital Press, 2001), and who proposed the development of this book. Were it not for exigent circumstances, this would have been a joint work.

Special thanks are also due to Theron Shreve (acquisition editor), Marje Pollack (compositor), and Rob Wotherspoon (copy editor) of Derryfield Publishing Services, LLC. What a pleasure to work with professionals who know the business and understand people!

Special thanks are due to Dan Strohschein, who worked on technical references, and Katherine Hancock, who verified the vendor list.

Finally, to those who have made significant contributions to my knowledge through the years: John Day, Chad Sessions, Stefan Joe-Yen, Rusty Topping, Justin Mortimer, Leslie Kain, Ben Hancock, Olivia Hancock, Marsha Foix, Vinnie, Avery, Toby, Tristan, and Maggie.

Chapter 1

What Is Data Mining and What Can It Do?

Purpose

The purpose of this chapter is to provide the reader with grounding in the fundamental philosophical principles of data mining as a technical practice. The reader is then introduced to the wide array of practical applications that rely on data mining technology. The issue of computational complexity is addressed in brief.

Goals

After you have read this chapter, you will be able to define data mining from both philosophical and operational perspectives, and enumerate the analytic functions data mining performs. You will know the different types of data that arise in practice. You will understand the basics of computational complexity theory. Most importantly, you will understand the difference between data and information.

1.1 Introduction

Our study of data mining begins with two semi-formal definitions:

Definition 1. Data mining is the principled detection, characterization, and exploitation of actionable patterns in data. Table 1.1 explains what is meant by each of these components.

Table 1.1 Definitive Data Mining Attributes

Attribute	Connotations
Principled	Rational, empirical, objective, repeatable
Detection	Sensing and locating
Characterization	Consistent, efficient, tractable symbolic representation that does not alter information content
Exploitation	Decision making that facilitates action
Actionable Pattern	Conveys information that supports decision making

Taking this view of what data mining is we can formulate a functional definition that tells us what individuals engaged in data mining do.

Definition 2. Data Mining is the application of the scientific method to data to obtain useful information. The heart of the scientific approach to problem-solving is rational hypothesis testing guided by empirical experimentation.

What we today call science today was referred to as natural philosophy in the 15th century. The Aristotelian approach to understanding the world was to catalog and organize more-or-less passive acts of observation into taxonomies. This method began to fall out of favor in the physical sciences in the 15th century, and was dead by the 17th century. However, because of the greater difficulty of observing the processes underlying biology and behavior, the life sciences continued to rely on this approach until well into the 19th century. This is why the life sciences of the 1800s are replete with taxonomies, detailed naming conventions, and perceived lines of descent, which are more a matter of organizing observations than principled experimentation and model revision.

Applying the scientific method today, we expect to engage in a sequence of planned steps:

1. Formulate hypotheses (often in the form of a question)
2. Devise experiments
3. Collect data
4. Interpret data to evaluate hypotheses
5. Revise hypotheses based upon experimental results

This sequence amounts to one cycle of an iterative approach to acquiring knowledge. In light of our functional definition of data mining, this sequence can be thought of as an over-arching data mining methodology that will be described in detail in Chapter 3.

1.2 A Brief Philosophical Discussion

Somewhere in every data mining effort, you will encounter at least one computationally intractable problem; it is unavoidable. This has technical and procedural implications, but it also has philosophical implications. In particular, since there are by definition no perfect techniques for intractable problems, different people will handle them in different ways; no one can say definitively that one way is necessarily wrong and another right. This makes data mining something of an art, and leaves room for the operation of both practical experience and creative experimentation. It also implies that the data mining philosophy to which you look when science falls short can mean the difference between success and failure. Let's talk a bit about developing such a data mining philosophy.

As noted above, data mining can be thought of as the application of the scientific method to data. We perform data collection (sampling), formulate hypotheses (e.g., visualization, cluster analysis, feature selection), conduct experiments (e.g., construct and test classifiers), refine hypotheses (spiral methodology), and ultimately build theories (field applications). This is a process that can be reviewed and replicated. In the real world, the resulting theory will either succeed or fail.

Many of the disciplines that apply to empirical scientific work also apply to the practice of data mining: assumptions must be made explicit; the design of principled experiments capable of falsifying our hypotheses is essential; the integrity of the evidence, process, and results must be meticulously maintained and documented; outcomes must be repeatable; and so on. Unless these disciplines are maintained, nothing of certain value can result. Of particular importance is the ability to reproduce results. In the data mining world, these disciplines involve careful configuration management of the system environment, data, applications, and documentation. There are no effective substitutes for these.

One of the most difficult mental disciplines to maintain during data mining work is reservation of judgment. In any field involving hypothesis and experimentation, preliminary results can be both surprising and exhilarating. Finding the smoking gun in a forensic study, for example, is hitting pay-dirt of the highest quality, and it is hard not to get a little excited if you smell gunpowder.

However, this excitement cannot be allowed to short-circuit the analytic process. More than once I have seen exuberant young analysts charging down the hall to announce an amazing discovery after only a few hours' work with a data set; but I don't recall any of those instant discoveries holding up under careful review. I can think of three times when I have myself jumped the gun in this way. On one occasion, eagerness to provide a rapid response led me to prematurely turn over results to a major customer, who then provided them (without review) to their major customer. Unfortunately, there was an unnoticed but significant flaw in the analysis that invalidated most of the reported results. That is a trail of culpability you don't want leading back to your office door.

1.3 The Most Important Attribute of the Successful Data Miner: Integrity

Integrity is variously understood, so we list the principal characteristics data miners must have.

- **Moral courage.** Data miners have lots of opportunities to deliver unpleasant news. Sometimes they have to inform an enterprise that the data it has collected and stored at great expense does not contain the type or amount of information expected.

  Further, it is an unfortunate fact that the default assessment for data mining efforts in most situations is "failure." There can be tremendous pressure to produce a certain result, accuracy level, conclusion, etc., and if you don't: Failure. Pointing out that the data do not support the desired application, are of low quality (precision/accuracy), and do not contain sufficient samples to cover the problem space will sound like excuses, and will not always redeem you.

- **Commitment to enterprise success.** If you want the enterprise you are assisting to be successful, you will be honest with them; will labor to communicate information in terms they can understand; and will not put your personal success ahead of the truth.

- **Honesty in evaluation of data and information.** Individuals that demonstrate this characteristic are willing to let the data speak for itself. They will resist the temptation to read into the data that which wasn't mined from the data.

- **Meticulous planning, execution, and documentation.** A successful data miner will be meticulous in planning, carrying out, and documenting the mining process. They will not jump to conclusions; will enforce the prerequisites of a process before beginning; will check and recheck major results; and will carefully validate all results before reporting them. Excellent data miners create documentation of sufficient quality and detail that their results can be reproduced by others.

1.4 What Does Data Mining Do?

The particulars of practical data mining "best practice" will be addressed later in great detail, but we jump-start the treatment with some bulleted lists summarizing the functions that data mining provides.

Data mining uses a combination of empirical and theoretical principles to connect *structure* to *meaning* by

- Selecting and conditioning relevant data
- Identifying, characterizing, and classifying latent patterns
- Presenting useful representations and interpretations to users

Data mining attempts to answer these questions

- What patterns are in the information?
- What are the characteristics of these patterns?
- Can meaning be ascribed to these patterns and/or their changes?

- Can these patterns be presented to users in a way that will facilitate their assessment, understanding, and exploitation?
- Can a machine learn these patterns and their relevant interpretations?

Data mining helps the user interact productively with the data

- *Planning* helps the user achieve and maintain situational awareness of vast, dynamic, ambiguous/incomplete, disparate, multi-source data.
- *Knowledge* leverages users' domain knowledge by creating functionality based upon an understanding of data creation, collection, and exploitation.
- *Expressiveness* produces outputs of adjustable complexity delivered in terms meaningful to the user.
- *Pedigree* builds integrated metrics into every function, because every recommendation has to have supporting evidence and an assessment of certainty.
- *Change* uses future-proof architectures and adaptive algorithms that anticipate many users addressing many missions.

Data mining enables the user to get their head around the problem space
Decision Support is all about . . .

- Enabling users to group information in familiar ways
- Controlling HMI complexity by layering results (e.g., drill-down)
- Supporting user's changing priorities (goals, capabilities)
- Allowing intuition to be triggered ("I've seen this before")
- Preserving and automating perishable institutional knowledge
- Providing objective, repeatable metrics (e.g., confidence factors)
- Fusing and simplifying results (e.g., annotate multisource visuals)
- Automating alerts on important results ("It's happening again")
- Detecting emerging behaviors before they consummate (look)
- Delivering value (timely, relevant, and accurate results)

. . . helping users make the best choices.

Some general application areas for data mining technology

- Automating pattern detection to characterize complex, distributed signatures that are worth human attention and recognize those that are not
- Associating events that go together but are difficult for humans to correlate
- Characterizing interesting processes not just facts or simple events
- Detecting actionable anomalies and explaining what makes them different and interesting
- Describing contexts from multiple perspectives with numbers, text and graphics
- Accurate identification and classification—add value to raw data by tagging and annotation (e.g., automatic target detection)

- o Anomaly, normalcy, and fusion—characterize, quantify, and assess normalcy of patterns and trends (e.g., network intrusion detection)
- Emerging patterns and evidence evaluation—capturing institutional knowledge of how events arise and alerting users when they begin to emerge
- Behavior association—detection of actions that are distributed in time and space but synchronized by a common objective: connecting the dots
- Signature detection and association—detection and characterization of multi-variate signals, symbols, and emissions
- Concept tagging—ontological reasoning about abstract relationships to tag and annotate media of all types (e.g., document geo-tagging)
- Software agents assisting analysts—small footprint, fire-and-forget apps that facilitate search, collaboration, etc.
- Help the user focus via unobtrusive automation
  - o Off-load burdensome labor (perform intelligent searches, smart winnowing)
  - o Post smart triggers or tripwires to data stream (anomaly detection)
  - o Help with workflow and triage (sort my in-basket)
- Automate aspects of classification and detection
  - o Determine which sets of data hold the most information for a task
  - o Support construction of ad hoc on-the-fly classifiers
  - o Provide automated constructs for merging decision engines (multi-level fusion)
  - o Detect and characterize domain drift (the rules of the game are changing)
  - o Provide functionality to make best estimate of missing data
- Extract, characterize and employ knowledge
  - o Rule induction from data and signatures development from data
  - o Implement non-monotonic reasoning for decision support
  - o High-dimensional visualization
  - o Embed decision explanation capability in analytic applications
- Capture, automate and institutionalize best practices
  - o Make proven enterprise analytic processes available to all
  - o Capture rare, perishable human knowledge and distribute it everywhere
  - o Generate signature-ready prose reports
  - o Capture and characterize the analytic process to anticipate user needs

1.5 What Do We Mean By Data?

Data is the wrapper that carries information. It can look like just about anything: images, movies, recorded sounds, light from stars, the text in this book, the swirls that form your fingerprints, your hair color, age, income, height, weight, credit score, a list of your likes and dislikes, the chemical formula for the gasoline in your car, the number of miles you drove last year, your cat's body temperature as a function of time, the order of the nucleotides in the third codon of your mitochondrial DNA, a street map of Liberal Kansas, the distribution of IQ scores in Braman Oklahoma, the fat content of smoked sausage, a spreadsheet of your household expenses, a coded message, a computer virus, the pattern of fibers in your living room carpet, the pattern of purchases at a grocery store, the pattern of capillaries in your retina, election results, etc. In fact: A *datum* (singular) is any symbolic representation of any attribute of any given thing. More than one datum constitutes *data* (plural).

1.5.1 Nominal Data vs. Numeric Data

Data come in two fundamental forms—nominal and numeric. Fabulously intricate hierarchical structures and relational schemes can be fashioned from these two forms.

This is an important distinction, because nominal and numeric data encode information in different ways. Therefore, they are interpreted in different ways, exhibit patterns in different ways, and must be mined in different ways. In fact, there are many data mining tools that only work with numeric data, and many that only work with nominal data. There are only few (but there are some) that work with both.

Data are said to be *nominal* when they are represented by a name. The names of people, places, and things are all nominal designations. Virtually all text data is nominal. But data like Zip codes, phone numbers, addresses, social security numbers, etc. are also nominal. This is because they are aliases for things: your postal zone, the den that contains your phone, your house, and you. The point is the information in these data has nothing to do with the numeric values of their symbols; any other unique string of numbers could have been used.

Data are said to be *numeric* when the information they contain is conveyed by the numeric value of their symbol string. Bank balances, altitudes, temperatures, and ages all hold their information in the value of the number string that represents them. A different number string would not do.

Given that nominal data can be represented using numeric characters, how can you tell the difference between nominal and numeric data? There is a simple test: If the average of a set of data is meaningful, they are numeric.

Phone numbers are nominal, because averaging the phone numbers of a group of people doesn't produce a meaningful result. The same is true of zip codes, addresses, and Social Security numbers. But averaging incomes, ages, and weights gives symbols whose values carry information about the group; they are numeric data.

1.5.2 Discrete Data vs. Continuous Data

Numeric data come in two forms—discrete and continuous. We can't get too technical here, because formal mathematical definitions of these concepts are deep. For the purposes of data mining, it is sufficient to say that a set of data is *continuous* when, given two values in the set, you can always find another value in the set between them. Intuitively, this implies there is a linear ordering, and there aren't gaps or holes in the range of possible values. In theory, it also implies that continuous data can assume infinitely many different values.

A set of data is *discrete* if it is not continuous. The usual scenario is a finite set of values or symbols. For example, the readings of a thermometer constitute continuous data, because (in theory), any temperature within a reasonable range could actually occur. Time is usually assumed to be continuous in this sense, as is distance; therefore sizes, distances, and durations are all continuous data.

On the other hand, when the possible data values can be placed in a list, they are discrete: hair color, gender, quantum states (depending upon whom you ask), head-count for a business, the positive whole numbers (an infinite set) etc., are all discrete.

A very important difference between discrete and continuous data for data mining applications is the matter of error. Continuous data can presumably have any amount of error, from very small to very large, and all values in between. Discrete data are either completely right or completely wrong.

Nominal to Numeric Coding of Data

Name	Class	Feature 1 (habitat)	Feature 2 (diet)	Feature 3 (integument)	Feature 4 (morphology)	Feature 5 (life cycle)
Bill	primates	land	omnivore	skin w/o feathers	biped no wings	live birth
Bubbles	fishes	sea	omnivore	scales	no wings, non biped	eggs w/o meta
Rover	domestic	land	carnivore	skin w/o feathers	no wings, non biped	live birth
Ringo	bugs	land	herbivore	exoskeleton	wings, non-biped	egss w. meta
Chuck	bacteria	parasitic	other	other	no wings, non biped	other
Tweety	birds	land	omnivore	skin with feathers	wings, biped	eggs w/o meta

Original Nominal Data

Within each column, establish a mapping to some numeric code for each nominal value. For example, in column 2, Class, we code mammals as "1" and non-mammals as "2":

Name	Class	Feature 1 (habitat)	Feature 2 (diet)	Feature 3 (integument)	Feature 4 (morphology)	Feature 5 (life cycle)
1	1	2	3	1	3	1
2	2	1	3	3	4	3
3	1	2	2	1	4	1
4	2	2	1	4	1	2
5	2	3	4	5	4	4
6	2	2	3	2	2	3

Final Coding: Categories mapped to numeric representations

Figure 1.1　Nominal to numeric coding of data.

1.5.3 Coding and Quantization as Inverse Processes

Data can be represented in different ways. Sometimes it is necessary to translate data from one representational scheme to another. In applications this often means converting numeric data to nominal data (*quantization*), and nominal data to numeric data (*coding*).

Quantization usually leads to loss of precision, so it is not a perfectly reversible process. Coding usually leads to an increase in precision, and is usually reversible.

There are many ways these conversions can be done, and some application-dependent decisions that must be made. Examples of these decisions might include choosing the level of numeric precision for coding, or determining the number of restoration values for quantization. The most intuitive explanation of these inverse processes is pictorial. Notice that the numeric coding (Figure 1.1) is performed in stages. No information is lost; its only purpose was to make the nominal feature attributes numeric. However, quantization (Figure 1.2) usually reduces the precision of the data, and is rarely reversible.

Numeric to Nominal (Quantization)

Original Values	After Quantization	Nominal Categories
$ 3245	$ 5000	A
$ 6187	$ 5000	A
$ 12876	$ 15000	B
$ 22453	$ 25000	C
$ 23855	$ 25000	C
$ 36706	$ 35000	D
$ 43732	$ 45000	E
$ 46666	$ 45000	E

Quantization Bins:

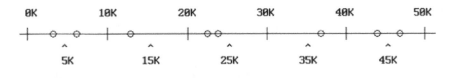

Figure 1.2 Numeric to nominal quantization.

1.5.4 A Crucial Distinction: Data and Information Are Not the Same Thing

Data and information are entirely different things. Data is a formalism, a wrapper, by which information is given observable form. Data and information stand in relation to one another much as do the body and the mind. In similar fashion, it is only data that are directly accessible to an observer. Inferring information from data requires an act of interpretation which always involves a combination of contextual constraints and rules of inference.

In computing systems, the problem "context" and "heuristics" are represented using a structure called a domain ontology. As the term suggests, each problem space has its own constraints, facts, assumptions, rules of thumb, and these are variously represented and applied.

The standard mining analogy is helpful here. Data mining is similar in some ways to mining for precious metals:

- **Silver mining.** Prospectors survey a region and select an area they think might have ore, the rough product that is refined to obtain metal. They apply tools to estimate the ore content of their samples and if it is high enough, the ore is refined to obtain purified silver.
- **Data mining.** Data miners survey a problem space and select sources they think might contain salient patterns, the rough product that is refined to obtain information. They apply tools to assess the information content of their sample and if it is high enough, the data are processed to infer latent information.

However, there is a very important way in which data mining is not like silver mining. Chunks of silver ore actually contain particular silver atoms. When a chunk of ore is moved, its silver goes with it. Extending this part of the silver mining analogy to data mining will get us into trouble. The silver mining analogy fails because of the fundamental difference between data and information.

The simplest scenario demonstrating this difference involves their different relation to *context*. When I remove letters from a word, they retain their identity as letters, as do the letters left behind. But the information conveyed by the letters removed and by the letters left behind has very likely been altered, destroyed, or even negated.

Another example is found in the dependence on how the information is encoded. I convey exactly the same message when I say "How are you?" that I convey when I say "Wie gehts?," yet the data are completely different. Computer scientists use the terms *syntax* and *semantics* to distinguish between representation and meaning, respectively.

It is extremely dangerous for the data miner to fall into the habit of regarding particular pieces of information as being attached to particular pieces of data in the same way that metal atoms are bound to ore. Consider a more sophisticated, but subtle example:

A Morse code operator sends a message consisting of alternating, evenly spaced dots and dashes (Figure 1.3):

● - ● - ● - ● - ● - ● - ● - ● - ● - ● - ● - ● - ● - ● - ● - ● - ● - ● - ● - ●

This pattern conveys NO INFORMATION because it exhibits no variation.

Figure 1.3   Non-informative pattern.

This is clearly a pattern but other than manifesting its own existence, this pattern conveys no information. Information Theory tells that us such a pattern is devoid of information by pointing out that after we've listened to this pattern for a while, we can perfectly predict which symbol will arrive next. Such a pattern, by virtue of its complete predictability is not informative: a message that tells me what I already know tells me nothing. This important notion can be quantified in the Shannon Entropy (see glossary). However, if the transmitted tones are varied or modulated, the situation is quite different (Figure 1.4):

This pattern conveys information BY VIRTUE of its variation (called <u>Modulation</u>)

Figure 1.4 Informative modulation pattern.

This example makes is quite clear that information does not reside within the dots and dashes themselves; rather, it arises from an interpretation of their inter-relationships. In Morse code, this is their order and duration relative to each other. Notice that by removing the first dash from O = - - - -, the last two dashes now mean M = - -, even though the dashes have not changed. This *context sensitivity* is a wonderful thing, but it causes data mining disaster if ignored.

A final illustration called the *Parity Problem* convincingly establishes the distinct nature of data and information in a data mining context.

1.5.5 The Parity Problem

Let's do a thought experiment (Figure 1.5). I have two marbles in my hand, one white and one black. I show them to you and ask this question: Is the number of black marbles even, or is it odd?

Naturally you respond *odd*, since one is an odd number. If both of the marbles had been black, the correct answer would have been *even*, since 2 is an even number; if I had been holding two white marbles, again the correct answer would have been *even*, since 0 is an even number.

This is called the Parity Two problem. If there are N marbles, some white (possibly none) and some black (possibly none), the question of whether there are an odd number of black marbles is called the Parity-N Problem, or just the Parity Problem. This problem is important in computer science, information theory, coding theory, and related areas.

Of course, when researchers talk about the parity problem, they don't use marbles, they use zeros and ones (binary digits = bits). For example, I can store a data file on disc and then ask whether the file has an odd or even number of ones; the answer is the parity of the file.

This idea can also be used to detect data transmission errors: if I want to send you 100 bits of data, I could actually send you 101, with the extra bit set to a one or zero such that the whole set has a particular parity that you and I have agreed upon in advance. If you get a message from me and it doesn't have the expected parity, you know the message has an odd number of bit errors and must be resent.

1.5.6 Five Riddles about Information

Suppose I have two lab assistants named Al and Bob, and two data bits. I show only the first one to Al, and only the second one to Bob. If I ask Al what the parity of the

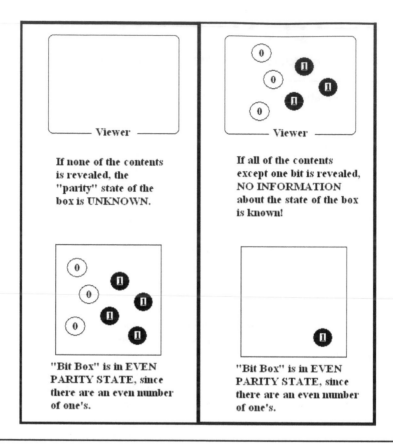

Figure 1.5 The parity problem.

original pair of bits is, what will he say? And if I ask Bob what the parity of the original pair of bits is, what will he say?

Neither one can say what the parity of the original pair is, because each one is lacking a bit. If I handed Al a one, he could reason that if the bit I can't see is also a one, then the parity of the original pair is even. But if the bit I can't see is a zero, then the parity of the original pair is odd. Bob is in exactly the same boat.

Riddle one. Al is no more able to state the parity of the original bit pair than he was before he was given his bit and the same is true for Bob. That is, each one has 50% of the data, but neither one has received any information at all.

Suppose now that I have 100 lab assistants, and 100 randomly generated bits of data. To assistant 1, I give all the bits except bit 1; to assistant 2, I give all the bits except bit 2; and so on. Each assistant has received 99% of the data. Yet none of them is any more able to state the parity of the original 100-bit data set than before they received 99 of the bits.

Riddle two. Even though each assistant has received 99% of the data, none of them has received any information at all.

Riddle three. The information in the 100 data bits cannot be in the bits themselves. For, which bit is it in? Not bit 1, since that bit was given to 99 assistants, and didn't provide them with any information. Not bit 2, for the same reason. In fact, it is clear that the information cannot be in any of the bits themselves. So, where is it?

Riddle four. Suppose my 100 bits have odd parity (say, 45 ones and 55 zeros). I arrange them on a piece of paper, so they spell the word "odd." Have I added information? If so, where is it? (Figure 1.6)

Riddle five. Where is the information in a multiply encrypted message, since it completely disappears when one bit is removed?

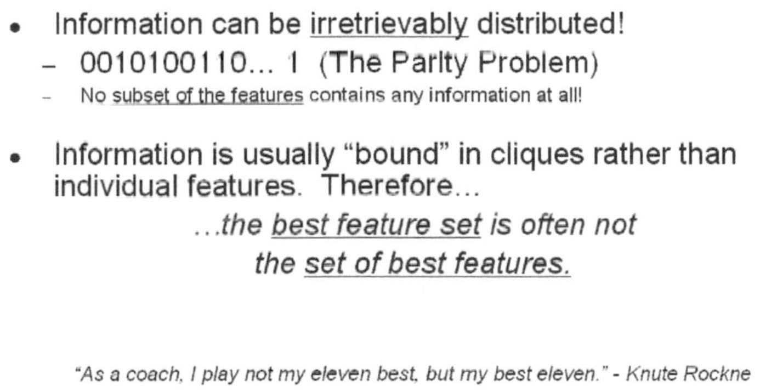

- Information can be <u>irretrievably</u> distributed!
  - 0010100110... 1 (The Parity Problem)
    - No <u>subset of the features</u> contains any information at all!

- Information is usually "bound" in cliques rather than individual features. Therefore...

  ...the <u>*best feature set*</u> *is often not*

  the <u>*set of best features.*</u>

"As a coach, I play not my eleven best, but my best eleven." - Knute Rockne

Figure 1.6   Feature sets vs. sets of features.

1.5.7 Seven Riddles about Meaning

Thinking of information as a vehicle for expressing *meaning*, we now consider the idea of "meaning" itself. The following questions might seem silly, but the issues they raise are the very things that make intelligent computing and data mining particularly difficult. Specifically, when an automated decision support system must infer the "meaning" of a collection of data values in order to correctly make a critical decision, "silly" issues of exactly this sort come up . . . and they must be addressed. We begin this in Chapter 2 by introducing the notion of a domain ontology, and continue it in Chapter 11 for intelligent systems (particularly those that perform multi-level fusion).

For our purposes, the most important question has to do with context: does meaning reside in things themselves, or is it merely the interpretation of an observer? This is an interesting question I have used (along with related questions in axiology) when I teach my Western Philosophy class. Here are some questions that touch on the connection between meaning and context:

Riddle one. If meaning must be known/remembered in order to exists/persist, does that imply that it is a form of information?

Riddle two. In the late 18th century, many examples of Egyptian hieroglyphics were known, but no one could read them. Did they have meaning? Apparently not, since there were no "rememberers." In 1798, the French found the Rosetta Stone, and within the next 20 or so years, this "lost" language was recovered, and with it, the "meaning" of Egyptian hieroglyphics. So, was the meaning "in" the hieroglyphics, or was it "brought to" the hieroglyphics by its translators?

Riddle three. If I write a computer program to generate random but intelligible stories (which I have done, by the way), and it writes a story to a text file, does this story have meaning before any person reads the file? Does it have meaning after a person reads the file? If it was meaningless before but meaningful afterwards, where did the meaning come from?

Riddle four. Two cops read a suicide note, but interpret it in completely different ways. What does the note mean?

Riddle five. Suppose I take a large number of tiny pictures of Abraham Lincoln and arrange them, such that they spell out the words "Born in 1809"; is additional meaning present?

Riddle six. On his deathbed, Albert Einstein whispered his last words to the nurse caring for him. Unfortunately, he spoke them in German, which she did not understand. Did those words mean anything? Are they now meaningless?

Riddle seven. When I look at your family photo album, I don't recognize anyone, or understand any of the events depicted; they convey nothing to me but what they immediately depict. You look at the album, and many memories of people, places, and events are engendered; they convey much. So, where is the meaning? Is it in the pictures, or is it in the viewer?

As we can see by considering the questions above, the meaning of a data set arises during an act of interpretation by a cognitive agent. At least some of it resides outside the data itself. This external content we normally regard as being in the domain ontology; it is part of the document context, and not the document itself.

1.6 Data Complexity

When talking about data complexity, the real issue at hand is the *accessibility* of latent information. Data are considered more complex when extracting information from them is more difficult.

Complexity arises in many ways, precisely because there are many ways that latent information can be obscured. For example, data can be complex because they are unwieldy. This can mean many records and/or many fields within a record (dimensions). Large data sets are difficult to manipulate, making their information content more difficult and time consuming to tap.

Data can also be complex because their information content is spread in some unknown way across multiple fields or records. Extracting information present in complicated bindings is a combinatorial search problem. Data can also be complex because the information they contain is not revealed by available tools. For example, visualization is an excellent information discovery tool, but most visualization tools do not support high-dimensional rendering.

Data can be complex because the patterns that contain interesting information occur rarely. Data can be complex because they just don't contain very much information at all. This is a particularly vexing problem because it is often difficult to determine whether the information is not visible, or just not present.

There is also the issue of whether latent information is actionable. If you are trying to construct a classifier, you want to characterize patterns that discriminate between classes. There might be plenty of information available, but little that helps with this specific task.

Sometimes the format of the data is a problem. This is certainly the case when those data that carry the needed information are collected/stored at a level of precision that obscures it (e.g., representing continuous data in discrete form).

Finally, there is the issue of data quality. Data of lesser quality might contain information, but at a low level of confidence. In this case, even information that is clearly present might have to be discounted as unreliable.

1.7 Computational Complexity

Computer scientists have formulated a principled definition of *computational complexity*. It treats the issue of how the amount of labor required to solve an instance of a problem is related to the size of the instance (Figure 1.7).

For example, the amount of labor required to find the largest element in an arbitrary list of numbers is directly proportional to the length of the list. That is, finding the largest element in a list of 2,000 numbers requires twice as many computer operations as finding the largest element in a list of 1,000 numbers. This *linear* proportionality is represented by $O(n)$, read "big O of n," where n is the length of the list.

On the other hand, the worst-case amount of labor required to sort an arbitrary list is directly proportional to the square of the length of the list. This is because sorting requires that the list be rescanned for every unsorted element to determine whether it is the next smallest or largest in the list. Therefore, sorting an arbitrary list of 2,000 numbers items requires four times as many computer operations as sorting a list of 1,000 numbers. This *quadratic* proportionality is represented by $O(n^2)$ read "big O of n squared," where n is the length of the list.

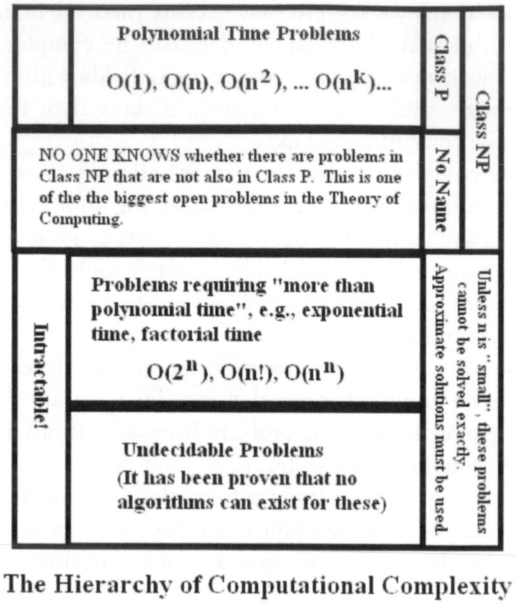
Polynomial Time Problems
O(1), O(n), O(n²), ... O(nᵏ)...
Class P
Class NP
NO ONE KNOWS whether there are problems in Class NP that are not also in Class P. This is one of the the biggest open problems in the Theory of Computing.
No Name
Problems requiring "more than polynomial time", e.g., exponential time, factorial time
O(2ⁿ), O(n!), O(nⁿ)
Intractable!
Undecidable Problems
(It has been proven that no algorithms can exist for these)
Unless n is "small", these problems cannot be solved exactly.
Approximate solutions must be used.
The Hierarchy of Computational Complexity

Figure 1.7 The hierarchy of computational complexity.

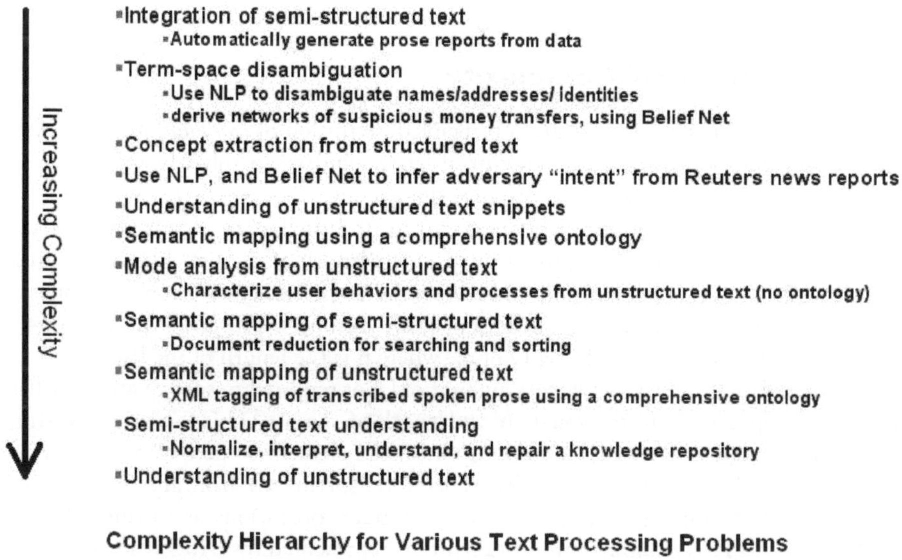
Increasing Complexity
▪Integration of semi-structured text
▪Automatically generate prose reports from data
▪Term-space disambiguation
▪Use NLP to disambiguate names/addresses/ identities
▪derive networks of suspicious money transfers, using Belief Net
▪Concept extraction from structured text
▪Use NLP, and Belief Net to infer adversary "intent" from Reuters news reports
▪Understanding of unstructured text snippets
▪Semantic mapping using a comprehensive ontology
▪Mode analysis from unstructured text
▪Characterize user behaviors and processes from unstructured text (no ontology)
▪Semantic mapping of semi-structured text
▪Document reduction for searching and sorting
▪Semantic mapping of unstructured text
▪XML tagging of transcribed spoken prose using a comprehensive ontology
▪Semi-structured text understanding
▪Normalize, interpret, understand, and repair a knowledge repository
▪Understanding of unstructured text
Complexity Hierarchy for Various Text Processing Problems

Figure 1.8 Complexity hierarchy for various text processing problems.

Lots of research has been conducted to determine the Big O complexity of various algorithms. It is generally held that algorithms having polynomial complexity, $O(n^p)$, are tractable, while more demanding Big O complexities are intractable. The details can't be addressed here, but we do note that many data mining problems (optimal feature selection, optimal training of a classifier, etc.) have a computational complexity that is beyond any polynomial level. In practice, this means that data miners must be content with solutions that are good enough. These are referred to as *satisficing solutions*.

Problems that are very computationally complex in their general case may fall into a class of problems referred to as *NP-Hard*. These problems, which have no known efficient algorithmic solutions, are frequently encountered in data mining work. Often problems in a domain are arranged in a hierarchy to help system architects make engineering trades (Figure 1.8).

1.7.1 Some NP-Hard Problems

- **The Knapsack Problem.** Given cubes of various sizes and materials (and hence, values), find the highest value combination that fits within a given box.
- **The Traveling Salesman Problem.** Given a map with N points marked, find the shortest circuit (a route that ends where it starts) that visits each city exactly once.
- **The Satisfiability Problem.** Given a boolean expression, determine whether there is an assignment of the variables that makes it true.
- **The Classifier Problem.** Given a neural network topology and a training set, find the weights that give the best classification score.

1.7.2 Some Worst-Case Computational Complexities

- Determining whether a number is positive or negative: $O(1)$ = constant time
- Finding an item in a sorted list using binary search: $O(\log(n))$
- Finding the largest number in an unsorted list: $O(n)$
- Performing a Fast Fourier Transform: $O(n*\log(n))$
- Sorting a randomly ordered list: $O(n^2)$
- Computing the determinant of an n-by-n matrix: $O(n^3)$
- Brute-force solution of Traveling Salesman Problem: $O(n!)$

1.8 Summary

The purpose of this chapter was to provide the reader with a grounding in the fundamental principles of data mining as a technical practice. Having read this chapter, you are now able to define data mining from both a philosophical and operational perspective, and enumerate the analytic functions data mining performs. You know the different types of data that arise in practice. You have been introduced to the basics of computational complexity theory, and the unavoidable presence of intractability. Most importantly, you have considered the important differences between data and information.

Now that you have been introduced to some terminology and the fundamental principles of data mining, you are ready to continue with a summary overview of data mining as a principled process.

Coming up

The next chapter presents a *spiral methodology* for managing the data mining process. The key principles underlying this process are summarized in preparation for the detailed treatments that follow later.

Chapter 2

The Data Mining Process

Purpose

The purpose of this chapter is to provide the reader with a deeper understanding of the fundamental principles of data mining. It presents an overview of data mining as a process of discovery and exploitation that is conducted in spirals, each consisting of multiple steps. A Rapid Application Development (RAD) data mining methodology is presented that accommodates disruptive discovery and changing requirements.

Goals

After you have read this chapter, you will be able to explain the more complex principles of data mining as a discipline. You will be familiar with the major components of the data mining process, and will know how these are implemented in a spiral methodology. Most importantly, you will understand the relative strengths and weaknesses of conventional and RAD development methodologies as they relate to data mining projects.

2.1 Introduction

Successful data mining requires the cultivation of an appropriate mindset. There are many ways that data mining efforts can go astray; even seemingly small oversights can cause significant delays or even project failure. Just as pilots must maintain situational awareness for safe performance, data miners must remember where they are in their analysis, and where they are going. All of this demands a principled approach implemented as a disciplined process.

The alternative to using a disciplined process is often expensive failure. "Data mining boys love their analytic toys"; directionless analysts can spend infinite time unsystematically pounding on data sets using powerful data mining tools. Someone who understands the data mining process must establish a plan: there needs to be a "Moses."

There also needs to be a "Promised Land." Someone familiar with the needs of the enterprise must establish general goals for the data mining activity. Because data mining is a dynamic, iterative discovery process, establishing goals and formulating a good plan can be difficult. Having a data mining expert review the problem, set up a reasonable sequence of experiments, and establish time budgets for each step of analysis will minimize profitless wandering through some high-dimensional wilderness.

There is still some disagreement among practitioners about the scope of the term *data mining*: Does data mining include building classifiers and other kinds of models, or only pattern discovery? How does conventional statistics fit in? and so on. There is also disagreement about the proper context for data mining: Is a data warehouse necessary? Is it essential to have an integrated set of tools? However, there is general agreement among practitioners that data mining is a process that begins with data in some form and ends with knowledge in some form.

As we have seen, data mining is a scientific activity requiring systematic thinking, careful planning, and informed discipline. We now lay out the steps of a principled data mining process at a high level, being careful not to get lost in the particulars of specific techniques or tools.

In computer science, development methodologies that repeat a standardized sequence of steps to incrementally produce successively more mature prototypes of a solution are referred to as *spiral methodologies*. Each cycle through the sequence of steps is one spiral.

An enterprise is any entity that is a data owner having an operational process. This includes businesses, government entities, the World Wide Web, etc. The following is an overview of a data mining project as a process of directed discovery and exploitation that occurs within an enterprise.

2.2 Discovery and Exploitation

As a process, data mining has two components: discovery and exploitation.

Discovery is an analytic process, e.g., determining the few factors that most influence customer churn. Exploitation is a modeling process, e.g., building a classifier that identifies the customers' most likely to churn based upon their orders last quarter. We can characterize these functionally by noting that during discovery, meaningful patterns are detected in data, and characterized formally, resulting in descriptive models. During exploitation, detected patterns are used to build useful models (e.g., classifiers).

- Discovery
  - o Detect actionable patterns in data
  - o Characterize actionable patterns in data

- Exploitation
  - o Create models
  - o Interact with the enterprise

Depending upon the complexity of the domain, the discovery process will have some or all of the components shown in Figure 2.1.

Once the discovery process has provided the necessary insight into how the data represent the domain, exploitation begins. It will have some or all of the major components in Figure 2.2, and might use some of the techniques suggested there.

This inclusive view of data mining is a bit broader than that currently held by some, who reserve the term data mining for what is here called the discovery component. They would refer to our exploitation component as predictive modeling. The broader view is taken here for three reasons:

1. The broader conception of data mining appears to be the direction things are headed in business intelligence (BI) circles, driven in part by tool vendors who continually increase the scope of their integrated data mining environments.
2. Some of the same tools and techniques are used for both discovery and exploitation, making discrimination between them somewhat subjective anyway (Are we exploiting yet?).
3. More and more, analysts want to engage in both discovery and exploitation using data mining tools and methods, going back and forth between the two during a project. Distinctions between discovery and exploitation are blurred in such situations.

Though an inclusive view of data mining is taken here, it should not be inferred that the distinction between discovery and exploitation is unimportant. For the purpose of managing a data mining project, selecting the right techniques, and keeping track of what we're doing now is essential to proper project management.

The data mining process will now be described as a sequence of steps, each having a specified purpose. The purpose, order, and content of each step are expressed in terms general enough to encompass those outlined in the well-known competing process standards.

Data mining projects are undertaken to solve enterprise problems. Some of these problems can be considered solved when insight is gained (e.g., What are the indicators of impending default?); others are solved only when this insight is made actionable by some application (e.g., Automatically predict default!). It's the difference between a question mark and an exclamation point: the descriptive models developed during the discovery phase address the "?", and the predictive models produced during the exploitation phase bring about the "!".

It is the enterprise goal that determines whether both discovery and exploitation are pursued for a particular data mining project. Typically, analysts and researchers want to discover, while managers and practitioners want to exploit.

Discovery is a prerequisite to exploitation. Sometimes though, there is sufficient knowledge of the domain to begin exploitation without undertaking an extensive

Data selection (defining the sampling frame)

Data cleansing

- Common data problems (outliers, gaps, time, consistency, collisions, imbalance)
- Identifying/handling outliers (statistical methods)
- handling missing fields (weak fill values, degapping, gap masking)
- handling temporal problems (aging, cycling, trends, non-stationarity, etc.)
- checking consistency (semantic filtering)
- handling class collisions
- handling class imbalance (replication, decimation)
- other

Data representation

- data syntax (precision, scale, format)
- nominal vs. numeric trades
- coding (nominal to numeric data)
- quantization (numeric to nominal data)

- **Feature extraction and transformation**
  - data registration
  - data normalization
  - feature synthesis

- **Feature enhancement**
  - feature salience (discriminating power of a feature)
  - feature independence (information contribution of a feature)
  - information-theoretic transforms (making information more accessible)

- **Data division**
  - sampling
  - stratifying
  - segmenting (creating training, calibration, validation, and holdback sets)

- **Configuration management**
  - nomenclature and naming conventions
  - documenting the workflow for reproducibility

Components of the Discovery Process

Figure 2.1   Components of the discovery phase.

Paradigms Selection
  -what it is, when to use it, how to create it, how to use it
  -neural networks (perceptrons, hopfield nets, recurrent nets, etc.)
  -knowledge-based expert systems
  -radial basis functions
  -adaptive logic networks
  -nearest-neighbor classifiers
  -support vector machines
  -decision trees, belief nets
  -others
Test Design
Model Construction
  -training (e.g., NN)
  -construction (e.g., KBES)
Meta-Schemes Development
  -bagging
  -boosting

• Model Evaluation (objective function)
  – accuracy (% correctness, precision/recall, RMS, etc.)
  – lift curve
  – confusion matrices
  – ROI
  – other
• Model Deployment
  – Web-based SOA, ASP
  – API, plug-ins, linked objects, file interface, etc.
  – other
• Model maintenance
  – retraining, stationarity
  – changing the feature set (adding/subtracting features)
  – other

Components of the Exploitation Process

Figure 2.2   Components of the exploitation process.

discovery effort. This is the approach taken, for example, by expert system developers who build intelligent applications using the knowledge already possessed by domain experts. Either way, every well-designed data mining effort includes an inquiry into what is already known about the domain.

2.3 Eleven Key Principles of Information Driven Data Mining

Included here to round out this introduction to data mining as a process are some foundational principles of the data mining process. Overlooking any one of them can lead to costly data mining project failure; ignore them at your peril. These are so important that we list them together for ready review before moving on to detailed treatments:

1. In order of importance: choose the right people, methods, and tools
2. Make no prior assumptions about the problem (begin as a domain agnostic)
3. Begin with general techniques that let the data determine the direction of the analysis (funnel method)
4. Don't jump to conclusions; perform process audits as needed
5. Don't be a one widget wonder; integrate multiple paradigms so the strengths of one compensate for the weaknesses of another
6. Break the problem into the right pieces; divide and conquer
7. Work the data, not the tools, but automate when possible
8. Be systematic, consistent and thorough; don't lose the forest for the trees.

9. Document the work so it is reproducible; create scripts when possible
10. Collaborate with team members, experts and users to avoid surprises
11. Focus on the goal: maximum value to the user within cost and schedule

2.4 Key Principles Expanded

These principles are the fruit of some of the author's own painful and expensive lessons learned the hard way. Working with these principles in mind will reduce the likelihood that you will make a costly and avoidable data mining error. Learn them; live them.

Key Principle Number One

Choose the right people, methods, and tools for your data mining effort

We place this principle first because it is the most important to the success of a data mining effort. Further, the three choices listed are in order of importance. If you have to compromise on something, it should not be the skill sets of the people involved in the mining effort. It is the aggregate skill set possessed by the team as a whole that will generate your success. The specific skills required for success will be discussed in Chapter 6.

Once the team has been put together, choosing the proper mining methods is next most important. Even people who really know what they're doing are less likely to be successful if the methods that they employ are not appropriate to the problem. By methods, we mean the mining goals, data sources, general methodology, and work plans.

Assuming that the right people and the right methods have been selected, the next most important item is the choice of appropriate tools. Fortunately, people well-versed in the procedures for conducting a data mining effort can often be successful even when they don't have the best toolsets. This is because many data mining activities rely on the analytic skills of the miner more than they rely on the efficiency provided by good tools.

Key Principle Number Two

Make no prior assumptions about the problem

This involves taking an agnostic approach to the problem. Assumptions are actually restrictions on what constitutes a reasonable hypothesis. Since you will not be a domain expert, you shouldn't have any of these. Often things that haven't been discovered about the problem space are unknown precisely because prior assumptions prevented people from perceiving them. If you make certain assumptions about what are viable solutions to a problem, you insure that certain approaches will not be carefully explored. If one of these excluded solutions is actually the solution for which you are mining, you will not discover it. Taking an agnostic approach to a data mining activity will initially leave the door open to undiscovered facts about the domain. If you don't have a solution in hand, it makes sense to at least consider approaches that might initially appear unpromising.

One of the implications of principle number two is that domain experts are often not the best people to carry out a data mining effort. The reason for this is that they already have a large collection of assumptions, many held unconsciously, about what's going to work and not work in the problem space. These assumptions will prevent them from investigating avenues of analysis that they "know won't work." A data mining effort led by a domain expert can be expected to discover all the things they already know about the problem space, and not much else. Someone not an expert in the problem will investigate areas an expert would let pass unexamined. It is generally much better to have someone who knows more about data mining than the problem space to be the technical lead on a data mining activity. The domain expert certainly is a necessary part of the team, but not as the leader.

Key Principle Number Three

Begin with general techniques that let the data determine the direction of the analysis

For problem areas that are not well understood, begin the project by pursuing several lines of general investigation. For example, initially employ two or more different analytic methods, toolsets, etc. Rather than putting all the eggs into one analytic basket, this holds open multiple lines of investigation long enough to determine which is likely to produce the best result. With this known, subsequent effort can be focused on that one best choice.

I refer to this as the *funnel method*, because work begins with a broad analytic attack, progressively narrowing as the problem is more fully understood. This method also provides a good way to make use of multiple team members, each using a different method and working in parallel until problem understanding is achieved. When that occurs, all of your working capital can shift over to the method found most likely to bear fruit in your problem domain.

Key Principle Number Four

Don't jump to conclusions; perform process audits as needed

This refers to a phenomenon that occurs often in data mining efforts, and is usually (though not always!) manifested by an inexperienced data miner. It is not unusual for an amazing analytic miracle to occur, a silver bullet that solves the problem. It is often the case, however, that huge breakthroughs on really hard problems are the deceptive fruit of some analytic mistake: some data have been mislabeled, ground truth has accidentally been added to the data set, or some data conditioning error caused an experiment to produce erroneous results.

The damage is usually limited to some embarrassment on the part of the claimant, but the real danger is that word of a breakthrough will find its way to a decision maker who will take it at face value. This can derail a data mining effort and at the very least, you'll have some explaining to do.

When results from a significant experiment differ radically from expectations, the proper approach is to perform *a process audit*: a thorough examination of the experiment to determine the facts. The most common errors are related to data preparation and use as follows:

1. Inappropriate data have been added to a training set (e.g. ground truth).
2. Validation has been done on the same data that was used to create the model (training data).
3. The data set has somehow been poisoned by additions and/or deletions in such a way that it misrepresents the problem.

Key Principle Number Five

Don't be a one widget wonder; integrate multiple paradigms so the
strengths of one compensate for the weaknesses of another

There is no perfect data mining tool or application; every tool and application is going to have certain strengths and weaknesses. There will be aspects of the problem a particular tool handles well, and others it does not handle well. This means that if you rely entirely on one or two tools to attack a complex data mining problem you'll probably not do the best job on all aspects of the problem.

An industry phrase for an analyst who relies entirely on one application is "a fool with a tool" (FWAT). The final product of a FWAT will consist of all the things their preferred tool does well, and none of the things it doesn't.

Key Principle Number Six

Break the problem into the right pieces; divide and conquer

A divide and conquer approach is often the key to success in difficult data mining problems. One of the factors that make some data mining problems difficult is the presence of several sub-problems, not all of which can be addressed by a single approach. For example, if the data contain disparate items from multiple sources that are at different levels of precision/accuracy, or are in very different forms (such as a mixture of nominal and numeric data), using multiple tools might be the only viable approach.

When a problem has these local disparities, it makes sense to consider breaking it into pieces and deploying different methods against the pieces. This allows the use of the best tool on each component of the problem. Just as you wouldn't fight a battle against a tank brigade using only infantry, you don't want to use a single approach against a problem that has multiple modes or aspects that require different approaches. Instead, divide and conquer: break the problem into appropriate pieces and attack them individually with methods suited to the various data terrains (Figure 2.3).

An additional benefit of problem segmentation is the ability to parallelize work by having different problem segments worked separately by different analysts. This can

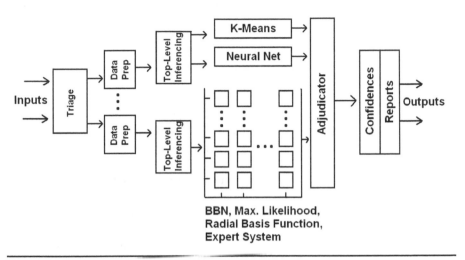

Figure 2.3 Multi-paradigm architecture.

sometimes shorten the overall project schedule, and can keep staff usefully engaged should there be slack periods in the project schedule.

Finally, it is often possible to automate the process of segmenting a difficult problem into natural chunks using unsupervised learning methods such as clustering (discussed in Chapter 10). It is often the case that some chunks will be the hard part of the problem, and others the easy parts. Separating these allows elementary methods to handle the easy problem instances, with more computationally complex methods being used only when necessary.

Automation can make a big difference in data mining activities, but its limitations must be recognized. Automation is good for handling rote tasks that humans don't do well, such as building histograms, computing correlation measures, grinding out bulk computations, doing clustering and matching, sifting through large quantities of data to perform repetitive statistical tests, and so on. But when it gets down to actually trying to squeeze the last bit of information out of a complex problem space, some reworking of the data is going to be required. By *reworking the data* we mean applying some mathematical transform, alternate normalization, or synthesis of altogether new features by combining some of the old. All of these provide fresh views of the problem space that can make information not yet extracted more accessible to your tools.

Key Principle Number Seven

Work the data, not the tools, but automate when possible

If you've run a data mining problem through several spirals and have not made sufficient progress, at some point you will begin thinking about new things to try. Questions that pop up in this situation are: Do I need to modify my tools? Is there some perfect collection of parameter settings for my modeling software that will produce large improvements? (There are times when this is exactly what is called for, but it is usually not when you are running low on tricks. This leads to planless tinkering, which is addressed in key principle number eight.)

When faced with the question of whether to work the tools or work the data, the correct answer is almost always <u>work the data</u>. This is because the information you are looking for is not in the tools; it is in the data. Experience has shown over and over again that in mining of all sorts, data mining and otherwise, you are more likely to get increased value from better dirt than you are from a better shovel. Resorting to data mining by twiddling dials on a tool is a lot like doing your taxes by rolling dice: it's just not the best approach.

Data mining is subject to the law of diminishing returns. Obvious patterns and principles are discovered early, but as information is mined from a data set, the rate of discovery will slow. The natural temptation when you're in the hunt for information with automated tools is to speed things up by tweaking the tools to get them to act more effectively against the data (changing settings and parameters, recalibrating them, adjusting sensitivity levels, configurations, vigilance factors, etc.). This will work for a while, but at some point it will stop bearing fruit. It is important to realize when this stage has been reached, and the experienced data miner will switch from working the tool to working the data.

If you are quite sure that you've done everything with the data that makes sense, tweaking tools is worth a try. But to give it a passable chance of success, you should automate. The number of random experiments you can try manually with a tool is relatively small, and you are probably searching a large space of possible parameter settings. A better approach is to select a small data set, and then create some kind of a script that rapidly tries ranges of settings. Recognize, though, that solutions obtained in this manner often generalize poorly. This is to be expected, given that the solution was obtained by gaming the sensitivity of your tools to find just the right arcane configuration for this particular training set.

Key Principle Number Eight

Be systematic, consistent, and thorough; don't lose the forest for the trees

It is very easy when you get into the heat of the information chase to begin trying long sequences of ad hoc experiments, hoping that something good will happen. When experimentation is run in an ad hoc manner, the risk is that the experimentation will not be systematic, won't adequately cover the problem space, and will miss discoveries by leaving parts of the problem unexplored. Documentation and other methods designed to reduce errors also tend to suffer. When operating in an ad hoc manner, it's easy to begin focusing on minutiae in the data, and lose sight of the fact that principled analysis is much more likely to be effective against a difficult problem than is luck. You don't choose a career by flipping coins, and you can't conduct good data science that way either.

Key Principle Number Nine

Document the work so it is reproducible

Just as in software engineering and hardware engineering, configuration management and version control is absolutely essential in data mining projects. In some ways it's even more important to apply good documentation standards and audit control to data mining efforts, because these are by nature experimental: procedures for reproducing particular processes don't yet exist. I've had the experience of making valuable discoveries in complex data sets, and then becoming so excited that I go into ad hoc mode before carefully documenting how I initially got them. Unless new processes are immediately documented, there is the very real possibility that you will be unable to reproduce the original breakthrough. This is a very frustrating position to be in: you know that the gold nugget is there; you've seen it and touched it but you can no longer find it.

To avoid this, when I do data mining work I keep a little notepad window open on my desktop so I can document the details of experiments as I perform them: what input files were used, what tool settings were made, what data conditioning sequence was applied, etc. This helps me reproduce any results obtained.

However, the best way to document work for reliable auditing and replication is to conduct the steps from script files that are executed automatically. In this way, not only is the process completely and unambiguously documented at the moment it is conducted, it's easy to rerun the experiment later if necessary.

Key Principle Number Ten

Collaborate with team members, experts and users to avoid surprises

We are not talking about good surprises here. Most surprises in science and engineering are not good. Data miners who are not domain experts will discover things that domain experts already know, and this is OK. The response to amazing discoveries must include review by a domain expert who can assess the practical value of pursuing them, because they might be well-known facts about the domain. If no mechanism for domain expert feedback is in place, lots of time will probably be spent rediscovering and documenting things that the expert already knows.

Another situation that can arise is the discovery of patterns in complex data that are real, but have no practical value in the solution of the users' problem. I remember an activity during which I discovered a number of interesting patterns I was fairly sure had not been seen before. After devoting a lot of time and effort to the extraction and characterization of these patterns, I brought them to a domain expert for review. The expert pointed out that the patterns I discovered were real patterns that did exist in the data, and they were not well-known. They also had no value because they were noise artifacts randomly created during the collection of this particular data set, and would never occur again.

You don't want to surprise the user too much. Even good surprises can have bad effects, because they disrupt plans and introduce technical uncertainty. It is important to keep both domain experts and users engaged as mining work proceeds, so that as progress is made through the prototyping cycles, everyone is carried along in their understanding at essentially the same level. In this way, when the final delivery is made, everyone knows what to expect because they have seen the results unfold, and have a stake in it because they were involved. The most certain way to produce satisfied customers is to meet their expectations. Those expectations can change during the course of the project, but there won't be a surprise if everyone is engaged.

Key Principle Number Eleven

Focus on the goal: maximum value to the user within cost and schedule

Data mining activities are undertaken to satisfy user needs. Data miners who love their analytics, their tools, and their methods can become distracted when interesting patterns are found or unexpected discoveries are made. These can initiate rabbit trails that cause the effort to go off track in pursuit of things that are interesting to the miner but not helpful to the user. It's important to remember that no matter what happens during the mining effort, the goal is to provide value to the user, and to do so within the constraints of cost and schedule.

2.5 Type of Models: Descriptive, Predictive, Forensic

Like every well-designed process, data mining proceeds toward a goal. For almost all data mining efforts, this goal can be thought of as a model of some aspect of the problem domain. These models are of three kinds: descriptive, predictive, and forensic. Understanding the differences brings us to the notion of a domain ontology.

2.5.1 Domain Ontologies as Models

For philosophers, an ontology is a theory of being. It is an attempt to conceptualize answers to certain fundamental questions such as: What is reality? Do things have meaning? What can be known?

In data mining, ontology has a similar meaning. Formally speaking, *an ontology for a data set* is a representational scheme that provides a consistent, coherent, unifying description of the domain data in context. Loosely speaking, an ontology for a data set is an interpretation of the data that reveals its meaning(s) by explaining its characteristics (sources, history, relationships, connotations). These representations are called *models*. Models represent ontologies in various ways: as consistent sets of equations describing data relationships and patterns (*mathematical models*), as coherent collections of empirical laws or principles (*scientific models*), etc.

When models merely describe patterns in data, they are called *descriptive models*. When models process patterns in data, they are called *predictive models*. When models discover or explain patterns in data, they are called *forensic models*. In practice, models often have elements of all three; the distinctions among them are not always clear.

The process by which scientists devise physical theories (the so-called scientific method) is a good example of a systematic development strategy for an ontology. The scientist comes to the experimental data with a minimum of a priori assumptions, intending to formulate and test a model that will explain the data. The scientific method is, in fact, one particular incarnation of the general data mining process.

Looking at how data has been used by scientists through history, we see an evolutionary development through three stages: descriptive use of data; predictive use of data; and explanatory use of data.

Early scientific models were long on description, short on prediction, and shorter on coherent understanding. In many ways, the maturity of a scientific discipline can be assessed by where it lies along this progression.

This is seen in its classic form in development of the cosmology of the solar system. The Pythagorean and Aristotelian models were mostly descriptive, with predictive and forensic components based mostly upon philosophical speculation. Ptolemy created a descriptive model that was useful for prediction, but it was ultimately made subservient to a philosophical model that hindered its development. It took a revolution in thought, begun by Copernicus and Galileo, and completed by Newton, to correct and extend Ptolemy's patchwork cosmology to a coherent system derivable in a rational way from first principles (Figure 2.4).

The same three modes (description, prediction, and explanation) that are operative in other instances of scientific reasoning are seen in data mining. They lie in the same natural hierarchy from simplest to most complex: descriptive, predictive, and forensic data mining.

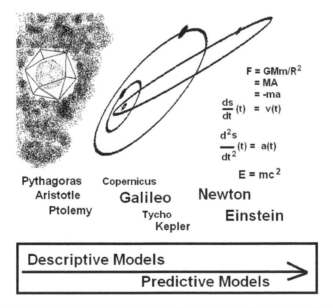

Figure 2.4 Cosmology of the solar system.

2.5.2 Descriptive Models

Descriptive applications are the simplest; they use data to describe its source or context. This is simple because it leaves the work of interpretation entirely to the recipient: descriptive data is what it is, and says exactly (and only) what it says. Data mining operating in this mode produces meta-data: descriptive statistics such as averages, counts, rates, charts, plots, etc.

2.5.3 Predictive Models

Predictive applications of data are somewhat more complex, in that they add to the data some external assumptions about repeatability and fidelity. Prediction is data in action, the observed facts of past experience moving into the present and future. However, prediction is almost always based upon mere correlation: when these data are observed, certain conditions often co-occur. The point is, while this might look like intelligence, it can be done quite well without having any authentic understanding of the data at all. David Hume, the British philosopher, referred to this kind of reliable coincidence as the "constant conjunction of ideas": it looks like implication or causation, but it is really an unexplained sequence for which exceptions have not yet been observed.

2.5.4 Forensic Models

Forensic applications are the most sophisticated data mining applications, because they interpret data in light of some context. This is an act of assigning meaning to symbolic patterns; in so doing, forensics generates semantic material from syntactic material. This is not just an enrichment process, but an elevation from one realm to another. This elevates data from the level of sense experience to understanding. This is data mining at its best.

2.6 Data Mining Methodologies

Like any process, data mining can be carried out either haphazardly or systematically. While there is no universally accepted data mining process standard, there are several contenders for the position of *de facto* standard. Among these, two are preeminent, due largely to their association with widely used products: Sample, Explore, Modify, Model, Assess (SEMMA), created by the SAS Institute and supported by the tool SAS Enterprise Miner; and CRoss-Industry Standard Process (CRISP) for data mining, created by a consortium consisting of NCR, Daimler-Chrysler, SPSS, and OHRA, and supported by the tool SPSS Clementine.

A review of the various data mining processes that have been proposed as industry standards leaves one with the impression that underneath it all, roughly the same process is being described in different ways. This conclusion is supported by the fact that proponents of competing process standards rarely debate the merits of their favored process. Instead, they focus on how well their favored process works when applied in conjunction with their favored data mining tool. This makes sense given that the creators of the most popular processes are closely associated with tool developers.

The principal implication of all this is that in actual practice, most data mining activities conducted by experienced analysts proceed in about the same general way: data is gathered, conditioned, and analyzed, giving descriptive models; then if desired, the results of the analysis are used to construct, validate, and field models. Each of these activities has multiple steps, requires the application of particular techniques, and has its own best practice. It is these steps, techniques, and practices that data mining process standards seek to specify.

Rather than sacrifice generality by describing the ad hoc details of just one of the competing standards, or blur the fundamentals by trying to survey them all, the following data mining process discussion will be conducted at a higher level of generality. With this done, each of the competing process standards will be seen as customizations for a particular problem type or tool set.

2.6.1 Conventional System Development: Waterfall Process

The standard development methodology used in many types of engineering is referred to as the Waterfall Process. In this process, projects proceed in order through a sequence of planning and development activities that culminates in the delivery of a capability specified by the user at the beginning of the effort.

This approach has some nice characteristics, and some shortcomings. On the plus side, it is inherently linear (in time), and has the look and feel of an orderly process that can be planned and managed. At each step along the way, you have some idea of how you are doing against the original plan, and how much work is left to do. It facilitates manpower and resource planning, and supports the prediction of project events. Because it has natural temporal and effort-level components, it supports cost estimation, and re-planning if necessary.

On the minus side, it requires important decisions to be made at a time in the project when the least information is available. Users must fully express their requirements before work begins, and the resources required to cope with unanticipated problems and risks must be estimated in advance. Often, assumptions must be made about critical issues before they are fully understood.

In particular, since data mining has investigative activities woven throughout, the Waterfall Process is not at all natural for data mining projects. How do you schedule discovery? What skill mix do you need to implement an algorithm that doesn't exist to solve a problem you don't know about? If a discovery halfway through the project proves that a completely new approach with new goals is needed, what do you do?

A development process that can accommodate the impact of changes in problem understanding and project goals is needed for data mining: a rapid prototyping process. This and related methods are referred to as examples of Rapid Application Development (RAD) methodologies.

2.6.2 Data Mining as Rapid Prototyping

In practice, data mining is almost always conducted in a Rapid Prototyping fashion. Data miners using this methodology perform project work in a sequence of time-limited, goal-focused cycles (called spirals). Before jumping into the details of each step of this methodology (which is done in subsequent chapters), we begin with a summary overview of the steps that constitute a generic spiral:

Step 1:   Problem Definition
Step 2:   Data Evaluation
Step 3:   Feature Extraction and Enhancement
Step 4a: Prototyping Plan
Step 4b: Prototyping/Model Development
Step 5:   Model Evaluation
Step 6:   Implementation

The order and content of these steps will vary from spiral to spiral to accommodate project events. This is very different from the Waterfall Process, and addresses most of the issues that make the Waterfall Process ill-suited to data mining projects. Most importantly, rapid prototyping enables data mining researchers and developers to accommodate and benefit from incremental discovery, and holds at abeyance final decisions on some requirements until they can be settled in an informed and principled way.

The flexibility inherent in a RAD methodology does not mean that data mining efforts are undisciplined. On the contrary, using a RAD methodology in an undisciplined manner usually results in the waste of resources, and perhaps project failure. This puts the onus on the program manager and technical lead to make sure that everything done during a spiral is done for a reason, that the outcomes are carefully evaluated in light of those reasons and that the team does not lose sight of the long term goal: satisfying user needs within cost and schedule.

2.7 A Generic Data Mining Process

More formal characterizations of the data mining process will be given in the next chapter. However, we will complete our informal characterization of a single spiral by reciting the process as a two paragraph narrative:

We begin by developing a clear understanding of what is to be accomplished in collaboration with the user. We then interview subject-matter experts using a (more or less formal) knowledge acquisition protocol. Next, we prepare the available data (evidence and hypotheses) for analysis. This involves inferring descriptive information in the form of meta-data (schemas), demographics (counts, ranges, distributions, visualizations), and data problems (conformation problems, outliers, gaps, class collisions, and population imbalance, all of which will be described in later chapters).

Based upon this descriptive modeling work, data are repaired if necessary, and transformed for analysis. Appropriate pattern processing methods and applications are used to extract and enhance features for model construction. Appropriate modeling

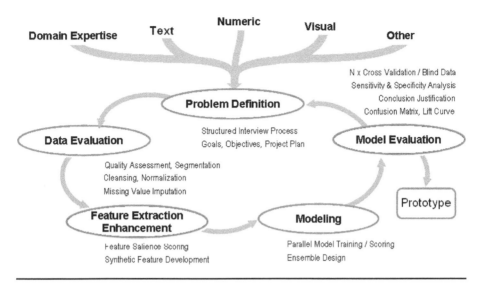

Figure 2.5   Spiral methodology.

paradigm(s) is/are selected (e.g., rule-based system, decision tree, support vector machine, etc.) and then integrated. The transformed data are then segmented, and models are built, evaluated, optimized, and applied. The results are interpreted in light of the goals for this spiral, and hypotheses and plans are adjusted. All work is documented and discussed with domain experts.

Each of the steps in a spiral advance us around the spiral found in Figure 2.5. The particulars of the lower-level procedures in the diagram will be discussed in later chapters.

Each of the steps in a RAD data mining methodology will be addressed in detail in the following sections. Keep in mind that RAD is intended to be a flexible process that enables researchers and developers to accommodate both new information and changing user requirements. It is not intended, nor is it recommended, that the work pattern described here be imposed in a rigid manner because to do so would eliminate its principal advantages.

2.8 RAD Skill Set Designators

In later discussions of the RAD methodology, we will have occasion to discuss specific skill sets as they are tasked during the steps of a RAD effort. For our purposes in understanding the RAD methodology, it is assumed these skills will be held by specialists designated by the following titles and their abbreviations:

CE: Cognitive Engineer (the data mining analyst)
DE: Domain Expert (usually a customer/end-user having in-depth operational knowledge of the domain)

DO: Data Owners (usually MIS personnel who collect/manage the user data)
PM: Program Manager (manager who can make cost/schedule decisions for the effort)
SE: Software/Database Engineer (application developer)

2.9 Summary

Having read this chapter, you now have a deeper understanding of the fundamental principles of data mining. You understand data mining as a process of discovery and exploitation that is conducted in multiple spirals consisting of multiple steps. You have been introduced to the steps that constitute a RAD cycle. Most importantly, you can explain the relative strengths and weaknesses of conventional and RAD development methodologies as they relate to data mining projects. Now that you have a summary understanding of data mining as a structured process, you are ready to begin your study of the individual steps that comprise it.

Coming up

The next chapter presents an extensive, annotated checklist of questions that must be addressed in Step 1 of a data mining spiral: Problem Understanding. Items from this checklist can serve as the basis for a knowledge acquisition interview with a domain expert.

Chapter 3

Problem Definition (Step 1)

Purpose

The practical purpose of this chapter is to specifically characterize the information to be collected and organized during the problem definition step of a data mining spiral. Rather than developing these ideas in prose from which the reader must extract actionable chunks, the material is presented as a topically organized checklist of questions to be addressed.

Goals

After you have read this chapter, you will know what information you must obtain before beginning a data mining spiral, and you will know why this information is useful. You will also know what follow-up questions to ask, and any special considerations that apply in that area.

3.1 Introduction

It is rare to see data mining problems defined in terms of formal performance requirements (though for long-term data mining system development efforts, this might make sense). Instead, the requirements are often expressed in terms of performance metrics for the processes they facilitate. It is common to see project goals along the lines of: "Use customer transaction data to generate decision support tools that enable operations managers to reduce churn by 30%." How this is to be done is usually left unstated.

3.2 Problem Definition Task 1: Characterize Your Problem

Data mining projects begin with an effort to understand the nature of the problem to be solved. As a collection of disparate analytic methods, data mining can proceed in a variety of ways, some of which are better suited to particular problems than others. A data mining project that does not begin with focused discussions with customers, domain experts, and system users is already in trouble.

The questions in this chapter are arranged topically. They are designed to elicit customer and user expectations, bringing the precise nature of the problem into focus. They are in a form that allows them to be carried into a meeting and used as a checklist to aid in arriving at a common understanding of the problem. Questions should be addressed to the right person (e.g., don't ask a business person detailed technical questions).

Of course, not all questions will apply to every data mining project, and spirals undertaken well into a project might begin with a very short list. Further, this checklist is necessarily somewhat generic. As you develop experience in data mining you will know which questions to ask, and will add focused questions specific to the problem domain. As much as anything else, this checklist serves as a reminder to the data miner about things not to forget!

3.3 Problem Definition Checklist

Question 1: What problem are we addressing (i.e., What is the output of the system?)?	
Why is this question important?	The default assessment of investigative efforts such as data mining is Failure. Without a clear understanding of the project's purpose, success is unlikely. Also, users might not clearly understand what data mining is, and have unspoken, and possibly unreasonable, expectations.
What is this question seeking?	The answer should be an operational definition of success for the project. It should list project deliverables and quantify elements of performance.
Likely responses and their meanings	Likely answers will be vague descriptions of desired ad hoc functions. If different users give widely divergent answers, the user organization probably doesn't know what it wants.
Follow-up questions	Ask for requirements of the same sort you would request on a conventional development. What, specifically, are the desired functions? What are the measures of performance? What are the project deliverables? How will success and failure be determined?
Special considerations	Get answers to these questions from the person(s) who will actually be evaluating the project. Their expectations are definitive.

This is the single most important question in the checklist, so it deserves some additional discussion.

Here is the kind of answer you might get to this question:
"We want something that predicts whether a customer is about to close their account."

Here is the kind of answer you need to this question:
"We want an automated model that will categorize each of our clients as falling into one of four account classes so that timely and appropriate customer retention measures can be taken."

Account Class 1—client will close account in less than 30 days
Account Class 2—client will close account in 31–90 days
Account Class 3—client will close account in 91+ days
Account Class 4—client will not close account

The project will use historical client data provided by the customer to build profiles of clients that fall into the different classes based on their feature values. A classifier to categorize the client account class will be built and scored by classification accuracy using blind examples. The preliminary project accuracy goal is 75% correctness of classification on the entire blind set. The classifier will ingest a feature data set, and produce as output a report giving the Account Class prediction for each customer in the input file. A certainty score To Be Refined (TBR) for each prediction will be included in the report.

You will usually get the vague answer first. Step 1 of a data mining spiral is devoted mostly to asking appropriate questions and making reasonable suggestions to help the customer generate something like the answer you really need, and get buy in from the customer organization.

Question 2: Describe the perfect solution for this problem.	
Why is this question important?	Too often, this question is not asked directly. Customer expectations must be fully understood. Presumably the perfect solution will satisfy these.
What is this question seeking?	Unspoken expectations that the customer has about the project.
Likely responses and their meanings	The first response is often something glib and vague. Press for details, particularly about measures of performance.
Follow-up questions	Ask about the business case for the project. Someone in the management chain is expecting a return on this effort; what are the specifics of those expectations in business terms?
Special considerations	Often there is some unsolved problem or must-have feature that drives the decision to undertake a data mining project. Try to determine what that is.

Question 3: How would you characterize the desired solution (classifier, estimator, associator, planner, reasoner?)?	
Why is this question important?	The user probably does not understand the difference between the functions and operation of these different solution paradigms. Asking this question gives you an opportunity to work through this decision with them. The last thing you want to do is solve the wrong problem.
What is this question seeking?	The answer to this question drives the choice of data mining process and architecture, since classifiers are designed and built differently from estimators, etc.
Likely responses and their meanings	Unless the user is sophisticated, the response will be puzzlement.
Follow-up questions	Ask about special features that might be needed in the solution (confidence factors, probabilities, tables, reports, etc.)
Special considerations	Most users will have little if any knowledge of this important aspect of planning. Be sensitive, and look for indications that additional explanation is needed.

Question 4: What makes this problem hard?	
Why is this question important?	Data mining is not the first thing most organizations try when they have a hard problem to solve. It is likely they have tried other things; find out what these are so you don't end up repeating a past failure.
What is this question seeking?	Knowing what hasn't worked can provide lots of information about the nature of the problem.
Likely responses and their meanings	Answers are often general and a little vague, since previous efforts might not be recent, or fully understood.
Follow-up questions	Ask about talking to those who have worked on the problem or the data before. These previous workers have knowledge that could save you time and trouble.
Special considerations	Questions about previous work that was only partially successful can be problematic. Be sensitive to organizational political considerations.

Question 5: What is the data domain (time, frequency, both, image, text, web, other)?	
Why is this question important?	This information is necessary to break the data out for encoding as features.
What is this question seeking?	Knowing what hasn't worked can provide lots of information about the nature of the problem.
Likely responses and their meanings	Metadata is usually available, though it is often not completely up to date. Be prepared to do some patching up.
Follow-up questions	Ask the user to extract the data and put it into a simple work ready format for you. They can do this more quickly than you can, and are less likely to make some naïve mistake that poisons the project. Ask to observe so that you can answer any questions that arise, understand how the extraction was done, and know specifically what data you have actually received.
Special considerations	Users invariably think that getting you access to their data is easier than it actually is. They also frequently over estimate its quality, completeness, and utility for data mining. This results in unexpected project delays. Have a backup plan should data delivery be slow (e.g., be prepared to construct simulated data from a schema so initial work on nonanalytic portions such as user interfaces can begin).

Note: You must know the units and intra-data relationships to properly extract and encode features for analysis. If the data are in a database, ask for a schema and data definition document that shows how the data are stored and linked.

Question 6: Describe the ground truth classes/range of estimates of plan templates, etc., for this domain.	
Why is this question important?	These items are the principle data outputs of any applications you develop. You must know what is expected.
What is this question seeking?	Specification of your output. How many classes is your classifier modeling? What are they? What are the units, precision, and range of estimator outputs, etc.?
Likely responses and their meanings	Users usually have a very good understanding of these matters, since they have probably had to generate and evaluate such outputs manually.
Follow-up questions	Ask for any written documentation that might exist on the output data elements.
Special considerations	Ask about the best way to present results to the user. This is driven by how the results will be used.

Question 7: What constitutes a data collect, and how many collects are there?	
Why is this question important?	You are looking for some notion of how individual records make it into the data. For example, If incoming chunks of data are organized or related in some way, it might be harmful to their information content to separate them.
What is this question seeking?	You are trying to see how the data represent the phenomena they are describing. This may suggest exploitable relationships among data items, or inspire additional questions about the problem domain.
Likely responses and their meanings	Users usually understand their data very well. Expect lengthy and highly detailed responses.
Follow-up questions	Ask for documents that describe the data collection process.
Special considerations	Some of this information might be proprietary; handle with care. Also, be alert for gaps in users' descriptions of their data; details may be missed or omitted in verbal descriptions.

Question 8: What constitutes a sample (e.g., a numeric measurement? a quality measure? a web page?)?	
Why is this question important?	A sample is usually a single unit of information, or measurement inside a record (e.g., a single data field.) However, it might be a larger collection of data.
What is this question seeking?	The internal organization of the data elements that constitute the various record type to be analyzed
Likely responses and their meanings	There are probably detailed documents on record structures; request these.
Follow-up questions	Make sure that data formats are clearly understood. Low level considerations like ad hoc encodings, parity, Endianness, ISO or IEEE standards, operating systems, etc., should be discussed.
Special considerations	When data are received conduct a "desk check" audit to verify.

3.3.1 Identify Previous Work

Question 9: What is the current level of performance?	
Why is this question important?	The current level of performance is the lower bound of the performance mark any solution must meet. An outcome that is only as good as that produced by the existing process will probably be regarded as a wasted effort.
What is this question seeking?	You have to determine the level of performance that constitutes success; it will certainly not be any lower than the current level.
Likely responses and their meanings	Sometimes users will specify unrealistic goals, but authentic domain experts often have a pretty good idea of what is possible to achieve in principle.
Follow-up questions	Ask for quantitative answers to the performance question. Vague responses that leave room for subjective interpretation leave you in danger of failing no matter how well you do.
Special considerations	Sometimes data just do not support the needed level of performance. Be prepared to acknowledge that the proposed data mining project might not have a viable business case.

Question 10: What is good performance, and what is bad performance?	
Why is this question important?	Just because you are able to improve the performance of an existing process does not mean that you have succeeded. The improvement must be sufficient to justify doing the work. Presumably, good performance rises to this level.
What is this question seeking?	We are trying to put a fine point on the users' expectations. A passing grade is nice, but an A or B is better.
Likely responses and their meanings	Answers will vary. There is a business answer and a technical answer. Know the difference.
Follow-up questions	Ask for quantitative answers to the performance question. Vague responses that leave room for subjective interpretation leave you in danger of failing no matter how well you do.
Special considerations	Sometimes data do not support the needed level of performance. Be prepared to acknowledge that the proposed data mining project might not have a viable business case.

Question 11: Have others worked on this problem? Who? When?	
Why is this question important?	Whoever worked on the problem before apparently did not solve it, but they can probably tell about things that won't work. It's always good to avoid repeating the mistakes of others.
What is this question seeking?	We are trying to determine who might have technical insight into the project problem.
Likely responses and their meanings	Often those who worked on a problem before are unavailable, or unwilling to help.
Follow-up questions	Is there some way you can talk to the people that worked on this problem before? What is their contact information?
Special considerations	When talking with previous researchers, avoid suggesting that they failed; this will cause them to shut down. Address them as experts, and ask for their advice.

Question 12: Did they use this data?	
Why is this question important?	While it might be the case that the problem has been worked before, if this was done using different data than that available to you, those results might not be relevant to your work.
What is this question seeking?	You want to know whether the problem you are working on is exactly like any previous efforts.
Likely responses and their meanings	Sometimes yes, and sometimes no.
Follow-up questions	How, specifically, is the data being supplied now, different from that used on previous data mining efforts?
Special considerations	Often, the differences in data from one effort to another appear minor (one or two data fields); but such differences can have a large impact on the information content of a source. It makes sense to assess the data involved and any differences first.

Question 13: What were their results?	
Why is this question important?	Since you might want to talk to previous researchers, you'll want to know whether they are speaking from a perspective of good results or bad results.
What is this question seeking?	Did previous researchers make headway on the problem? If they were competent and made little progress, this probably means the problem is hard.

(Continued on following page)

Question 13: What were their results? (*Continued*)	
Likely responses and their meanings	Answers to these questions are usually vague and anecdotal, but sometimes provide very useful information.
Follow-up questions	Is documentation from previous efforts available for review?
Special considerations	Previous efforts might be regarded as proprietary and not releasable to you.

3.3.2 Data Demographics

Question 14: How much bulk data are we talking about (KB, MB, GB, TB, PB)?	
Why is this question important?	The scale of the data to be mined often determines which tools and methods are feasible. Data sets that are very small probably shouldn't be mined using sampling methods; data sets that are very large (petabytes?) might require schedule extensions, special hardware/software, etc.
What is this question seeking?	This question is trying to assess the data complexity of the data mining problem.
Likely responses and their meanings	Answers to this question are usually very precise; users understand their metadata pretty well.
Follow-up questions	Is documentation available on the data?
Special considerations	The rate at which the data set is growing/shrinking should be known, and is relevant to whether your work will scale.

Question 15: How is this data currently stored, and how do we get it?	
Why is this question important?	This question is really asked to initiate a discussion of how the data will be made available to you.
What is this question seeking?	How will you get the data, and in what form will it be? If possible, get the user to extract working data for you. Ask to be present.
Likely responses and their meanings	You usually don't get complete answers to this the first time you ask. They'll probably have to get back to you.
Follow-up questions	Are there existing tools that you can use to extract the data, or must you create access tools from scratch?
Special considerations	The fact that data exist doesn't mean you can get access to it. There might be security concerns, proprietary issues, privacy issues, and even turf wars within the user's organization. Be prepared for delays.

Question 16: What are the baseline sample rates and sizes (samples per second, bits per sample)?	
Why is this question important?	You must know the data formats and structure to properly interpret them.
What is this question seeking?	This question is asking for information on the data collection rate. This can be a performance driver for a predictive model that must run in real time.
Likely responses and their meanings	Ingest rates are usually precisely known.
Follow-up questions	What factors affect the samples rates?
Special considerations	There might be multiple legacy versions of the system that operate at different rates. Ask for documentation.

Question 17: What is the number of samples in a record?	
Why is this question important?	You need to know the data scale.
What is this question seeking?	How many samples constitute a record, for example?
Likely responses and their meanings	Ingest rates are usually precisely known.
Follow-up questions	What factors affect the number of samples in a record?
Special considerations	There might be multiple legacy versions of the system that have different numbers of samples in a record. Ask for documentation.

Question 18: What is the duration/rate of the sampling activity that produced the data you will be using?	
Why is this question important?	Asking this question provides an opportunity to sanity check the answers to other questions on rates and scales.
What is this question seeking?	You are trying to get another view of the scale of the problem that allows you to cross-check the others.
Likely responses and their meanings	Answers to this question are usually imprecise.
Follow-up questions	Is data available for a range of dates and durations? If the data available to you for mining are all from a single collection, they might not be representative.
Special considerations	Asking for the date of the collection lets you know whether the data are current or not. Have there been changes?

Question 19: Were collections taken under varying conditions?	
Why is this question important?	Authentic variety in the data is an essential requirement for building high fidelity models, and generalizable results.
What is this question seeking?	Do the data include instances of all cases? What scenarios or modes are not represented?
Likely responses and their meanings	Domain experts will be able to answer this question. Sometimes it is not possible to obtain data for multiple collections, and you have to work with what you get.
Follow-up questions	If the available data do not cover all scenarios, how will this be taken into account during the evaluation of this data mining project? Will you be graded on parts of the problem you did not see?
Special considerations	It might be necessary to build some mechanism to bring data from different scenarios or modes into conformation.

3.3.3 User Interface

Question 20: What kind of user interface is currently used?	
Why is this question important?	Data mining results will probably be fed back to the user by means of this interface.
What is this question seeking?	Does the interface support presentation of graphics, tables, hyperlinked prose? Or is it a primitive text interface? Is there a standard means to use it (e.g., an API)?
Likely responses and their meanings	Users can often describe the user interface in detail, and might be able to demonstrate it. Ask for a demo.
Follow-up questions	Ask for copies of any user interface documents that might exist. Also, how would the user like data mining results presented?
Special considerations	Modifying a user interface is usually politically too hard, since this affects all users. Sometimes it is better to provide results in a data mining report the user can open in a browser or editor.

Question 21: Who are the end users, and how sophisticated are they?	
Why is this question important?	If the end users are technical experts, they might be interested in detailed technical results.
What is this question seeking?	You are trying to determine how detailed data mining reporting should be. In particular, more sophisticated users might want to interact directly with data mining applications to specify complex displays and reports, etc.
Likely responses and their meanings	Users usually know whether detailed technical information from a data mining application will be useful to them.
Follow-up questions	What is the general level of education/training of the average user?
Special considerations	It is usually a good idea to hide complexity from the user unless they express an interest or need for it.

Question 22: How do users use the system?	
Why is this question important?	You want to get a feel for the manner in which user systems are operated, who uses them, and for what purposes.
What is this question seeking?	The most important information to get here is about the amount of interaction the user expects. Will they need status updates frequently? How often? What action will these updates enable?
Likely responses and their meanings	This question can usually be answered in detail.
Follow-up questions	It might be possible for you to see the system in operation. Also, request any documentation that describes the system's Concept of Operation (CONOP).
Special considerations	Ask to watch a user in an actual work situation.

Question 23: How will the data mining solution be integrated?	
Why is this question important?	You will need to know whether you are creating applications/models/methods that will be integrated into the operational flow, and how. Will it be by DLLs, stand-alone applications, server-based network access, web-enablement, Application Programming Interfaces (API), operational changes, etc.?
What is this question seeking?	The method of integration will determine how your work is handed to the system.

(Continued on following page)

Question 23: How will the data mining solution be integrated? (*continued*)	
Likely responses and their meanings	Users generally want data mining applications to run separately from their operational systems (to reduce operational cost and risk). This means that data mining results are usually placed in machine readable reports, or written to a database rather than sent directly to the user.
Follow-up questions	Is there an API for the system?
Special considerations	The biggest problem encountered in modern integration efforts is configuration control of interface specs and software versions. Be sure to get information of versions of drivers and database releases with which you have to interact.

Question 24: In what form do users want the output: visualization, reports, soft/hard copy?	
Why is this question important?	Users need information in a form that is compatible with their work processes; they will not accept unwieldy or incompatible help that causes them additional work.
What is this question seeking?	You want to know how to add value to the workflow, or, at least, how not to impede it.
Likely responses and their meanings	This can vary from user to user. Talk to several and look for a good compromise.
Follow-up questions	Ask for examples of output styles and formats that users like.
Special considerations	In some cases, it might make sense to consider personalization; that is, adjusting the output style for each user according to a profile. But this can be expensive to implement.

Question 25: Do users want/need confidence factors or Conclusion Justification Reports (CJR's)?	
Why is this question important?	People might be reluctant to make critical decisions based upon the advice of a machine unless they have some notion of the basis of the machine's recommendation.
What is this question seeking?	Is a conclusion justification report of some kind needed as part of the output? What information should it provide? Must numeric confidence be provided, and how should this be expressed (e.g., as a probability, a %, etc.)?
Likely responses and their meanings	Different users will give different answers. Discuss with the chief expert.

(*Continued on following page*)

Question 25: Do users want/need confidence factors or Conclusion Justification Reports (CJR's)? (*continued*)	
Follow-up questions	If numeric measures of confidence are desired, ask how they will be used. This will help determine how they should be computed.
Special considerations	Users probably don't have a deep knowledge of probability theory; do not expect them to be able to correctly interpret complex information; reporting incomprehensible information does more harm than good.

3.3.4 Covering Blind Spots

Question 26: Why hasn't this problem been solved?	
Why is this question important?	If the problem is important to the user, they have probably tackled it before. If there is some heretofore insurmountable obstacle, you want to know that.
What is this question seeking?	You don't want to retry things that are known not to work. You want to be able to talk to others who have worked the problem previously.
Likely responses and their meanings	Sometimes failure has political/logistical causes, such as insufficient resources or lack of data. Realize that if the problem is technically difficult, the user might not know why previous work was unsuccessful.
Follow-up questions	Ask whether the user has a proposed solution to any political/logistical challenges.
Special considerations	Answers to this question can provide insight into areas most likely to be trouble spots; this can help with project planning.

Question 27: What are the three most important things to know about this problem?	
Why is this question important?	Vague questions like this flush out issues you don't know enough to ask about.
What is this question seeking?	You are trying to determine what the user thinks is most important about the project.
Likely responses and their meanings	Answers will either be a reiteration of what you've already been told, or complete surprises.
Follow-up questions	If something new pops up in the answer to this question, chase it down with additional questions.
Special considerations	This is a shot in the dark, but it can uncover some valuable information that might otherwise be overlooked.

Question 28: What questions have I not asked that I should have asked?	
Why is this question important?	This is another vague question intended to draw out issues not yet discussed.
What is this question seeking?	You are trying to determine what the user thinks is most important about the project.
Likely responses and their meanings	Answers will either be a reiteration of what you've already been told, or complete surprises.
Follow-up questions	Issues that are often overlooked are Organizational (i.e., political) Considerations; Data security (need for anonymity, proprietary content, classification); and Legal Considerations (e.g., redlining, age/gender/cultural/religious discrimination)
Special considerations	This is a shot in the dark, but it can uncover some valuable information that might otherwise be overlooked. Be sure to ask specific questions to subject matter experts when in depth knowledge acquisition interviews cannot be performed.

3.3.5 Evaluating Domain Expertise

Question 29: What is your job?	
Why is this question important?	You want to position this expert within the domain. Do they have broad and deep experience? Are they a decision maker?
What is this question seeking?	Can this person speak definitively? Do they understand the needs of the user? Should I trust everything they tell me?
Likely responses and their meanings	Usually a job title, which is not very helpful.
Follow-up questions	Ask them to describe their workday duties and activities, and how these relate to the work of others.
Special considerations	Be careful not to offend; avoid making statements that might be interpreted as disparaging assessments of a person's role.

Question 30: What ten words best describe what you do?	
Why is this question important?	This is an open-ended question designed to give you some insight into this expert's view of the problem without requiring you to have any domain knowledge yourself.

(Continued on following page)

Question 30: What ten words best describe what you do? (*continued*)	
What is this question seeking?	This question often elicits lots of helpful information. Take particular note of what they say first, and anything they say more than once.
Likely responses and their meanings	Answers will vary widely.
Follow-up questions	Listen for acronyms, jargon, and unfamiliar terms. Ask for definitions.
Special considerations	This is one of the best starter questions you'll ever find.

Question 31: What skills are required to do your job?	
Why is this question important?	This question will give you insight into the complexity of the domain and some information about the level of sophistication of the user.
What is this question seeking?	If users need complex or special skills, you will probably need more contact with the domain expert.
Likely responses and their meanings	This will usually consist of a list of educational requirements and prior job experience.
Follow-up questions	Ask about the availability of training materials that are used to educate new domain experts. This could be useful.
Special considerations	Sophisticated users often want access to more detailed technical feedback from an application and more control over its operation. They also want to be able to limit feedback from an application when they don't need it.

Question 32: In what ways is your domain changing?	
Why is this question important?	This is a question about future proofing. You want to develop a solution that will not be quickly broken by foreseeable changes in the domain (e.g., switching operating systems, major hardware upgrades, and changes in operational procedures or organizational goals).
What is this question seeking?	You want to implement a solution in a way that ensures it will provide lasting value.
Likely responses and their meanings	Answers are usually vague, which is good.
Follow-up questions	Be sure to ask follow-up questions about any known changes.
Special considerations	Technical staff is not always fully informed on organizational plans.

3.3.6 Tools

Question 33: How would you describe your work area (tools, books, layout, etc.)?	
Why is this question important?	Experts often keep useful backup tools in their workspace. They usually won't mention these unless they are specifically asked.
What is this question seeking?	Is there some document, book, or software tool that would help you understand the domain better?
Likely responses and their meanings	Experts usually like to talk about their favorite tools.
Follow-up questions	Get document references (URLs, and ISBN numbers, etc.).
Special considerations	It is probably worth taking a look at an expert's workspace if you have time. You might see something worth asking about (books, papers, etc.).

Question 34: How would you describe the perfect system (look, feel, functionality, performance, etc.)?	
Why is this question important?	You can uncover lots of hidden expectations with this question.
What is this question seeking?	What kind of user experience would be ideal? Is there some killer app function that you might be able to incorporate into your solution? Is there a preferred color scheme? (Sometimes this really matters to people, but they'll rarely say so.)
Likely responses and their meanings	You can often flush out unstated requirements this way. Listen carefully.
Follow-up questions	This is a question worth asking again later in the project.
Special considerations	Be sure to ask about anything said that is mysterious or unclear.

Question 35: How do your current systems fall short of the perfect system?	
Why is this question important?	What is the current system lacking?
What is this question seeking?	You will need to know what the current system can't do so that you don't build a solution that expects it to exceed its capabilities.
Likely responses and their meanings	No, the system is perfect. The usual response is short and vague.
Follow-up questions	If some unexpected limitation is mentioned, ask about it.
Special considerations	The answers to this question will be anecdotal.

3.3.7 Methodology

Question 36: How would you describe your typical workday?	
Why is this question important?	This will help you understand the expert's work load, work process, resource set, and problem solving methods.
What is this question seeking?	Intelligent systems must mesh with the work style of the user. Understanding this style will help you create applications that do this.
Likely responses and their meanings	Domain experts usually give excellent renditions of their daily activities.
Follow-up questions	Ask for definitions of unfamiliar terms, acronyms, processes, or names that come up.
Special considerations	Be cognizant of the sensitive nature of this question.

3.3.8 Needs

Question 37: Do you have enough time to do what you need to do?	
Why is this question important?	This will let you know the level of availability of experts.
What is this question seeking?	If people are already pressed for time, you don't want to provide a time consuming solution, even if it is technically sound.
Likely responses and their meanings	Expect an honest answer.
Follow-up questions	If time allowed to do required work is not enough, ask why. This might provide some useful insight into system inefficiencies.
Special considerations	Be cognizant of the sensitive nature of this question.

Question 38: What are five things that are impossible in your domain?	
Why is this question important?	If the domain expert thinks something is impossible, it probably is (though not always).
What is this question seeking?	You want to avoid incorporating impossible processes into your proposed solution!
Likely responses and their meanings	Domain experts usually have a couple of examples of this.

(Continued on following page)

Question 38: What are five things that are impossible in your domain? (*continued*)	
Follow-up questions	Ask for details if it isn't clear why something is impossible; there could be useful information there.
Special considerations	That which is impossible to one expert, may only be a challenge to another expert.

Question 39: If you controlled the R&D budget, what kind of developments would you fund?	
Why is this question important?	This will tell you what this domain expert believes is most important.
What is this question seeking?	You might have a serendipitous opportunity to do something about this problem.
Likely responses and their meanings	Most domain experts will have a pet problem they would like to see addressed.
Follow-up questions	Follow up if there seems to be value there.
Special considerations	Be cognizant of the sensitive nature of this question.

Question 40: What is the biggest obstacle to success in your domain?	
Why is this question important?	If there are hidden obstacles, the sooner you know about them the better.
What is this question seeking?	Are there precautions that should be taken to avoid unseen problems?
Likely responses and their meanings	Answers are more likely to be related to logistics and policy than technology.
Follow-up questions	Ask for specific examples of non-obvious obstacles to success.
Special considerations	Remain cognizant of the sensitive nature of this question. Answers should probably not be shared with others.

Question 41: What data are most useful? Least useful? Why?	
Why is this question important?	Domain experts often have a good feel for which data are most informative.
What is this question seeking?	Which features are most likely to be helpful, and which are least likely to be helpful.

(*Continued on following page*)

Question 41: What data are most useful? Least useful? Why? (*continued*)	
Likely responses and their meanings	Domain experts can usually answer this question, but their answers might not be accurate with respect to data mining.
Follow-up questions	You might ask the domain expert to list the five or more best features.
Special considerations	Keep in mind that what is useful to a human might not be useful to a black-box algorithm, and vice versa.

Question 42: What are your three most difficult problems?	
Why is this question important?	This will give insight into the things that are most difficult in the problem domain.
What is this question seeking?	We would like to know what is difficult even for the human to do.
Likely responses and their meanings	Could be just about anything, but usually involves more logistic and policy problems than technology problems.
Follow-up questions	Are any of these addressed by our data mining project?
Special considerations	Domain experts are skeptical of claims that automation can solve problems they cannot. Better not to insult them with unfounded claims.

3.4 Candidate Solution Checklist

3.4.1 What Type of Data Mining Must the System Perform?

Data mining processes operate on data to provide two basic types of decision support. First, they help the user obtain domain understanding; and, second they enable appropriate user action. Underlying these operations are various types of machine reasoning, each implemented by a particular type of reasoner. Each reasoner has an architecture that is driven by the type of reasoning it must perform. To determine what type of system should be built, we must determine what type of reasoning it will have to do. If this question isn't answered properly, the data mining effort is unlikely to succeed.

Here we briefly describe five pure reasoners, and suggest hybrids for particular types of reasoning problems.

Reasoner	Description
Classifiers	Classifiers ingest a list of attributes, and determine into which of finitely many categories the entity exhibiting these attributes falls. Automatic target recognition and next-event prediction are examples of this type of reasoning.
Estimators	Estimators ingest a list of attributes, and assign some numeric value to the entity exhibiting these attributes. The estimation of a probability or a risk score is an example of this type of reasoning.
Semantic Mappers	Semantic mappers ingest symbolic data (usually structured text, unstructured text, or both), and generate a data structure that gives the meaning of the text. Automatic gisting of documents is an example of this type of reasoning (i.e., the Google search engine is an example of a relatively weak semantic mapper). Semantic mapping generally requires some kind of domain ontology.
Planners	Planners ingest a scenario description, and formulate an efficient sequence of feasible actions that will move the domain to the specified goal state.
Associators	Associators sample the entire corpus of domain data, and identify relationships among entities. Automatic clustering of data to identify coherent subpopulations is a simple example. A more sophisticated example is the forensic analysis of phone, flight, and financial records to infer the structure of money laundering networks.

3.4.2 Multifaceted Problems Demand Multifaceted Solutions

Hard problems are often hard because their solutions cannot be readily obtained by pure reasoners, and because the integration of multiple pure reasoners is problematic.

Suppose that a machine reasoner is being built to perform/support a complex recognition problem for which some data have been collected. We would like it to be a multifaceted application that provides full or partial answers to the following kinds of questions:

1. What kind of entity (e.g., customer) is present here? (Classifier categorizes this event based upon available features)
2. Is all of the evidence consistent, or is something unusual here? (Estimator generates novelty score, tags unusual facts)
3. Is there relevant content in this corpus of web traffic? (Semantic Mapper gists unstructured text)

4. What are the likely next events in the domain? (Planner extends the scenario into the immediate future)
5. Has this set of facts been observed before? When and Where? (Associator performs complex fuzzy spatiotemporal match)

A system able to automatically handle all of these questions would integrate certain aspects of each of the five pure reasoners described above. In fact, even pair wise combinations of pure reasoners can provide benefit (e.g., integrating a classifier with a semantic mapper yields a system that can categorize entities, and justify its reasoning.)

3.4.3 The Nature of the Data

Once the problem to be addressed has been characterized, we turn our attention to the raw material available for its solution: domain data. Information can be bound in data in different ways, and data come in many forms. The domain data must be characterized so that proper methods and tools are selected. Because we are still in the Problem Definition Step of the data mining project, the data characterization being described here is mostly a paper exercise, supported perhaps by an informal descriptive analysis of the data. Refinement of this characterization by deeper analysis comes in a later step. This section is focused on the question "What is the nature of the data that will support the reasoning?"

Here are some starter questions that we have about each data field. Most are just short answer (e.g., one or two words), some require discourse, and some might be irrelevant for some data fields.

Question 43: What is the enterprise source of this data field (e.g., database, application, guess)?	
Why is this question important?	This is your entry to ask questions about the pedigree of the data.
What is this question seeking?	Do the data come from one source along one path? Or, do they arrive from different sources, perhaps at different times? In particular, is the data repository distributed? If so, there might be conformation and/or synchronization problems.
Likely responses and their meanings	This is usually well documented.
Follow-up questions	Ask for documentation on the data sources and paths.
Special considerations	This information might be proprietary. Handle it with care.

Question 44: What does this data field mean?	
Why is this question important?	You are looking for some intuitive explanation of the data field; field names tend to be jargonized, and this question will help you make sure you know what the field actually is.
What is this question seeking?	If you know what the field means, you are more likely to detect erroneous data, and more likely to be able to form synthetic features that make physical sense.
Likely responses and their meanings	Domain experts can usually give good answers to this question.
Follow-up questions	Ask for documentation on the data that goes to the level of individual data fields.
Special considerations	If unfamiliar terms are used, ask about them.

Question 45: What are the possible values for this data field (nominal/numeric, ranges)?	
Why is this question important?	You will want to incorporate some kind of range checking into your data validation methodology.
What is this question seeking?	What are the valid ranges for each data item?
Likely responses and their meanings	This is usually well known to domain experts. Ask for data format and schema documentation.
Follow-up questions	Be sure to ask about units being used (i.e., there are about ten different ways to express latitude and longitude).
Special considerations	If any unfamiliar terms are mentioned, ask about them.

Question 46: Why is this data field collected?	
Why is this question important?	This will help you understand more precisely what kind of information this data field conveys.
What is this question seeking?	This is a question to help you develop an intuitive understanding of the type of information contained in each data field.
Likely responses and their meanings	Domain experts might know the answer to this question. But particular data fields might be used in different ways by different people.
Follow-up questions	Ask for data documentation.
Special considerations	If any unfamiliar terms are mentioned, ask about them.

Question 47: Who uses this data field, and how?	
Why is this question important?	This gets at the type of information the feature carries.
What is this question seeking?	Is this feature valuable?
Likely responses and their meanings	Domain experts will be able to answer this question.
Follow-up questions	If this feature has special significance for some application, try to determine what that is.
Special considerations	If any unfamiliar terms are mentioned, ask about them.

Question 48: Is this data field related to other data fields? What are these relationships?	
Why is this question important?	Interrelationships between data fields signal opportunities for dimension reduction by either discarding one if they are highly correlated, or merging them to synthesize a single, more powerful feature.
What is this question seeking?	Is there a way to exploit known relationships among the data?
Likely responses and their meanings	Domain experts will have an intuitive sense of this, but will probably not be able to quantify it.
Follow-up questions	Run descriptive statistics to directly measure inter-feature correlation.
Special considerations	If any unfamiliar terms are mentioned, ask about them.

Question 49: Does this data field always have a value? What does it mean when this field is missing?	
Why is this question important?	The answer to this question will drive your degapping strategy.
What is this question seeking?	What should I do when this data field is empty?
Likely responses and their meanings	Answer will be different for each data field.
Follow-up questions	What does it mean if this data field is empty?
Special considerations	Sometimes the fact that a data field is empty is itself meaningful.

Question 50: How is this data field collected (e.g., customer form, verbal, data entry)?	
Why is this question important?	The collection methodology is a good indicator of data fidelity (accuracy, completeness)
What is this question seeking?	How reliable is this data? If it is unreliable, it should not become a pivotal feature in a model.
Likely responses and their meanings	This is usually understood by domain experts.
Follow-up questions	Ask for documentation on data collection processes.
Special considerations	This information is probably proprietary. Handle it with care.

Question 51: How was the raw data for this data field coded/transformed/formatted?	
Why is this question important?	If the data have been altered or conditioned in some way, you'll want to know.
What is this question seeking?	Naïve data conditioning can destroy information content; you might have to ask for the raw data.
Likely responses and their meanings	Experts might misunderstand this question, since the definition of "raw" is a matter of perspective.
Follow-up questions	Ask for documentation of the data conditioning process.
Special considerations	If any unfamiliar terms are mentioned, ask about them.

Question 52: How repeatable is this data field (if it was collected again, would we get the same value?)?	
Why is this question important?	Are the data stable? That is, do they vary significantly in range, type, variability, etc., over time? For example, are there seasonal or other known trends? If not, getting repeatable models using them will be difficult.
What is this question seeking?	How volatile is the domain, and how reliable is the data collection?
Likely responses and their meanings	This is a good time to ask questions about data collection problems such as noise, fidelity, precision, etc.
Follow-up questions	Ask for documentation on the phenomenology that the data are quantifying.
Special considerations	If any unfamiliar terms are mentioned, ask about them.

3.5 Problem Definition Task 2: Characterizing Your Solution

Having characterized the domain problem and the data available, we are now in a position to characterize our solution. We want to know: What will an effective solution look like?

This will include a description of the desired operation of the solution (Concept of Operation, or CONOP), but must go farther. A structured sequence of questions for selecting the best paradigm for solving an intelligent system problem is in chapter 6 (presented by the author at the 2003 International Data Mining Conference of the Society of Industrial and Applied Mathematics).

3.5.1 Candidate Solution Checklist

Question 53: What is the concept of operation of the current system?	
Why is this question important?	Any solution that you provide will have to be interoperable with current system components.
What is this question seeking?	This will provide insight into the ways that applications are expected to interact with the system and the user.
Likely responses and their meanings	Domain experts will be able to give detailed answers to this question.
Follow-up questions	There are sometimes CONOP documents. Ask for this.
Special considerations	It is often helpful to see a live demonstration of the system in operation. Ask about this.

Question 54: What is the ground truth (e.g., class names/categories, numeric scores)?	
Why is this question important?	What is the nature of the answer the data mining solution is expected to provide?
What is this question seeking?	Is it providing a classification? A numeric score? A plan? What do these look like?
Likely responses and their meanings	Ask for any documentation that might be available on the desired ground truth datum.
Follow-up questions	Is the definition of ground truth likely to change in the future, say, with the addition of new classification categories, or plan types?
Special considerations	If any unfamiliar terms are mentioned, ask about these.

Question 55: Should the system produce confidence factors with each decision?	
Why is this question important?	If they want confidence factors, you will have to provide them.
What is this question seeking?	Is a method for computing confidence factors needed? What type of confidence does the user need (probability, quality score, etc.)?
Likely responses and their meanings	Users probably haven't given this any thought. Don't expect an immediate answer.
Follow-up questions	What type of quality metrics should your application provide?
Special considerations	If any unfamiliar terms are mentioned, ask about them.

Question 56: Should the system be able to explain its decisions (CJR)?	
Why is this question important?	In critical decision support situations, user might need insight into how an automated recommendation was made.
What is this question seeking?	What kind of explanation facility must your application provide?
Likely responses and their meanings	Users probably haven't given this much thought. You might have to show them examples of the types of reports you can produce.
Follow-up questions	Must explanations be provided only for the recommended choice, or for all choices (i.e., why certain choices were not_recommended)?
Special considerations	If any unfamiliar terms are mentioned, ask about them.

Question 57: What would cause the user to accept/reject the system?	
Why is this question important?	If there are any functional or performance show stoppers, you want to know.
What is this question seeking?	You want to make certain you don't make a design decision that guarantees failure even if your solution works technically.
Likely responses and their meanings	Domain users will have some suggestions.
Follow-up questions	Try asking several users about this.
Special considerations	If any unfamiliar terms are mentioned, ask about them.

3.6 Problem Definition Case Study

This case study shows an initial but relatively detailed four part description of a predictive modeling effort put together as a problem definition statement. This is an extensive and detailed case study covering all of Section 3.6. The project was to analyze the historical behaviors of the clients of a large, international company, and create signatures and a computer model that could be used to predict which clients might be about to drop their accounts (that is, were about to *attrit*). This was intended to be an early warning system that would enable account managers to proactively engage quiet but unhappy clients.

   This four part statement served several purposes:

1. It helped the data mining researcher document what seemed to be a reasonable approach to the project in a form that could be passed around and critiqued by others.
2. It established a general scope of work that was used to help determine cost, schedule, and staffing for the effort
3. It established a set of talking points as the basis for additional discussions with the customer.

   It opens with a glossary, lays out the project concept, proposes two very general use cases, describes project technical and administrative roles, and offers a summary description of the fundamental technologies being considered for the project: an expert system and a Radial Basis Function (RBF) classifier.

3.6.1 Predictive Attrition Model: Summary Description

3.6.2 Glossary

Term	Definition
AJL	Attrition Jeopardy List: list of clients and corresponding numeric attrition risk scores
CEM	Cognitive Engineering Methodology
CH	Case Histories: summary reports of past outcomes for various RM actions
CJR	Conclusion Justification Report: prose explanation system belief that client is at risk
CONOP	Concept of Operations: way that client and system will usually interact; similar to a script
ICA	Independent Component Analysis
IE	Inference Engine: component of KBES that selects and applies rules
KBES	Knowledge-Based Expert System: system that reasons using rules generated by humans

3.6.2 Glossary (continued)

Term	Definition
KE	Knowledge Engineering: methodology for constructing effective KBES
ATM	Attrition Model
PCA	Principal Component Analysis
RAL	Recommended Action List: case-appropriate actions for RM to avert attrition
RM	Retention Manager: expert assigned to reduce attrition for particular clients
TBD	To Be Determined
TBR	To Be Refined

3.6.3 The ATM Concept

Before proceeding with a detailed look at the advanced technology underlying the ATM implementation, the system is described from the user's point of view. This operational functionality determines how the system looks and feels to the user.

Operationally, the RM (Retention Manager) will select all or part of their assigned clients to assess for current attrition risk. The ATM system will process these clients using the most recent available information. An Attrition Jeopardy List (AJL) will be prepared, showing the selected clients ordered by current relative attrition risk, with numeric risk scores displayed. Optionally, a Conclusion Justification Report (CJR) can be automatically prepared by ATM explaining the rationale for any selected client in the AJL. Optionally, a Recommended Action List (RAL) for the RM to take can be prepared for any selected client in the AJL. Optionally, available Case Histories (CH) for similar past scenarios and their outcomes can be retrieved for any selected client in the AJL.

3.6.4 Operational Functions

The ATM system has two principal goals: analyze available information to identify clients at risk of attrition, and provide support for system administration. Retention managers will be assessing attrition risk, while the ATM system administrator will be managing the system.

Risk. This is the operational path followed by the general user: specify a group of clients to assess, perform the attrition risk assessment for a specified subset of those clients accessible to the user, display the CJR (Conclusion Justification Report), display the Recommended Action List (RAL), retrieve CH reports on similar cases, and create complex reports.

Administration. This is the path followed by the system administrator in performing maintenance functions: run diagnostics (conventional and cognitive), manage user accounts, maintain the database, process system logs, and retrain the cognitive engine.

- Concept of Operation (CONOP)
- General User (usually RMs)

The general user's goal is to obtain information that can be used to reduce client attrition. This includes identification of clients at risk of attrition; review, evaluation, and selection of preventive action; and the production of risk assessment reports.

A typical general user scenario is:

1. Login (provide password which determines level of access and privileges)
2. RISK
   a. Select a subset of accessible clients for risk assessment
   b. Set processing parameters (number of AJL entries, AJL inclusion conditions, AJL format preference)
   c. Process the selected list to obtain the AJL (Attrition Jeopardy List), which is a list of N clients having the greatest attrition risk, formatted/sorted according to user preference.
   d. Display/print CJR for selected AJL list members
   e. Display/print RAL for selected AJL list members
   f. Display/print CH for selected AJL list members
   g. Specify and create complex reports
3. EXIT (cleanup, save, close)

Items 1, 2a – 2d, and 3 are created during build 1; implementation of items 2e – 2g will be part of later builds.

System Administrator

The system administrator's goal is to maintain the system for the general users. This includes creating and managing user accounts, review of system logs, maintenance of the database, performance of diagnostics, and retraining of cognitive components as required.

A typical system administration scenario is:

1. Login (provide password which determines level of access and privileges)
2. ADMIN
   a. Review logs for operational anomalies
   b. Create/delete user accounts
   c. Adjust scope and privileges of user accounts
   d. Application software maintenance (TBR)
   e. Database maintenance (TBR)
   f. Cognitive diagnostics (TBR; e.g., regression tests)

      g. Select training set
      h. Retrain cognitive engine(s)
      i. Create administrative reports
  3. EXIT (cleanup, save, close)

Build 1 will provide items 1, 2a – 2i, and 3. Implementation of items 2d – 2f will be part of later builds.

GUI. Top level screens

The system will use a Motif Graphical User Interface (GUI). The main screen will have a master toolbar with the following buttons: RISK, ADMIN, EXIT, HELP, ABOUT

The RISK display will appear when the RISK button is selected on the main screen.

The RISK display will have a toolbar with the following buttons: SELECT, PROCESS, CJR, ACTION, HISTORY, REPORTS.

The ADMIN display will appear when the ADMIN button is selected on the main screen. The ADMIN display will have a toolbar with the following buttons: ACCOUNTS, DIAGNOSTICS, LOGS, DBASE, and RETRAIN.

Selecting EXIT on the main screen causes the application to terminate, returning the user to the operating system monitor.

Selecting the HELP button will activate context sensitive help (TBR).

Selecting the ABOUT button will cause a message box with versioning information to appear.

3.6.5 Predictive Modeling and ATM

One of the most attractive facets of modern data mining applications is the insight they give into the business process, making possible the development of predictive models. Predictive models can use human knowledge and historical data to make forecasts about future states and conditions of the systems they represent. For example, predictive models can use historical client behaviors to estimate the relative likelihood of attrition during the next prediction period. In a complex competitive market, a model that anticipates client attrition enables retention managers to focus their attention on valuable at-risk clients in time to reduce the probability that their accounts will be lost.

    Predictive models can use conventional methods (control charts, GANNT charts, spreadsheets, etc.), but these are largely manual. The ATM system will use an automated cognitive engine for high-end predictive modeling, and will employ both knowledge-based and neural network techniques:

- **Knowledge-Based Expert System (KBES).** Rule-based systems which use heuristics obtained from human domain experts to codify expert knowledge for incorporation into predictive models. These models capture rare, perishable human expertise in executable form, so that it can be retained, copied, and enhanced by successive generations of human experts. This *brain power in a box* will work in any location (or every location), and can run 24 hours a day. If built with the ability to explain its decisions, such a system can also be used as a training tool. KBES can be constructed with the ability to explain their decisions to human users.
- **Radial Basis Functions (RBF)—Predictive models based upon one of the many RBF paradigms.** Partitions of unity, restricted coulomb energy methods and adaptive taxonomic classifiers, etc.; these models can be retrained to take changing market conditions into account. KBES and neural systems are technically mature, natural choices for attrition risk estimation. Used in combination, they are very effective.

3.6.6 Cognitive Systems and Predictive Modeling

Cognitive systems—an overview. One of the great advantages that humans have over conventional technology automated systems is their ability to learn by experience. Using cognitive engineering methods, machines can be given this ability. Machine learning may be defined as the *organization of domain knowledge into formal, machine resident, executable structures.* An automated system which implements such machine learning, and which uses the executable structure so obtained to solve domain problems, is a *cognitive system.*

Cognitive systems acquire human knowledge in two ways: through passive learning, and through active learning. In passive learning, a Knowledge Engineer (KE) or domain expert manually encodes problem specific, expert level knowledge into a cognitive system, usually as rules. In active learning, the system itself organizes its experience during a training period.

In both active and passive learning, domain knowledge is bound into fundamental units of a type corresponding to the paradigm selected by the system developer. ATM will be constructed using two cognitive paradigms: the KBES, and the RBF. The KBES will apply known risk assessment heuristics, while the RBF will analyze the clients' complex historical behaviors. These two assessments will be combined using an aggregation rule, and the results reported to the user.

3.6.7 The ATM Hybrid Cognitive Engine

The cognitive engine for ATM will consist of two components: a Knowledge-Based Expert System (KBES), and a Radial Basis Function (RBF). The KBES uses rules derived from the experience and insight of human experts. Because this insight is intuitive to human users, this component is a white-box component. (White-box and black-box systems will be discussed in a later chapter.)

The RBF will use pattern recognition methods to exploit subtle and complicated historical patterns in client behaviors. Because these are not intuitive to human users, this component is a black-box component. For a given client, the risk assessment of the KBES will be combined with the risk assessment of the RBF to yield the client's final numeric attrition risk score.

KBES maintenance—rule editing. If business conditions change dramatically, or new factors are discovered that affect attrition assessment, it may be desirable to modify the rules used by the ATM KBES. This is accomplished using a rule editor.

- RBF for Attrition Modeling
- RBF Maintenance: Retraining

A retraining function will be included as an embedded function in ATM. The system administrator will prepare a structure containing the training data, and invoke the RETRAIN function. No other information or parameters are necessarily required to retrain the RBF.

3.6.8 Testing and Validation of Cognitive Systems

Cognitive systems are tested for software integrity using normal testing techniques (desk checking, path testing, domain testing, etc.). They are tested for functionality principally by blind testing. The purpose of testing is to insure that the engine is giving the right answers for the right reasons. For the ATM hybrid system, three testing regimens will be employed. The KBES will be tested separately, the RBF will be tested separately, and the hybrid will be tested as a unit. KBES testing will verify that the proper rule sequences are being executed, and that belief is properly aggregated and reported. Conflicts between rules will be resolved, and non-contributing rules will be eliminated. RBF testing will assess confusion matrices for test sets, and insure that belief is properly aggregated and reported.

Testing of the total hybrid engine will verify that the aggregation rule is functioning properly. In blind testing, subsets of data not used for development are processed by the engine, and the results compared with known outcomes. This kind of testing can be performed by general software developers; no special modeling expertise is required.

3.6.9 Spiral Development Methodology

Knowledge acquisition and integration. Knowledge acquisition and integration is part of the development cycle for cognitive systems, and is not repeated during normal maintenance. Changes in attrition indications can be modeled in ATM by editing KBES rules and retraining the RBF.

Knowledge acquisition occurs in interviews with human experts. The objective of the KA activity is the acquisition of unbiased domain knowledge pertinent to client retention. The domain experts will be customer personnel. Classical knowledge acquisition techniques will be used for the interview activities.

3.7 Summary

Having read this chapter, you know what information you must obtain before beginning a data mining spiral, and you know why this information is useful. You have been alerted to certain special considerations that apply in some situations, and you know what follow-up questions to ask. You now have a list of questions that you could carry into a meeting with a customer, domain expert, or user. You have also seen an example of a problem definition document in the Problem Definition Case Study.

Coming up

The next chapter presents an extensive, annotated checklist of questions that must be addressed in Step 2 of a data mining spiral, data evaluation. Items from the checklist can serve as the basis for a knowledge acquisition interview with a domain expert. Specific methods for data conditioning will be presented.

Chapter 4

Data Evaluation (Step 2)

Purpose

The practical purpose of this chapter is to characterize the information to be collected and organized during the data evaluation step of a data mining spiral. Rather than developing these ideas in prose from which the reader must extract actionable chunks, the material is presented as a topically organized checklist of questions to be addressed.

This chapter also describes some techniques for conducting the preliminary analysis of domain data (analysis that is done before the feature extraction step).

Goals

After you have read this chapter, you will know what information you must obtain using simple data analysis methods before beginning the feature extraction step of a data mining spiral. Most importantly, you will learn the basics of how to interpret *clustering* in a data set. This fundamental skill is essential to understanding how many data mining algorithms work.

4.1 Introduction

The following checklist describes what the data miner must discover about the data before feature extraction can be done. Some of the questions can be answered by a domain expert. But unlike the questions in previous checklists, many of these questions won't be posed for customers, users, or even domain experts. These questions have to be answered by the data itself, or by the data miner, using analytic techniques applied to the data.

Purpose of Data Evaluation: Produce an effective representation of the domain (data ingest and format)

Principal Participants and Their Tasks	
SE	Ingest data (e.g., plug in JAZ drive, download, spool, etc.)
SE	Format data (e.g. RDBMS, .CSV, etc.)
SE/CE	Validate, ingest, and format operations
CS/SE	Randomize record order
CS/SE	Sample data
CS/SE	Partition data

4.2 Data Accessibility Checklist

Question 1: Are the data Accessible, Correct, Salient, and Complete?	
Why is this question important?	You can't use data you can't get. You don't want to use data that are inaccurate. Data that are not relevant contain no information. Data that are incomplete produce solutions that are lacking.
What is this question seeking?	You want to know the semantic deficiencies of the data.
Likely responses and their meanings	Users' answers to this question are usually vague and unreliable. But this question exposes issues.
Follow-up questions	If specific issues are raised in any of these areas, you should follow up with additional questions.
Special considerations	Press for specifics. If you are told that data is available, ask "When, and from whom?" Get dates and names.

Question 2: How much data is available?	
Why is this question important?	This information is needed to determine the data scale of the effort. It drives the selection of tools and techniques, and affects cost and schedule.
What is this question seeking?	You are trying to determine the infrastructure needed to perform project work.
Likely responses and their meanings	Answers to this are usually vague at first, and become for specific a couple of weeks into an effort.

(Continued on following page)

Question 2: How much data is available? (*continued*)	
Follow-up questions	Ask for a data dictionary/database schema, and any metadata documents that might be available.
Special considerations	Low-level data issues can arise that are unlikely to be mentioned unless you ask about them specifically (Big/Little Endian, signed/unsigned integers, parity, line and record terminators, field delimiters, etc.) Ask about these.

Question 3: How much data is needed for the project?	
Why is this question important?	Users will have some notion of how much data would be needed, for example, to address certain analysis tasks manually.
What is this question seeking?	You want an initial estimate of how much data will be needed to achieve results.
Likely responses and their meanings	Answers will generally be underestimates of what is needed for data mining, because experts won't be allowing for validation sets, bad records, etc. Take what they give you and double it.
Follow-up questions	Are there multiple versions of the data? Do we need data from every version?
Special considerations	The physical management of large data can be costly and time consuming.

Question 4: How often is the data updated, if ever? How and why is this done?	
Why is this question important?	The tempo of the data (collection times, refresh rates, age) introduces a time element into the mining process that must be taken into consideration.
What is this question seeking?	You are trying to determine how stable the data are. For example, If you are given old data, is it still valid for mining? Also, events like system upgrades often ripple through the data. Has this happened? When might it happen again?
Likely responses and their meanings	You are trying to guard against data synchronization problems, and against temporal infeasibility (Chapter 1).
Follow-up questions	What events might trigger a data update/correction? Are the data synchronized/replicated across multiple systems? If so, does this affect the data mining project?
Special considerations	Date-time tags in data can be used to help establish a data pedigree; this can be very useful in mining.

Question 5: Is data needed to cover a range of parameters? (times, locations, types, situations)	
Why is this question important?	If there are ad hoc requirements on the problem, these must be known.
What is this question seeking?	You want to make sure you get data that cover the problem you are being asked to address.
Likely responses and their meanings	Answers must be unambiguous and specific, clearly describing the scenarios of interest.
Follow-up questions	Ask for documentation describing the operational modes of interest for the project. Get contact information for experts you can contact with questions.
Special considerations	Ad hoc requirements add substantial risk, and are cost drivers.

4.3 How Much Data Do You Need?

This is the same sort of question asked when someone says, "How much ore must you mine to get rich?" Answer: "It depends on the ore, your tools, and what *rich* means." In reality, this is a question that you can't answer with much definiteness until you get into the problem. What do you do?

A first-cut heuristic for the minimum number of data samples for modeling is something I call the *Six-M-N Rule* (written 6MN). It has all the strengths and weaknesses of any simplistic rule of thumb, but it works pretty well as a way to establish a lower bound on the number of data records needed for a data mining effort about which not much is known.

Let N be the number of ground truth classes if the data mining effort is building a classifier. If this isn't known, use the number of general categories of entities being studied. If this isn't known, let N = 2.

Let M be the number of data fields that are available for use as features. If this is unknown, let M be the number of records in the data divided by 16 (i.e., some of the data will be 8-bit characters, some will be 16-bit integers, and some will be 32-bit floats).

The 6MN Rule says you need a minimum of 6MN records to expect analysis to produce meaningful results. For example, suppose you are trying to build a classifier to distinguish between 4 different classes of customers, and each record has 10 fields of customer information that is feature worthy (e.g., don't count non-feature data such as phone numbers, etc.). Then I would set N = 5 (4 customer types, plus 1 for *other*), M = 10, and 6MN = 6×5×10 = 300 records. Knowing nothing else about the problem space, this is what I would propose as a minimum number of records for beginning analysis.

The rationale for this rule is that we want to have a mean and standard deviation in each data field for each class: demanding 3 values for a standard deviation for each of M fields gives 3*M, and doing this for every category gives 3MN. Doubling things for good measure gives 6MN.

Crude? Yes. Unprincipled? Definitely. However, an answer to the "How Much Data Will You Need" question is always demanded long before there is any rational basis for answering it. I have always found this simple estimate to provide a sufficient basis for being able to say something that is somewhat meaningful about a problem. Will this amount of data be sufficient to build a comprehensive, high-fidelity predictive or forensic model? Probably not, but it is usually enough to start minimally productive work. It will also allow you to work out interface and formatting issues, and start to generate some meaningful questions for later discussions.

4.4 Data Staging

Data must be organized, or staged, for feature extraction. This includes three activities: randomization, sampling, and partitioning.

Randomization refers to any process that eliminates associations that are side effects of the data collection and storage process. For example, if data are in a flat file (e.g., a spreadsheet) that has been sorted on some primary key (such as collection date, location, alphabetically, etc.), records will be ordered in a manner that could produce biased sets if they are sampled in a naïve way.

The randomization process could be as simple as resorting data on a field populated with random numbers. However, this is a critical process that should be given careful thought, because mistakes here could invalidate an entire project.

Sampling is the process of selecting a subset of the population (a *sample*) for analysis. It is important that each sample represent the entire population in an unbiased way. This can be a challenging problem; using large sample sizes provides some insulation against most errors. As with randomization, this must be done with extreme care.

Partitioning (Figure 4.1) is the principled division of data into subsets that are representative of the population. It is recommended that the data be partitioned into at least four groups as follows:

Partitioning of Data	
Calibration Set	This set serves as the basis for validation of meta-data, and derivation of descriptive statistics: means, variances, correlations, feature ranges, data quality estimates, etc. It is usually then added into the analysis set.
Analysis Set	This set is used for model development. Any classifiers, detectors, decision support applications, etc., will be developed using this data. It is the "training data."
Validation Set	This set is used to verify any discoveries made during analysis, and to determine the performance of any models created.
Hold-Back Set	This set is held by the user for blind testing of the delivered application, model, or conclusions. This set will only be present when there is plenty of data available.

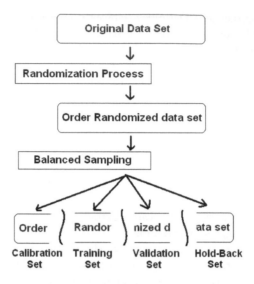

The Data Partitioning Process

Figure 4.1 The data partitioning process.

Each of these sets must be representative samples of the problem space within which the data mining results will be applied. This generally means that they are numerically balanced in the way they represent the problem, and are not skewed by sampling bias. For example, they will have the same proportion of each ground truth class as the population.

4.5 Methods Used for Data Evaluation

The Step 2 data evaluation is done for the purpose of developing intuition about the data. This is done prior to feature extraction. It should begin with actually looking at the data (at least some of it) using an editor or reader of some sort. I am still surprised by how few people do this, just blindly assuming that whatever was done to generate the data couldn't possibly have produced a file full of garbage.

Once we know that we actually have data, data evaluation is a matter of running a sequence of relatively simple tests that produce descriptive outputs. This usually includes generation of meta-data; estimation of correlation among the various data fields within the records; and coarse measures of data adequacy. Here is a notional list; in practice, this is domain dependent:

- Amount of data (number of files, number of records, number of fields in records, number of bytes in fields)
- Data types
- Data precisions
- Instances of missing data (outlier detection is discussed in Chapter 5)
- Simple charts and graphs (scatter plots, histograms, etc.)

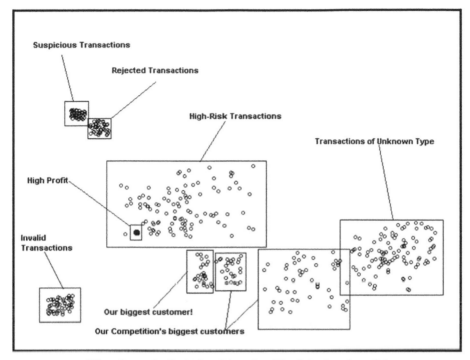

Suspicious Transactions

Rejected Transactions

High-Risk Transactions

Transactions of Unknown Type

High Profit

Invalid
Transactions

Our biggest customer!

Our Competition's biggest customers

When "meaning" can be determined for "clusters," useful patterns and discriminators can sometimes be revealed.

Figure 4.2   Pattern recognition and visualization.

As noted in Chapter 1, information is bound to data through some kind of variation/modulation, giving rise to informative patterns. The presence of patterns can be determined mathematically, but few automated pattern detectors can compete with what the human visual system does. This makes visualization an important indicator of the existence of patterns that might be exploitable. For two or three-dimensional data, clusters can sometimes be detected using simple scatter plots; for higher dimensional data, data can be plotted pair wise, or clustering algorithms can be used to characterize patterns that have extent in many dimensions (Figure 4.2).

4.6 Data Evaluation Case Study: Estimating the Information Content Features

This case study describes how a simple clustering algorithm can be used in a supervised learning mode to assist with feature selection. Because this is a very important aspect of data mining that really needs some automation, we will go into more detail than usual.

Recall that features are just measurements in some problem domain. For this discussion, we will assume:

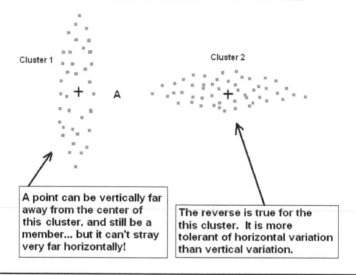

Here are two "clusters" of points in Euclidean space, each having its own shape. Each can be thought of as allowing a point to vary from the cluster center (+) by a certain amount and still be a member of the cluster.

Cluster 1

Cluster 2

A

A point can be vertically far away from the center of this cluster, and still be a member... but it can't stray very far horizontally!

The reverse is true for the this cluster. It is more tolerant of horizontal variation than vertical variation.

Figure 4.3   Clustered representation of selected feature set.

1. The data is in a comma-delimited spreadsheet (a CSV file). Each row is a feature vector (one data samole); each cell is one feature.
2. The data are numeric.
3. Column 1 provides row numbers used to identify the records (1, 2, 3, etc.).
4. The last column contains a positive integer that is a ground truth assignment for the row. Therefore, this data can be used for supervised learning (Chapter 9).

When many columns of data are available (i.e., each vector has many features), choosing the right ones to use is hard for a number of reasons:

1. Lots of columns means lots of dimensions when viewed geometrically.
2. The data in the columns can interact in complicated ways. For example, two weak pieces of evidence together sometimes provide more information than one strong piece of evidence alone.
3. There are a huge number of possible combinations in which columns could be chosen/rejected as features for a data mining project, so it is time-consuming (or impractical) to check them all. For example, if there are 30 columns, there are 2^{30}-1 > one billion ways to choose which subset of features to use for mining/modeling.

There are many ways to assess a subset of features for information content. A notional description of a Monte Carlo approach is now described. The information assessment begins by reading in the data to be analyzed, and computing the mean and standard deviation for each feature for each of the ground truth classes. That is, the mean and standard deviation are computed for each column for all the rows that are in ground truth class 1, giving the center and variability of the class 1 data; then, for class 2 data, and so on.

To determine which columns contain information useful for classification of the data into its ground truth classes, we test many possible subsets of the available columns while selecting subsets randomly, and keep track of which subset gives the best results for a weighted nearest neighbor classifier (described later). The process operates as follows:

Algorithm Phase A	
Step 1	Read in the data file.
Step 2	Segment into calibration, training, and validation files (row order randomized).
Step 3	Compute centers and standard deviations for each class in the calibration segment.

Algorithm Phase B	
Step 1	Select a subset of the columns to test (a *clique*)
Step 2	Use the centers and standard deviations computed in Phase A for the clique to assign each data point in the training segment to a class (weighted nearest-neighbor classifier).
Step 3	Compute performance statistics for this clique, i.e., its classification accuracy (% correct) on the training segment.

Repeat Phase B for many feature cliques. The features in the best clique (highest accuracy score on the test set) are the ones that, as a group, have the most useful information for classification of those tested. This winning team comprises our selected feature set. Figure 4.3 shows how cluster shape is related to how informative particular features are. Cluster 1 is tall and thin, and cluster 2 is short and wide.

A weighted nearest-neighbor classifier is based upon well-known statistical principles. It was chosen for this application for several reasons, but the most important is that no retraining is required when a new feature clique is to be evaluated; features not selected are ignored in the calculation. This makes it possible to run a large number of clique tests very quickly.

Consider a point located as position A. Should it be assigned to cluster 1 or cluster 2? A slightly harder example is depicted in Figure 4.4, along with an objective measurement that will help us answer this question.

To take the shape of each class into account, the standard deviation, denoted by the Greek letter Sigma (σ) is computed for each class, along each feature (Figure 4.5). This is a built-in computation in many spreadsheets. The standard deviation expresses the variability in a data set, and is often used for data normalization (z-scores) and detection of outliers in data (discussed later in this chapter).

The cluster on the left is less tolerant of variation along the horizontal direction than the cluster on the right, because the left cluster is narrower along this direction. Similarly, the right cluster is less tolerant of vertical variation, because it is shorter vertically.

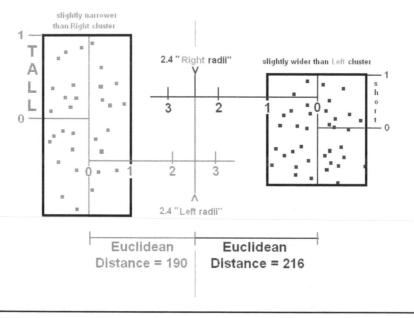

Figure 4.4   Tolerance of variation in clusters.

Using the standard deviations in each feature for a class cluster, a weighted distance can be computed from the center of that class to any point in the feature space (Figure 4.6). If the data cluster in a natural way, this weighted distance can be used to determine how a point should be classified: just assign it to the class that has the closest cluster in this weighted distance (Figure 4.7).

If the data classes do not form nice clusters, some pathological conditions can arise. This method of evaluating features is fast and simple, but not perfect (Figure 4.8).

To create a numeric measure of the classification power of a subset of the available features, this very fast weighted nearest-neighbor classifier is run repeatedly on a calibration set with various sets of features, and the best collection is remembered. Also, if the same feature appears in many high-performing feature sets, we conclude that it is probably good. In this way, the clustering algorithm described here is used to game feature sets in a *Monte Carlo* fashion.

This particular application prints out a spreadsheet report giving the classification power of various feature sets (Figure 4.9). In the figure below, 1 means the column feature was present in that set, while 0 means it was not. The application has tried all 32 of the possible feature cliques for this 5-dimensional data. This output gives the performance measures for all of them so the user can see the value of including/excluding the various feature combinations.

The performance of each feature clique is shown in a row of Figure 4.9; a 0 means the feature was excluded, and a 1 means the feature was included. For example, row 23 shows that it is possible to get 86.13% of the points correctly classified using only features 2, 3, and 5.

4.7 Some Simple Data Evaluation Methods

When working in new domains, it can be difficult to determine the best technical approach. Rather than trying to make all the methodological, tool selection, staffing, and algorithmic decisions before the data are understood, it is sometimes best to begin a spiral development using several approaches in parallel, and comparing their results before making a commitment to any single data mining strategy (Figure 4.10).

As demonstrated in Figure 4.9, this auditioning process can be used for feature selection. This process can be used for making all sorts of choices for which there is no clear cut decision process (Figure 4.10). To see how this method can be applied to a slightly different problem, a bulleted procedure is given for obtaining an empirical answer to the following question: if a new data source becomes available, will using it make an existing model better, or not?

The elements of the plan are arranged in the order in which they are to be carried out, beginning with experiment definition. For specificity, the goal in this example is to

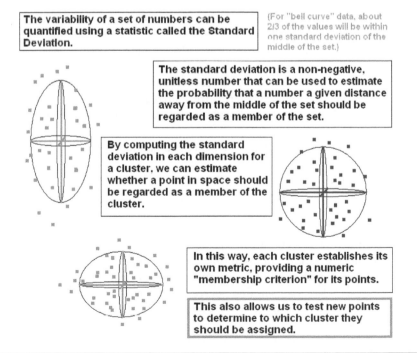

Figure 4.5   Standard deviation and variability of data.

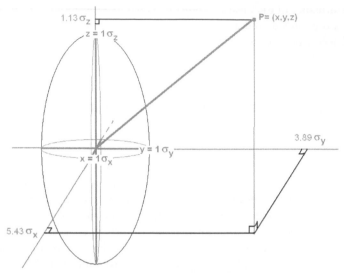

In the coordinate system established by this cluster,

$$P(x,y,z) = (5.43\,\sigma_x, 3.89\,\sigma_y, 1.13\sigma_z)$$

The distance from P to the cluster center, therefore, is:

$$\sqrt{(5.43^2 + 3.89^2 + 1.13^2)} = 6.77$$

Figure 4.6   Weighted distance computation for points in feature space.

determine whether adding data from a new source, call it B, to the existing feature data from source A can improve model performance. Cubist and C5 are rule induction applications: they learn classification rules directly from data that is tagged with ground truth.

- Experiment definition—assess the benefits of adding a new data source to an existing classifier.
  - o Choose the number of features, N, to use for the experiment.
  - o Aggregate data from the sources to be tested, A and B. Extracting and mixing features from these sources will give various views of the problem.
- Create three views of the problem.
- Extract three data sets for modeling.
  - o One uses N features, all taken from source A. It is view A.
  - o One uses N features, all taken from source B. It is view B.
  - o One uses N features, some from source A and some from source B. It is view AB.
  - o Segment each of the three views (permute and split into disjoint training and blind sets).
  - o Rebalance data sets by class if necessary (decimation, replication, synthesis).
- Experiment 1. No preprocessing of features (e.g., no normalization, scaling, etc.).
  - o Perform feature analysis on each of the three modeling views.
  - o For each of the three unnormalized views, apply feature selection applications.

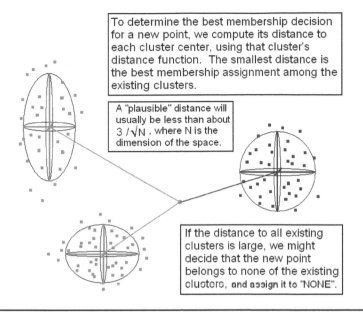

To determine the best membership decision for a new point, we compute its distance to each cluster center, using that cluster's distance function. The smallest distance is the best membership assignment among the existing clusters.

A "plausible" distance will usually be less than about $3/\sqrt{N}$, where N is the dimension of the space.

If the distance to all existing clusters is large, we might decide that the new point belongs to none of the existing clusters, and assign it to "NONE".

Figure 4.7   Point classification to nearest cluster.

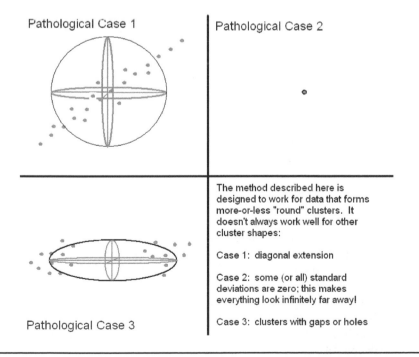

Pathological Case 1

Pathological Case 2

Pathological Case 3

The method described here is designed to work for data that forms more-or-less "round" clusters. It doesn't always work well for other cluster shapes:

Case 1: diagonal extension

Case 2: some (or all) standard deviations are zero; this makes everything look infinitely far away!

Case 3: clusters with gaps or holes

Figure 4.8   Data cluster pathologies.

	A	B	C	D	E	F	G	H
	Feature 5	Feature 4	Feature 3	Feature 2	Feature 1	Precision	Recall	Accuracy
2	0	0	0	0	1	0	0	14.34574
3	0	0	0	1	0	0	0	17.34694
4	0	0	0	1	1	0	0	60.02401
5	0	0	1	0	0	0	0	17.34694
6	0	0	1	0	1	0	0	57.56303
7	0	0	1	1	0	0	0	59.96399
8	0	0	1	1	1	0.845931	0.77053	83.85354
9	0	1	0	0	0	0	0	16.9868
10	0	1	0	0	1	0	0	57.26291
11	0	1	0	1	0	0	0	58.46339
12	0	1	0	1	1	0.839805	0.787703	85.11404
13	0	1	1	0	0	0	0	59.78391
14	0	1	1	0	1	0.839721	0.78471	83.97359
15	0	1	1	1	0	0.849963	0.772561	84.69388
16	0	1	1	1	1	0.949595	0.911047	93.9976
17	1	0	0	0	0	0	0	18.66747
18	1	0	0	0	1	0	0	58.22329
19	1	0	0	1	0	0	0	55.64226
20	1	0	0	1	1	0.830776	0.768066	83.13326
21	1	0	1	0	0	0	0	57.32293
22	1	0	1	0	1	0.845648	0.772357	84.15366
23	1	0	1	1	0	0.866735	0.809079	86.13445
24	1	0	1	1	1	0.953746	0.920376	94.41777
25	1	1	0	0	0	0	0	60.62425
26	1	1	0	0	1	0.86853	0.807823	85.65426
27	1	1	0	1	0	0.854971	0.806307	86.4946
28	1	1	0	1	1	0.963149	0.954443	96.03841
29	1	1	1	0	0	0.866156	0.808867	85.17407
30	1	1	1	0	1	0.955888	0.938771	94.71789
31	1	1	1	1	0	0.957486	0.93918	95.2581
32	1	1	1	1	1	0.987769	0.981775	98.4994
33	1	1	1	1	1	0.989064	0.984782	98.67947

Figure 4.9 Classification power of feature sets.

- o For each of the three unnormalized views, apply clustering applications.
- o For each of the three unnormalized views, apply rule induction applications (e.g., Cubist/C5).
- Experiment 2. Basic preprocessing of features (e.g., normalization).
- o Normalize the feature sets for all three views (e.g., z-score, PCA).
- o Perform feature analysis on each of the three modeling views.
- o For each of the three normalized views, apply feature selection applications.
- o For each of the three normalized views, apply clustering applications.
- o For each of the three normalized views, apply rule induction applications (e.g., Cubist/C5).
- Construct a prototype from each view using appropriate paradigms (e.g., C5).
- Finally, the objective decision that answers the question: Do views B or AB give sufficient improvements over views A or AB to consider adding data from source B to the model?

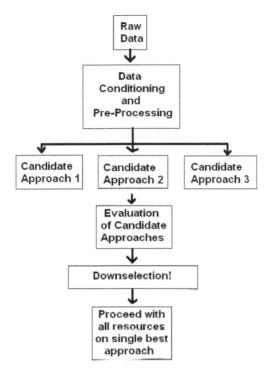

Making feature selection and paradigm
choices through an "audition" process

Figure 4.10   Data mining candidate audition process.

4.8 Data Quality Checklist

Question 6: How is data currently evaluated and validated?	
Why is this question important?	Domain experts know their data very well, and will understand pathologies that make it unusable.
What is this question seeking?	You want to be able to recognize corrupt data when you see it.
Likely responses and their meanings	Answers are often jargonized.
Follow-up questions	Ask for careful explanations of data quality metrics used by the experts. Examples are very helpful.
Special considerations	A sound validation methodology is usually relatively complex. This question gives you a chance to assess the robustness of your customer's method.

Question 7: What is the source of the data?	
Why is this question important?	If the data come from multiple sources, they might be of variable quality, and might arrive at different times.
What is this question seeking?	Is there a data conformation risk? Are we at risk of temporal infeasibility? (Chapter 1)
Likely responses and their meanings	Answers to this question are usually very precise, and carefully documented.
Follow-up questions	Ask for interface control documents (ICDs), data dictionaries, and meta-data. Ask whom to contact if there are detailed technical questions about the data.
Special considerations	If possible, consider talking with those who manage the data.

Question 8: What are the measures of data quality?	
Why is this question important?	You want to include the users' own metrics in your assessment of the data, because they will already understand these.
What is this question seeking?	You want to know how to be able to recognize corrupt data. You want to use metrics the user understands and believes.
Likely responses and their meanings	Answers are usually very specific.
Follow-up questions	Ask for any documentation that addresses data quality. Also ask what the most common data quality issues are, how often they come up, and how they are handled.
Special considerations	Missing data is a special case of low quality; does the user have a policy for handling missing data/gaps in data?

Question 9: What level of quality is needed for the project?	
Why is this question important?	This is a question about the level of performance you must meet; it is the basis for the customer's business case.
What is this question seeking?	Will the available data support the application we are trying to develop?
Likely responses and their meanings	Users might not have specifics on this; they usually respond with ad hoc examples of "bad data."
Follow-up questions	Ask for samples of good and bad data.
Special considerations	People who don't actually have to use raw data (MIS support staff, Managers) usually think the data is much better than it actually is. Domain experts know the truth. Take into account who is answering this question.

Question 10: Will it be necessary to pre-process data to improve its quality for this project?	
Why is this question important?	Data repair is a significant cost and schedule driver. It is time consuming and prone to error.
What is this question seeking?	To develop an accurate project plan, you must know how much data rework is required before mining can begin.
Likely responses and their meanings	It is likely that some data (hopefully not all) will require tweaking that is related to the way it is collected, transmitted, and stored. Get details on which data require what adjustments.
Follow-up questions	Ask for any data correction applications that already exist.
Special considerations	Reformatting, rescaling, registration, normalization, etc. will probably have to be applied to most data fields. This should be automated up front.

4.9 Summary

Having read this chapter, you know what information you must obtain using simple data analysis methods before beginning the Feature Extraction Step of a data mining spiral. You have also learned the basics of how to interpret clustering in a data set, a critical skill that is fundamental to understanding how many data mining algorithms work.

Coming up

The next chapter presents a treatment of principled feature extraction. It includes a number of checklists and case studies. Feature extraction methods and more sophisticated data conditioning methods are discussed.

Chapter 5

Feature Extraction and Enhancement (Step 3)*

Purpose

The practical purpose of this chapter is to describe in some detail the process of deriving features from *raw data* (feature extraction), and conditioning them so that their latent information is as accessible as possible (feature enhancement).

This is the most important step in the data mining process, since it is what ultimately determines the success or failure of a data mining project. It is also the single most time consuming step.

Goals

After you have read this chapter, you will know how to select data items for use as features with a data mining project. You will understand how to correct dimensionality and sampling deficiencies (data that is too large or too small), and solve certain data quality problems. You will know how to synthesize additional features from existing ones.

5.1 Introduction: A Quick Tutorial on Feature Space

Once features have been developed for a data mining application, it is customary to arrange them in an ordered list called a *feature vector*. For example, if the features

---

* *Note:* Due to the mathematical nature of this topic, readers might find some portions of this chapter challenging.

for a credit risk estimation problem were annual income, credit score, and number of bankruptcies, the feature vector for a particular person might be the ordered 3-tuple (45000, 680, 0).

The mathematical theory for the numerical manipulation of ordered n-tuples of real numbers is called linear algebra. If there are two numbers in the tuple, we can regard it as representing a point or vector in the two-dimensional plane. The first number is the x-coordinate of the point, and the second is the y-coordinate of the point. The credit risk example above uses a third coordinate, z, making it a 3-tuple point in three-dimensional space. If we have a data base with these three pieces of credit information for many people, we can extract many of these 3-tuples, producing a point cloud in three-dimensional space. We analyze this point cloud during mining and model construction.

For n>3, n-tuples represent points in higher-dimensional spaces, but many of the same mathematical ideas still hold. In this way, the numerical attributes of a feature vector are identified with locations in a feature space, all governed by the principles of linear algebra. We can compute mathematical distances and angles between vectors in feature space, for example. These measurements give us information about the domain entities represented by the n-tuples; for example, entities whose n-tuples are close together in space are probably similar. It is customary to use the term "feature space" to refer to the set of all possible n-tuples of feature values for a particular problem domain.

5.1.1 Data Preparation Guidelines

Data preparation is the principled conditioning of a data set to preserve and make more accessible its latent information, while reducing the effects of non-informative artifacts. Data rarely come out of the pipe ready to mine, and usually require some kind of preparation. Unfortunately, this crucial step in data mining is often done in an ad hoc way that varies from time to time and analyst to analyst. This can affect the consistency, quality and accessibility of latent information in unpredictable ways.

Some data preprocessing (referred to here as *simple preprocessing*) is the natural reformatting required to satisfy the input requirements of data mining tools and systems. This includes such operations as simple conformation (placing data into a common framework of units, scale, synchrony, and precision), range checking, reformatting, coding, quantization, normalization, registration, and the like.

Real-world data usually require another level of preprocessing (referred to here as *complex preprocessing*) to handle data problems and enhance the accessibility of latent information. Some aspects of this process were discussed in Chapter 4. Complex preprocessing often uses a domain ontology and machine learning techniques. Done poorly, it can reduce the accessibility of latent information; done *very* poorly, it can remove authentic information, and add spurious information (Yes, been there, done that!).

Other data issues addressed in this chapter relate to matters of *scale*: conditioning data that are either too large (i.e., too many dimensions); too small (e.g., undersampled, not full rank, too few exemplars), and unbalanced by class (some categories of data occur much more frequently in the available data than others). Specific attention will be given to feature analysis (determining how the information is bound to the data stream) and feature enhancement (expressing the problem in a way that makes the latent information more accessible).

Conventional techniques for complex data conditioning generally rely on distributional methods (i.e., statistics). The mathematical models underlying these techniques are both mature and well understood. Robust implementations exist that are efficient and effective. Difficulties arise, however, when the assumptions that justify the use of conventional models are violated. Real-world data often have arcane distributions, do not satisfy assumptions of independence, are not stationary (their statistics vary), do not form coherent clusters, contain discontinuities and non-linearity, and have either too many or too few attributes.

The computational complexity of data mining algorithms (e.g., classifiers and detectors) can be affected dramatically by these conditions. When data are conditioned under assumptions that do not apply, poor results can be expected.

5.1.2 General Techniques for Feature Selection and Enhancement

Feature selection is the process of determining which of the available data will be used for mining. *Feature enhancement* refers to the process by which features are conditioned/transformed to make their information content more accessible.

The first steps are usually to register and normalize the data. *Registration* is the process of bringing the data into proper alignment. The precise nature of this depends upon the data. For example, if the data is raw video footage, registration would detect the boundaries between frames so individual images are grabbed for analysis. If the data are two aerial photographs of a ground scene, these must be overlaid such that corresponding locations coincide before, say, trying to conduct change detection. Or, if the data is a sequence of messages, these should be sorted onto a common unifying timeline before being interpreted. If boundary markers are present in the data, these can be used to automate registration. If not, registration can be done manually; edge detection algorithms might be used; or more advanced methods using convolutions and various other filtering might be used.

Normalization is the process of scaling a set of data so the range of variability is controlled. This can be thought of as a unit conversion process. For example, if the data are two aerial photographs of a ground scene, these have to be brought into the same scale before they can be usefully compared. Typical methods are z-scoring, and Principal Component Analysis (PCA) (see the Winnowing Case Study).

There are many techniques for trying to reduce the dimension of a feature space without destroying its representational power. These fall into two broad categories:

Category 1

Techniques that identify a subset of the original feature set for subsequent processing. The mathematical term for this feature subset operation is *orthographic projection*. This is easy to implement; you simply discard some of the dimensions. The trick of course, is to determine which features to keep.

The underlying technology for this category consists of distributional and information theoretic techniques that measure the joint information content of features. A subset of features that retains a significant amount of the discriminating power of the original feature set is selected for use.

A bottom-up accretive approach to dimension reduction sometimes gives good results. In this method, rather than selecting dimensions to remove, we select dimensions to retain; this is done in such a way as to end up with the lowest dimensional set that covers the known data. This technique proceeds roughly according to the following sequence of steps:

1. For each feature, a separate classifier is trained using only that single feature.
2. These classifiers are sorted according to their accuracy on the remaining data (initially, this will be the entire data set).
3. The feature having the highest accuracy has its feature added to the retained set.
4. All the vectors correctly classified by the last best feature are removed from the remaining data.
5. Steps 2 through 4 are repeated until the desired level of coverage is obtained, that is, until a negligible number of vectors remain.

This technique is not designed to find the best individual features for the purpose of classification, but rather the smallest set of features that explains most of the data. And it should not be inferred that the features not retained are of no value. On the contrary, as additional feature vectors are obtained, it is expected that the relationships among all features will be clarified, facilitating the development of improved models.

These techniques have the advantage that the resulting lower-dimensional feature sets consist of features that are already understood: their original meaning is intact. These techniques have the disadvantage that unless the discarded features are irrelevant to the problem (data noise), they generally do not enhance patterns of interest. Dimension reduction is their only benefit.

Category 2

These techniques transform (rather than merely project) the original features into a new space having lower dimension. The underlying technology for this category consists of regression and optimization techniques that merge features in some way, resulting in a lower dimensional space. PCA is such a technique; it determines a linear transform from the data itself used to rotate and rescale the data in each feature to obtain a more efficient representation. Only the first few features in each vector are retained, and the rest are discarded.

These techniques have the advantage that they can concentrate the information content of the data, making patterns more apparent. They have the disadvantage that they are computationally more expensive, and the resulting synthesized features generally have no intuitive meaning to users.

Within each of these two categories of techniques, there are methods that take ground truth class assignments into account, and those that do not. The former we refer to as *class sensitive*, and the latter, *class agnostic*.

5.2 Characterizing and Resolving Data Problems

- **Outlier detection and mitigation.** The term *outlier* can refer either to data that are invalid due to some error (e.g., sensor error, corrupted during storage), or to data that are valid but assume unexpected values. The former we call *bad*; the latter we call *anomalies*. The problem of missing data is addressed below.

  Telling the difference between bad data and anomalous data is challenging, because the determination is really an assessment of cause rather than effect. For example, "the observed data are not nominal" is an observed effect. If the cause of this effect is not determined, it will be difficult to handle outliers in a principled way.

- **Detection of outliers.** For our purposes, an outlier is a datum having a value that is not consistent with the established pattern. Outliers are pattern breakers. This definition is a bit vague, suggesting that the term outlier is subjective . . . and so it is. One data miner's outlier is another's nominal datum. This subjectivity arises because what is consistent and established in one context need not be so in another; it really depends upon how the data are being used.

  Outlier detection is important in data mining because the presence of data that violate the pattern make the pattern harder to detect, characterize, and exploit. Part of proper data conditioning includes the consideration of whether certain records are invalid, and should be removed so that authentic patterns are not obscured.

Methods for definitive outlier tests do exist in some problem domains by virtue of their having gained acceptance among domain experts. This is certainly true for domains requiring unambiguous definitions, such as medicine and law.

For most data mining efforts, though, the data miner must establish their own definition of an outlier, and construct their own outlier tests. There is no universally applicable outlier test, but there are principled outlier tests. Here are five different methods (objective and subjective) that together cover many data mining situations.

Objective Methods:

- **Range checking.** Establish reasonable minimum and maximum values for each feature. Values that fall outside this range are outliers.
- **Z-scores.** Using the Calibration set, compute the mean and standard deviation for each feature. To determine whether an instance of that feature is an outlier, use these to compute its z-score. If the feature value is less than the minimum acceptable z-score, or greater than the maximum acceptable z-score, it is an outlier. A standard choice for the minimum and maximum allowable z-scores are -3 and +3, respectively.

Subjective Methods:

- **Visualization.** Plot the data. Data that don't fit the visual pattern are possible outliers.
- **Clustering.** Use a clustering algorithm to aggregate the data into clusters. Clusters that have very few members (e.g., one), might consist of outliers.
- **Contextualization.** Establish outlier rules that can be applied to check for known inconsistencies. For example, suppose a medical record says a patient's gender is male, and their diagnosis is gestational diabetes (i.e., the patient is a pregnant man). These feature values cannot both be correct, so an outlier has been detected.

The *objective* methods are nice because they don't really require an understanding of the domain, and can be performed quickly and automatically. The *subjective* methods are more powerful and discriminating, but require time and domain knowledge to apply.

Anomaly Detection

For our purposes, an *anomaly* is a valid datum having a value that is assumed very rarely. Notice that a distinction is being made here between outliers and anomalies. Outliers are bad data; their frequency of occurrence is irrelevant. Anomalies are good data that are rare; they are not outliers. Deciding which you have in a particular case is a judgment call (domain experts often have heuristics for this). Knowing the difference is important if outliers and anomalies must be handled differently.

There are two types of anomaly detection problems: Closed Corpus and Open Corpus. Closed Corpus problems are those for which there is a known, a priori list of anomalous patterns. Software virus detection is an example: an anomalous version of a program is detected by scanning it for the presence of known bad code.

Closed Corpus anomaly detectors characterize *anomalous* patterns (by keeping a list). This approach characterizes *abnormal* patterns, and creates detectors for *similarity* to these patterns.

Strengths:

- Good track record (e.g., virus and spam detection).
- Supervised learning can be used, because examples of every target pattern can be generated.

Weaknesses:

- The corpus must be regularly updated.
- Patterns that are not (yet) in the corpus will not be detected.

Open Corpus problems are those which must detect anomalies that have never been seen before: there is no a priori list to check. In this situation, anomalous data must be detected by examination of its attributes. An example is a bot detector on a web page. You are asked to prove that you are human by typing in a partially garbled word presented in a thumbnail image. The web site doesn't have a list of all humans, but it does know what humans can do that bots can't.

Open Corpus anomaly detectors have a known, a priori collection of historical patterns constituting normalcy. This approach characterizes *normal* patterns, and creates detectors for deviation from these patterns.

Strengths:

- Good track record (e.g., change detection, control systems).
- Previously unseen patterns might be detected.

Weaknesses:

- More complex and therefore more difficult to build and use.
- Unsupervised learning must be used, because it is not known a priori what anomalous patterns must be detected.

Open Corpus anomaly detection is usually regarded as the more difficult of the two problems. It can be performed in a number of ways. One method is an application of unsupervised learning combined with continuous regression.

The concept is simple. If a pattern consisting of several parts is not unusual, then it should be possible to hide some of its parts, and use pattern matching to infer these hidden parts from those that are not hidden. In a certain sense, parts that can be inferred in this way conform to what is expected, and are not novel. However, when some part of a pattern cannot be inferred from the others, it must in some way be unusual in the context of the whole pattern.

This suggests a method for using pattern matching to detect novel items. For each part of a pattern, a learning engine is created to infer that part from the others. Items are run through the engine to determine whether all of their parts make sense in context. Items that contain many parts that cannot be inferred by the engine are deemed novel. Using scores computed during processing by the learning engine, items are ranked by novelty. The most novel items are flagged for manual review.

5.2.1 Outlier Case Study

This experiment shows that it is sometimes possible to detect weak features and remove (winnow) them without degrading the information content of the data as a whole. In some cases, feature winnowing can actually improve the performance of the classifier.

5.2.2 Winnowing Case Study: Principal Component Analysis for Feature Extraction

This case study describes a laboratory experiment designed to illustrate the use of PCA for dimension reduction and feature extraction. We describe what PCA is, and its strengths and weaknesses as a dimension reduction and feature extraction technique.

The most important issue to consider when using PCA for dimension reduction is its effect on the ability of the new features to distinguish between ground truth classes.

Addendum [1] at the end of this case study suggests a methodology for developing nonlinear transforms manually; and Addendum [2] describes a real-world use of nonlinear encoding for feature enhancement.

5.3 Principal Component Analysis

The dimension of the data set being processed dramatically affects the computational complexity of pattern processing algorithms (e.g., classifiers and detectors). For many algorithms, there is a practical upper bound on the number of dimensions that can be handled in a reasonable amount of time and space. For this reason, techniques that reduce the dimension of a data set *without damaging its information content* can be very useful.

The phrase, "without damaging its information content" is the key. If all we want to do is compactly represent a data set, then the information content is preserved if the variation is captured. This is what PCA does. In this sense, PCA is an ideal method for representing data compactly.

However, when the goal is to build a classifier, the information content usually has little to do with how variation in the data is encoded. Rather, we seek a representational scheme that preserves the class identities given by the ground truth. This is not a question of variation, but discrimination. For difficult problems, the variations that define the differences between two target classes are often quite small. These can be exactly the variations that are discarded during PCA dimension reduction as described above.

Class Agnosticism (an important limitation of PCA as a feature extraction method)

PCA is a class agnostic winnowing method: it does not consider the ground truth assigned to feature vectors in selecting its representation. We now describe a critical limitation that arises from this fact when using PCA during feature extraction.

PCA is a method for efficiently accounting for the variation in a data set. The underlying mathematics provides a mechanism for detecting, characterizing, and quantifying variation in the given data. This information is then used to formulate a new representation of the data that concentrates as much of the variation as possible in as few terms as possible. The vectors that define this new representation are called *principal components*. They are completely determined by the data.

It is customary to order the principal components of a data set in decreasing order by the amount of variation they explain. For many data sets, the first few principal components account for a large percentage of the total variation in the data set. When this occurs, dimension reduction can be achieved by simply discarding the components from some point on, since these do not account for a significant amount of the variation. The number of terms to retain can sometimes be determined by reference to

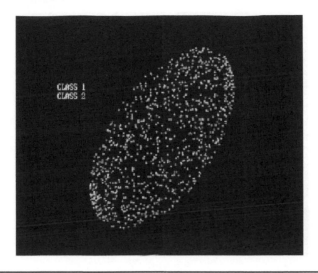

Figure 5.1 Three-dimensional scatter plot of two classes.

factors (computed during the PCA process) that quantify each component's explanatory power. More frequently, some experimentation is required.

In summary, PCA is designed to pack as much of the variation of a data set into as few dimensions as possible. It does this by systematically isolating and discarding insignificant forms of variation. This is done agnostically: ground truth assignments are not consulted, so the dimension reduction is done with complete disregard for how class distinctions might be affected. In the following intuitive example, we show what PCA can do when the distinctions between classes are small relative to the dynamic range of the data.

Consider a set of 1,000 three-dimensional data points, constituting two ground truth classes (Figure 5.1).

Figure 5.1 is a scatter plot showing two thoroughly mixed and overlapping classes. We can't tell which class each point is in, and it looks like a single cluster. The viewer is seeing the data plotted in the first two coordinates x (horizontal axis) and y (vertical axis). The third coordinate, z, is coming out of the page toward the viewer. From this perspective, nothing can be known about the third dimension. This view clearly shows that the two visible coordinates x and y by themselves do not provide a good basis for distinguishing between the two classes: class 1, and class 2.

Considering only x and y, the principal components of this data set are depicted by the lines, the first principal component points to "2 o'clock", and runs along the line that accounts for most of the variation in the data. The second principal component runs along the line that accounts for most of the variation that remains after the contribution of the first principal component has been removed. In the example above, the second principal component gives the line that points to "10 o'clock" (Figure 5.2).

For data having many dimensions, this process is repeated until all of the variation in the data has been accounted for. The procedure is deterministic, and guaranteed to

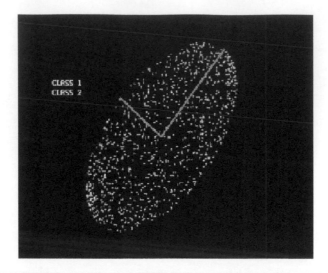

Figure 5.2 Direction of principal data set components.

terminate after at most N steps, where N is the dimension of the feature space. The principal components will be mutually orthogonal (perpendicular to each other).

Once the directions of maximum variation (the principal components) have been determined, the data are rescaled along each component (Figure 5.3)

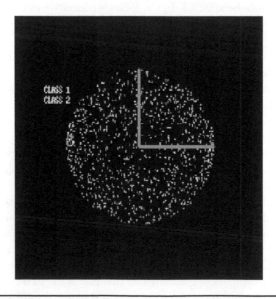

Figure 5.3 Rescaled data aligned with new axes.

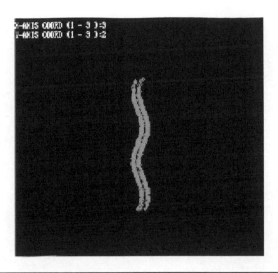

Figure 5.4   Nonlinear representation of two classes.

It is customary to think of the data being expressed in terms of the principal components, so the variation in the data aligns with the new axes.

Return now to considering the original data before PCA is applied. If we move around to look at the data from a perspective perpendicular to the z-axis, the problem of distinguishing between the mixed classes does not appear quite so hopeless. Close examination shows there is still quite a bit of overlap between the two groups in this view, but some of the data can be distinguished (Figure 5.4). This tells us that the third feature, z, carries some information that was not present in x and y by themselves.

Here we see the data plotted as y vs. z; y is on the vertical axis, and z is on the horizontal axis. From this perspective, it is clear that the problem of separating the two classes can be completely solved by carefully drawing a wavy boundary between the two sets. We have found a feature set (y and z) that will solve the problem. Because of the wave in the data, a nonlinear boundary will be required.

Having seen the data from all three perspectives, we now realize that it consists of two sheets that are elliptical in x and y, and that are slightly separated, interlocked sinusoids in y and z (sort of like two ruffled potato chips locked together; Figure 5.4).

Variation in the z coordinate is small relative to the ranges of x and y. As a result, PCA will see elimination of the contribution of z as providing an opportunity to enhance the efficiency of data representation.

Applying PCA, we obtain a new representation of the data. In keeping with our goal of using PCA for dimension reduction, we keep the first two principal components and discard the third. The resulting data set is plotted below. The first principal component is horizontal, the second, vertical (Figure 5.5).

After PCA, the data still appear as a single aggregation. Nothing has been gained, but a price has been paid: much of the discriminating power in z has been removed, because this accounted for only a small portion of the overall variation in the data. As

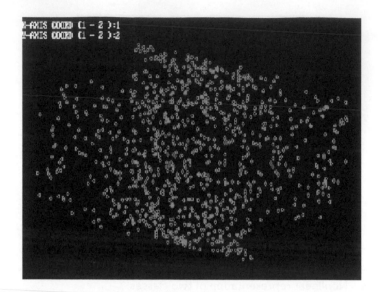

Figure 5.5   Application of PCA to data set.

we saw above, it is this variation in z that is needed to fully solve the problem. After PCA, we are left with a data set that still has the two classes confounded, and there is no longer a third dimension available to resolve the conflict. Because the scale of variation is a function of the units of measurement used, we see that it would be possible for PCA to ruin a data set, for example, just because one of the measurements was expressed in minutes rather than seconds!

Nonlinear PCA for Feature Extraction

Conventional Principal Component Analysis (i.e., Karhunen-Loeve PCA[1]) is a linear technique: it develops an efficient basis for representing data using linear regression, and then applies an *affine* transformation to encode the data. Linear and affine mappings are unable to model many complex relationships encountered in real-world data. PCA leaves this complexity intact, passing all the work of discrimination on to subsequent processes. As seen above, it may destroy information, guaranteeing the failure of subsequent techniques.

The use of nonlinear regression for representation of feature data can (in theory) convert complex problems into simple ones. In practice, dimension reduction can sometimes be realized by the application of nonlinear transforms to features, even though linear transforms fail. This amounts to the creation of a nonlinear basis for the feature space. Because these transforms can be created with ground truth assignments in mind, the new representation may yield a simpler classification problem.

Independent Component Analysis (ICA) is a methodology for transforming data so that class distinctions (rather than data variation as in PCA) are the driving consideration. In a more general sense, the whole field of feature extraction and enhancement addresses the problem of representing a problem space in such a way that classes are coherent and distinct.

As an example, we refer again to our three-dimensional data set. The two classes in this problem are distinct, but not coherent. Any linear transform applied to this data set will leave us with an abutting curved interface between the classes, that is, it will fail to reduce the complexity of the classification problem.

However, the application of a (contrived) nonlinear transform can yield the following result. The transformed problem is trivial (Figure 5.6):

The nonlinear transform threaded a wavy boundary between the two potato chips, dragged them apart, and shaped them into nice, round discs.

In practice, the characterization of a transform for determining nonlinear components is difficult (in fact, determining *optimal* components is equivalent to the classification problem itself). Sometimes a process of trial and error is successful, but sometimes the use of some kind of automated optimization scheme is required. An excellent treatment of nonlinear PCA using neural networks is *"Image Compression by back propagation: An example of extensional programming,"* ICS Report 8702, UCSD, February, 1987.[2]

It must be kept in mind that PCA of whatever sort is data driven, not problem driven. That is, if transforms are being sought to compress data, no ground truth is needed. If transforms are being sought to prepare the data for analysis or modeling, distinctions between ground truth classes are at risk.

Class discrimination aside, there is often value in using nonlinear PCA agnostically to reduce dimensionality and mitigate complexity. The result is a low-dimensional representation of the problem having a simplified phenomenology.

Conventional PCA is a useful first cut technique for dimension reduction. It is designed for efficiency of linear representation, and does not consider a priori class

Figure 5.6 Application of nonlinear transform.

assignments. As a linear agnostic technique, it can damage the power of a data set to support class discrimination.

There are nonlinear techniques for feature selection and transformation that are designed to reduce data dimensionality and enhance its ability to discriminate between a priori classes. The selection of such a technique in a particular problem domain generally requires special tools and expertise.

5.3.1 Feature Winnowing and Dimension Reduction Checklist

Question 1: How much bulk data are we talking about (KB, MB, GB or TB)?	
Why this question is important?	Data scale is a cost and complexity driver.
What is question seeking?	Is your existing infrastructure and tool set adequate for this project?
Likely responses and their meanings	Likely answers and their meanings: This answer can usually be answered pretty precisely.
Follow-up questions	If specific issues are raised in any of these areas, you should follow up with additional questions.
Special considerations	The customer probably already has some data access and conditioning tools. Ask about these.

Question 2: What is the dimensionality/complexity of the entire feature space?	
Why this question is important?	Sometimes data is kept in multiple distributed repositories, and records are never actually brought together in one place in the operational system.
What is question seeking?	The user might not realize how wide one record is. They also might not know whether distributed data are synchronized. If not, you might have to do this.
Likely responses and their meanings	Usually a domain expert will know the specifications of all the separate repositories.
Follow-up questions	Ask for data definition documents, data base schema's, and meta-data descriptions for all distributed repositories.
Special considerations	There might be conformation problems across a distributed data set (e.g., the same value in different units).

Question 3: What is the dimensionality/complexity that can be supported?	
Why this question is important?	Performing a data join across multiple repositories might not be feasible.
What is question seeking?	You want to make sure that your solution does not require a level of resources that is not available.
Likely responses and their meanings	Domain experts usually know the limitations of their computing systems well, and will share these.
Follow-up questions	Ask for system specifications describing scale and speed.
Special considerations	Be cautious about architecting a solution that might require long load times, or bog down an operational network. It might be necessary to run your processes offline after-hours, or on some kind of schedule to avoid interfering with operational activities.

Question 4: Are there data elements whose use is mandated (either by policy or legacy processes)?	
Why this question is important?	Sometime users have a hard intellectual commitment to certain data items. They are convinced that these items MUST be used by any analytic process that hopes to succeed.
What is question seeking?	If there are some data elements you must use to be credible, then use them. When this happens, it is usually because part of the repository is data that has been purchased at someone's behest.
Likely responses and their meanings	If they want you to use certain data, they will tell you if you ask.
Follow-up questions	Ask why certain data is deemed to be essential; perhaps it is, and for reasons that you need to know.
Special considerations	Be sensitive to the customer's politics and psychology.

Question 5: Must data be retained in its native form during processing (either by policy or legacy processes)?	
Why this question is important?	There are some shops that have policies requiring (usually for legal or liability reasons) that certain data not be altered from its original form.
What is question seeking?	If such a policy exists, most data conditioning methods cannot be used (e.g., PCA, z-scoring, amplitude normalization, coding, quantization, histogram equalization, some types of registration, imputation of missing values, etc.).
Likely responses and their meanings	Policies usually only apply to certain data. You will need to know which ones.
Follow-up questions	Ask for any policy documents that are available.
Special considerations	Do not violate your customers' data use policies.

Question 6: What are appropriate feature winnowing strategies in this domain (high rho, low correlation with GT, low quality, dimension reduction)?	
Why this question is important?	Sometimes domain experts will already know the best ways to condition their data.
What is question seeking?	You want to benefit from what is already known.
Likely responses and their meanings	Domain experts usually know the answer to this question from an operational perspective. However, keep in mind that they probably do not understand the considerations relevant to data mining.
Follow-up questions	Are there existing tools for data selection/ feature winnowing?
Special considerations	This is a reasonable place to ask the domain expert for their opinion about which features are most and least informative.

Addendum [1]. Figure 5.7 is a flow chart that illustrates the trial and error approach to selecting a nonlinear transform for data representation. The goal is to find a transform that recasts the problem as an approximately linear problem.

Addendum [2]. A simple real-world example of how a nonlinear transform simplified a hard problem. This example describes the application of a nonlinear transform to the conditioning of a feature set for forecasting hourly demand for electric power. The available data consisted of annual average electrical loads, date/time for prediction, and forecasted weather.

The weather data consisted of:

- Wet-bulb temperature (degrees Celsius)
- Dry-bulb temperature (degrees Celsius)
- Relative humidity (%)
- Wind direction (degrees of bearing)
- Wind speed (knots)
- Cloudiness (numeric rating from 0 to 9)

The final prototype required about 2 hours to train, and performed the prediction of an hour's load in about 300 milliseconds (i.e., 7.2 seconds to predict a 24-hour day's worth of loads). The completed model was evaluated by processing the entire 365 days of feature vectors (including the 14 bad days), constituting a test that was about 80% blind, with 4% real-world anomalous input.

It was hypothesized that the month of the year should be a useful feature as part of a model for predicting the demand for electrical power. Instead of just coding the month

Steps in Regression Analysis Procedure

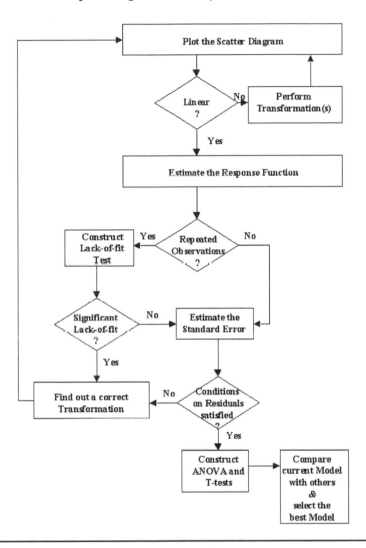

Figure 5.7   Steps in regression analysis procedure.

as January=1, February=2, etc., the month was coded as the average temperature during that month for the previous year. In this scheme, January=39, February=35, August=88, etc. Figure 5.8 is a bar chart having twelve pairs of bars; the first bar of each pair is the coded month value, and the second bar is the average electrical demand during that month. Because of the disparity in the units of measure, these are of very different heights. Notice that the electrical demand peaks in February and August, while the coded month peaks only in August. In this presentation, it is difficult to see and clear relationship between the coded month and the electrical demand for that month.

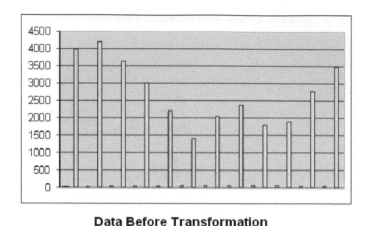

Data Before Transformation

Figure 5.8   Data before transformation.

Reasoning that residential electrical demand would be high when the temperature was extreme (air conditioning! heating!), and that electrical demand would be low when the temperature was moderate, the following nonlinear transform was applied to the coded month:

$$NEWCODE = 4500|OLDCODE-68|$$

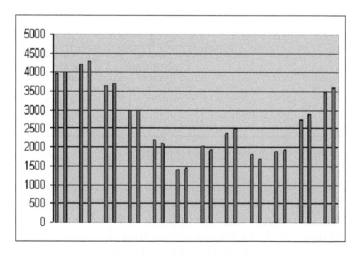

Data After Transformation

Figure 5.9   Data after transformation.

Here the data infer that 68 degrees appeared to be the critical temperature above and below the electrical demand, and 4500 was a unit scale factor. After applying this nonlinear transform to the coded month, the coded month is seen to be an excellent predictor of the average electrical demand during that month (Figure 5.9).

The nonlinear transform, which was inferred from the data, allowed us to turn a single mediocre feature into an excellent predictor of the base value of the variable to be predicted.

5.3.2 Checklist for Characterizing and Resolving Data Problems

Run this checklist to make sure that data problems have been addressed.

Question 7: What are the likely data problems (outliers, missing data, timeliness, precision, etc.)?	
Why this question is important?	What are the data pathologies that will have to be addressed during the project?
What is question seeking?	Data problems are cost and complexity drivers. They must be understood formally, and quantified numerically.
Likely responses and their meanings	Answers will be anecdotal.
Follow-up questions	Ask for samples illustrating particular types of data errors.
Special considerations	Some data problems are more expensive to fix than others.

Question 8: What data problems does the user report (outliers, missing data, timeliness, precision, etc.)?	
Why this question is important?	The users are the best source of reliable information on data errors that cause operational problems.
What is question seeking?	Add the problems reported by users to the list of problems to be addressed.
Likely responses and their meanings	Sometimes error phenomenology is documented, but this is rare. You will probably not get a comprehensive list.
Follow-up questions	Ask for estimates of rates of occurrence for the various types of known errors.
Special considerations	Some errors are more serious than others. The fact that an error is present does not necessarily mean it should be fixed; it might make more sense to discard the record.

5.4 Synthesis of Features

Feature synthesis is the merging of several existing features to obtain one or more new features. This is done by applying a mathematical transform to the raw features, or combining features in some intuitively meaningful way. Synthesis of features is usually undertaken when the existing features are individually weak. By combining them with other features, two benefits might be realized:

1. Synthesized features can be more powerful because they combine the information content of several features.
2. If the original, weak features are removed and only the synthesized feature is kept, the dimension of the data is lower.

Good Features

It is desirable to have features that are correlated with the ground truth to be predicted/estimated, and uncorrelated with each other. When this is the case, each feature is itself highly informative, and provides an information stream that is not redundant with other features.

Making Good Feature Sets From Bad Ones

It is rare for data mining practitioners to be able to specify the data provided for their effort. They usually receive data that was collected for some other purpose, but happens to be available for a data mining effort. In practice, this can put the data mining researcher in the challenging position of trying to get useful information out of not so useful data. A process that can help is feature synthesis.

Whether a particular type of feature synthesis will be helpful depends strongly on the particulars of the data itself, so it doesn't make sense to attempt an extended treatment here; the reader is referred to the excellent detailed treatments found in "*Data Preparation for Data Mining,*" Dorian Pyle,[3] and encouraged to read the case study below.

Feature synthesis can include things like replacing the two features *total revenue* and *advertising expenditures* by their ratio to obtain the synthesized feature *revenue dollars per advertising dollar*, which might be more meaningful in some applications. Or, it might replace 6 features of monthly sales with the slope of the trend line for those six months, which in one number indicates whether things are getting better or getting worse, and how rapidly.

5.4.1 Feature Synthesis Case Study

This case study examines the details of a predictive modeling project to predict the worker's compensation liability incurred by a state government. The goal was to build a model that could ingest the claims submitted during a month, and estimate the total payout on each claim over the following six months.

The available data consisted of a disparate collection of mostly nominal features. Initial predictive modeling experiments using numerical codes for the nominal features did not give good results.

The features were taken from the worker's compensation claim forms submitted for payment. In an attempt to perform relatively high-precision estimation (within $1000 on each claim), it was decided to synthesize some additional features from those supplied. In particular, it was believed that transforms that computed a variety of weighted sums, ratios, and nonlinear combinations of the existing discrete features might expose some subtle information encoded in the distribution of feature values within each claimant's record.

Further, for this case study, three ground truth variables were selected by the customer; one of these had to be synthesized (as a difference) of claimant data fields.

The Original Data

A commercial source provided 12,130 worker's compensation claim records (comp records) for the pre-study effort. Each record contained 85 fields, any or all of which could be used as features. These data were sampled from claims filed in a single state over a five-year period. Supporting documentation was also provided which included a data concordance, coding tables, and a description of the sampling methodology.

Several Problems Were Addressed:

1. Is it possible to predict from comp record phenomenology the total incurred medical expense?
2. Is it possible to predict from comp record phenomenology the duration of disability?
3. Is it possible to predict from comp record phenomenology which claims will result in litigation/adjudication?

Preliminary Analysis of the Data

Preliminary analysis was performed to determine general population parameters. The distribution of outcomes (in terms of medical dollars) is heavily skewed to the low end: over 99% of the claims had valuations under $100,000.

Single-factor Bayesian analysis, scientific visualization techniques, and covariance measures showed that most of the features were not correlated with each other. Many vacant fields were found in the supplied data. In order to insure that any results obtained could be applied in practice, attention was restricted to only those fields present in virtually all records.

Preliminary cluster analysis indicated that the supplied estimates of future medical costs were very poor. Further, the system being developed should aim to improve on current estimation techniques rather than replicate their shortcomings. In subsequent work, attention was restricted to closed cases only.

Feature Extraction

The features satisfying the above conditions, which were intuitively correlated with total medical cost, were selected. Some of these were synthesized from multiple comp record fields by weighted summation, differencing, or other transformations:

1. Type of injury
2. Part of body
3. Person's age at time of injury
4. Gender
5. Marital status
6. Age of policy at time of injury
7. Employment status at time of injury
8. Attorney been retained?
9. Claim ever contested by carrier?
10. Type of employment
11. Traumatic, occupational, or cumulative injury?
12. Pre-injury weekly wage

These features were z-scored and sorted by correlation with outcome valuation, and PCA was applied. The data set was divided into four smaller sets: A, B, C, and D. Each of these smaller sets held approximately 1100 normalized case records.

Training Methods

A neural network was applied to the feature sets A and C. This was done in both a supervised and unsupervised training mode. For sets A and C (those used in training), individual case valuations could consistently be predicted to within $1000 over 98% of the time. In other words, the ground truth assignments can be learned for a given data set. For both sets A and C, it was possible to predict total medical expense for the training sets themselves to within 10%. When applied as blind tests against sets B and D (which were not part of the training data), the prediction of total population claim value was within 15% on the whole sets.

Data analysis indicated that the involvement of an attorney strongly de-correlated the data. A simple stratification was performed to remove cases involving attorneys and contested claims, and the procedures above repeated. (*Note:* the trained machine could correctly predict the involvement of an attorney over 80% of the time.)

After stratification, the blind test set results improved to estimation of total cost to within 0.5% on set B, and 7% on set D. However, individual case estimates were still poor.

Conclusions

Results based upon the limited effort applied were promising for population estimation. Additional stratification and feature enhancement was considered, but indications were that the data provided do not support prediction of individual cases.

The Need for Additional Data

It appeared that further progress would be constrained by the limitations of the supplied data set. Missing fields in the supplied data set forced consideration of only a few of the 85 collected features. Aggregate results were consistently much better than individual results. The data set had to be subdivided to obtain blind test sets. These facts, coupled with the high resolution ($1000 bins) desired on the output side indicate that the supplied data set does not adequately cover the universe of discourse.

5.4.2 Synthesis of Features Checklist

Run this checklist to insure that issues related to feature synthesis have been considered.

Question 9: Will I synthesize features?	
Why this question is important?	This question reminds you to consider feature synthesis as a way to reduce complexity and improve performance.
What is question seeking?	Does it make sense to merge some of the features, either to reduce their number or increase their power?
Likely responses and their meanings	Some experiments should be performed trying various synthesis methods.
Follow-up questions	Are there policy restrictions that require features to be retained in their native form during processing?
Special considerations	Feature synthesis algorithms should be automated.

Question 10: What is my feature synthesis strategy?	
Why this question is important?	Because feature synthesis alters the view of the problem space, detection of problems is made more difficult. There are inherent risks; in particular, it is during synthesis that certain bad things (like Trojan Horsing) can happen, for example, by synthesizing the wrong data due to a software bug.
What is question seeking?	Do we have a sound synthesis strategy? A sound strategy will include validation methods.
Likely responses and their meanings	The synthesis strategy should be included in the project final report.
Follow-up questions	Does the synthesis strategy violate any data policies for example, does it use any *forbidden fields* (e.g., race, gender, age, etc.)?
Special considerations	Feature synthesis algorithms should be automated.

5.5 Degapping

Data analysis and pattern processing are hindered when some records contain fields that are empty or corrupt. This situation occurs for many reasons, including data measurement errors, data transmission errors, elimination of a data source, and the use of improper data conditioning methods. The process of inferring an appropriate replacement value (fill value) for a suspect datum is called *imputation*.

Sometimes missing or corrupt data values can be recovered by simple automatic mechanisms such as table lookups and hard-coded values. More often, missing or corrupt data can only be replaced through time consuming and error-prone manual estimation of correct replacement data.

High data volume and heavy user workloads usually make manual imputation impractical. As a result, the only feasible alternatives are to either discard entire data records, or retain the data record as is with missing or corrupt data values in place. This is a dilemma: discarding an entire data record destroys the potentially valuable information that it does contain; but leaving in place records containing gaps makes subsequent analysis more difficult and error prone.

Data gaps and inconsistencies cannot be fully understood without considering the context supplied by other values in the record. Therefore, context free, gap-filling techniques such as plugging holes with naïve replacement values (e.g., averages) are not very effective. Robust methods for handling gaps and inconsistencies must use context.

Data are sometimes missing from a record for a reason; other gaps are merely random occurrences. To distinguish between the various categories of data gaps (a necessary precursor to robust imputation), and account for the data context of a gap, an imputation strategy must be developed. This strategy first characterizes missing data by its cause: systematic (data holes that occur consistently under certain conditions), random (gaps occur sporadically), intentional (e.g., applicant leaves out number of bankruptcies on a credit application), and others depending upon the domain. The imputation strategy then invokes an imputation procedure appropriate to the cause of the gap.

Imputation procedures are often ad hoc, since they are unique to the data mining problem being considered, and the data involved. Clearly, nominal data must be degapped differently than numeric data.

Intra-vector imputation methods restore missing values within a record by analyzing other values in that same record. *Inter-vector* imputation methods restore missing values in a record by analyzing other records that do not have missing values.

A number of commercial tools perform context-sensitive degapping (e.g., QUBIST). Certain degapping techniques work well for some problems, and not at all for others. If all features in a vector are statistically independent of each other, an intra-vector technique will not work (since independence means that features contain no information about each other). If, however, the features within a vector are correlated (perhaps nonlinearly), an intra-vector technique is probably preferred. Modern sophisticated approaches to degapping typically operate in one of two ways:

Distributional Approach

Supply fill values for missing fields in such a way as to preserve global population information measures (e.g., entropy, covariance, maximum likelihood).

Ontological Approach

Posit an ontology for the domain (a world model) and supply fill values in such a way that the ontology is preserved (e.g., the resulting degapped set is consistent in the ontology). Both of these approaches have weaknesses.

Weaknesses of the Distributional Approach

These approaches perform degapping by selecting fill values that preserve global distributional characteristics of the data set. This preservation of available information is desirable when subsequent analysis is primarily statistical in nature.

The principle weakness of this approach is that it assumes that the distributional characteristics of the *gappy* data are representative of the population, and forces degapped sets to preserve them. This might not be a valid assumption.

A secondary weakness of the distributional approach is that it overlooks the fact that fields might be missing for a reason, and the pattern of missing fields could itself be important, and should be used in assigning fill values. An ontological model could help here.

Weaknesses of the Ontological Approach

The ontological approach assumes a model for the domain, and then supplies fill values in a manner that produces degapped set consistent with this model. This approach is very effective when consistency is absolutely essential to subsequent processing (e.g., in cases where lives are at stake).

The principal weakness of the ontological approach is the difficulty of building a sufficiently comprehensive model of a non-trivial real-world system. There will always be omitted cases, exceptions, and outliers. Further, as the complexity of the ontology increases, so does the likelihood that the model itself contains complex errors arising from internal relationships.

A secondary weakness of ontological models is that they provide little help when there are many consistent assignments for a fill value. If diagnosis=pregnant, then gender=female; but an ontological model will not provide much insight into a fill value for height. A distributional model could help here.

A Degapping Algorithm for Numeric Data

One simple inter-vector imputation method is to replace missing values with their population means, a $O(n)$ process. This naïve approach is simple, but ignores context within the record. For numeric data, a more sophisticated method is the nearest neighbor normalization technique. This can be applied efficiently even to large data sets with many dimensions (in a brute force approach this is a $O(n^2)$ process). The following is an explanation of how the nearest neighbor normalization method works. This technique proceeds in the following manner for each missing feature in a given vector, V_1:

1. From a degapping set of feature vectors, find the one, V_2, which:
   a. Shares a sufficient number of populated fields with the vector to be degapped (this is to increase the likelihood that the nearest vector is representative of the vector being processed).
   b. Has a value for the missing feature, F_m.
   c. Is nearest the vector to be degapped (possibly weighted).
2. Compute the weighted norms of the vector being degapped, V_1, and the matching vector found in step 1, V_2, in just those features present in both.
3. Form the normalization ratio $R_n = |V_1|/|V_2|$.
4. Create a preliminary fill value $P = R_n {}^*F_m$.
5. Apply a clipping (or other) consistency test to P to obtain F'_m, the final, sanity checked fill value.
6. Fill the gap in V_1 with the value F'_m.

This method is based upon the idea that someone who is expensive/cheap in several areas is likely to be expensive/cheap in others, and by about the same ratio. The nearest neighbor normalization technique can be applied to nominal data, but in that application the available symbol in the matching vector is usually copied directly over without further processing.

5.5.1 Degapping Case Study

This case study illustrates two approaches to missing data:

1. Fill gaps using some kind of estimation algorithm.
2. Construct a classifier that ignores missing data and does the best it can with the data that are present.

The case study involves the use of data mining to estimate the financial risk in extending credit to applicants in the form of a monthly service contract.

The client supplied 33,000 applicant records tagged with ground truth (paid for service vs. did not pay for service). All of these were for applicants who actually received contracts and became customers; the sample was a mixture of *good applicants* and *bad applicants*. A good applicant was one who became a paying customer, and a bad applicant was a serviced customer who defaulted. The purpose of this data mining project was to predict, based upon a service application and a credit report, which applicants would become good customers, and which would not.

The client also supplied over 120,000 untagged customer records, which were used for the computation of descriptive statistics, and various sampling and calibration experiments. Hence, there was a sampling problem with the training data: it was drawn not from the population to the model will be deployed, but from a population of applicants who appeared to be considered *good* at the time they applied. The client recognized and appreciated this problem.

Approximately 89% of the applicants in the data having ground truth were good customers, and the other 11% were bad customers. This is an unbalanced sample, so special measures were taken in developing the predictive model.

The order of the data records was randomized so that linear resampling could be used to extract unbiased samples. Thirty-eight numeric features were extracted from the data (they specifically omit customer age and gender, since gender and age discrimination are illegal in the target industry). About half-a-dozen coded nominal features were added to this set.

There Were Lots of Missing Data

About half of the total features in the sample were absent (empty strings), and not presented in any systematic way. Very few records had all features present. The missing data problem had to be addressed as part of any extensible solution, since each applicant can be expected to have some fields and not others, and varying data *cleanliness*. A lot of effort was devoted to identifying and marking missing data with a special code so that processing software could recognize and handle it.

For the regression experiments, good customers were tagged as class 1, and bad customers were tagged as class 2. A Type I error occurs when a good customer is turned away. A Type II error occurs when a bad customer is accepted. All experimental work was done in a specially equipped working environment that provided the scientist access to tools appropriate to the current stage of development.

Before modeling began, the missing data issue had to be addressed, at least conceptually. To this end, three experiments on the hole-laden data were conducted and documented. The first two experiments required some software development.

Experiment 1

Build a predictive model after filling in missing data using degapping software. Because about half of the features were missing, the degapping software had little information to use for estimating fill values.

Nevertheless, 3667 feature vectors were degapped, giving 3036 usable feature vectors (631 vectors were so sparse they could not be degapped at all). The degapping process required 20 hours of machine time (approximately 40 million vector manipulations in 38-dimensional space were required). The degapped file was split into three equal parts by linear resampling. One part was used for calibration (e.g., z-scoring), one part was used for training, and one part was used for blind testing.

Note: During the degapping, normalization and training processes, ground truth was removed from the files to prevent "Trojan Horsing" the ground truth into the training data. After file preparation, the ground truth was reattached for use in training. The overall classification accuracy on the blind test set was 76%.

The working environment was used to develop a Radial Basis Function (RBF) classifier. The overall accuracy of classification was 76.9%. The confusion matrix was:

class 1's classified as class 1: 756	class 1's classified as class 2: 118
class 2's classified as class 1: 116	class 2's classified as class 2: 22

Conclusion: Degapping this data does supply usable fill values.

Experiment 2

Do not degap the data. Modify the training and execution software to ignore missing data, building a predictive model using only those features actually present in each feature vector.

The suggested software modifications were made to the classification software to allow it to process feature vectors that have missing fields. An 11,000 feature vector training file, and an 11,000 feature vector blind test file were z-scored using statistics from an 11,000 feature vector calibration file. All three files had missing data in place.

The working environment was used to develop an RBF. The overall accuracy was 80.0%. The confusion matrix was:

class 1's classified as class 1: 8452	class 1's classified as class 2: 1287
class 2's classified as class 1: 909	class 2's classified as class 2: 352

Probability of Type I error: 11.7% Probability of Type II error: 8.3%

Analysis of the regression errors and the associated confidence factor values indicated that results could be improved by adding a post-processing rule which reversed the classification decision when the output was class 2 and the confidence was below 0.15. The RBF was rerun with this post-processing rule in place. The overall accuracy of classification rose to 85.3%. The confusion matrix was:

class 1's classified as class 1: 9212	class 1's classified as class 2: 527
class 2's classified as class 1: 1096	class 2's classified as class 2: 165

Probability of Type I error: 4.8% Probability of Type II error: 10.0%

Conclusions: The classic trade between Type I and Type II errors is clearly seen in this experiment. We can turn away fewer good customers at the expense of accepting more bad ones. These results are an improvement over the results of experiment one, since the business model in this industry is more sensitive to Type I errors.

5.5.2 Feature Selection Checklist

Feature selection can be performed in a multitude of ways. Assessing the ability of the resulting feature set to support effective data mining requires answering five questions:

Question 11: Did the original attributes themselves contain minable information?	
Why this question is important?	Data mining tools and methods do not create information; they uncover it. It makes no sense to mine for information that is not there.
What is question seeking?	Does this project have a reasonable chance of success?
Likely responses and their meanings	Some sense of this can be obtained from domain experts, and descriptive analysis of the data.
Follow-up questions	Do I have the tools and methods to extract the latent information from this data?
Special considerations	Operational timelines can be show stoppers. Sometimes is it possible to get information out, but not at a rate that makes the effort worthwhile.

Note: If not, no feature extraction process will produce a minable feature set. Feature selection never creates information; it merely makes information already present more accessible.

Question 12: Did the method chosen to convert the attributes to features preserve the information content of the attributes?	
Why this question is important?	Did we select and condition the data in a way that preserves the latent information?
What is question seeking?	Or, does the data conditioning methodology need to be reformulated?
Likely responses and their meanings	This requires some analysis, and a process audit. Data visualization is often very helpful in assessing what conditioning has done to the data.
Follow-up questions	Were the data conditioned by entirely automated means? How is the customer's processing validated?
Special considerations	Data conditioning should always be automated early in the project.

Note: Careless conversion can destroy latent information.

Question 13: Can the features produced be used by the mining tool(s) and technique(s) to be applied?	
Why this question is important?	This is looking at whether the data and tools are compatible.
What is question seeking?	Do we need new tools? Should the data be refactored?
Likely responses and their meanings	Consider conducting some tests using samples of conditioned data.
Follow-up questions	Make a list of features that must be transformed.
Special considerations	Data transformation can damage information content in ways that are not obvious (e.g., loss of precision).

Note: It is pointless, for example, to represent attributes as character strings if the available mining tools require numeric input.

Question 14: At the time a model must run, which data elements are present, and which are not?	
Why this question is important?	This question is asked to avoid temporal infeasibility (Chapter 1).
What is question seeking?	Will all the features being used in our model be available at the time the model will be run?
Likely responses and their meanings	This requires some understanding of the operational process.
Follow-up questions	Are there any data synchronization problems that must be considered?
Special considerations	This is more likely to be a problem if the data are held in a distributed repository. Assessment of data quality should address the following questions: 1. Is the data set complete? 2. Does the data set contain errors? 3. Does the data set contain empty or unvarying attributes? 4. Does the data set contain incorrectly derived attributes? 5. Does the data set contain missing values? 6. Does the data set contain values that are out of range?

5.6 Summary

Having read this chapter, you know how to select data items for use as features for a data mining project. You understand how to correct dimensionality and sampling deficiencies in the data (data that is too large or too small), and certain data quality problems (e.g., gaps and outliers). You know how to synthesize additional features from existing ones.

Coming up

The next chapter treats paradigm selection and model development. It includes a number of checklists and case studies. It also contains a notional decision rule for choosing the right model for various data mining problems. Various types of modeling are presented.

Chapter 6

Prototyping Plan and Model Development (Step 4)

Purpose

The purpose of this chapter is to describe the practical aspects of planning and carrying out a data mining prototyping effort, Step 4 in our RAD development methodology. We will discuss the selection of project personnel in terms of the skill mix. A detailed discussion of paradigm selection is presented with a supporting case study. A discussion of prototyping is presented with a supporting case study.

Goals

After you have read this chapter, you will understand the practical aspects of planning and carrying out a data mining prototyping effort. You will understand the process of paradigm selection along with the necessary trades, and you will be familiar with the process of data mining model construction.

6.1 Introduction

Step 4 is presented as two sub-steps: Step 4A, during which the prototyping effort is planned (including paradigm selection); and Step 4B, during which the plan is executed and a prototype model is constructed.

6.2 Step 4A: Prototyping Plan

Purpose: Develop a technical plan for a data mining modeling task based upon enterprise goals that covers the essential technical elements: tool selection, experiment formulation, team skill set, schedule, and methodology

Refer to Figure 6.1. During Step 4A, the modeling strategy is finalized, making this a planning step. Based upon the work done in tasks 1–3, analysis is formalized as a sequence of experiments. Experiments that can be performed in parallel can be assigned to different members of the development team. Because discovery breeds discovery, this step will probably be executed several times during the analysis cycle.

A Sample Project Plan

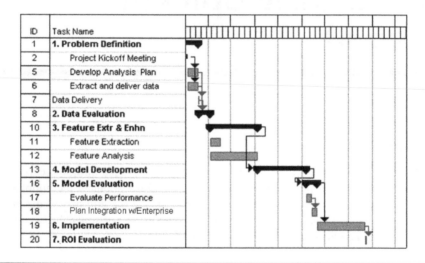

ID	Task Name
1	1. Problem Definition
2	Project Kickoff Meeting
5	Develop Analysis Plan
6	Extract and deliver data
7	Data Delivery
8	2. Data Evaluation
10	3. Feature Extr & Enhn
11	Feature Extraction
12	Feature Analysis
13	4. Model Development
16	5. Model Evaluation
17	Evaluate Performance
18	Plan Integration w/Enterprise
19	6. Implementation
20	7. ROI Evaluation

Figure 6.1   Sample project plan.

6.2.1 Prototype Planning as Part of a Data Mining Project

Rapid prototyping efforts aren't linear, so the schedules below consist of lists of tasks that are done in spirals, with the total effort allocated to each.

Notice that the amount of effort dedicated to data conditioning (tasks 2 and 3 in Figure 6.1), constitute the lion's share of the analytic effort. This is an important point: if lack of time or resources demands that some task be cut short, make it task 4, Model Development. At least this way the results obtained will be valid. Skimping on tasks 2 and 3 in Figure 6.1 is one of the principal causes of failure for data mining projects: the analysis of poorly conditioned data almost guarantees poor results.

Typical data mining efforts involve 1–5 people and take anywhere from 1 month to 1 year, depending on the scope and complexity of the problem being addressed. Projects longer than 6 months are usually on-going efforts that are tracking developments in some evolving domain of great interest to the user.

It is not unusual to precede a large data mining effort (e.g., 5 people for a year) with a small proof-of-concept effort (e.g., 2 people for 2 months). This allows enterprise managers to estimate the Return-On-Investment (ROI) for an extended effort based upon a realistic estimate of what the data will support.

It is also not unusual for the smaller exploratory efforts to be conducted by IT people and domain experts in-house, with larger follow-on's contracted out to experts. If the work done during the small effort is well documented, it can jump-start a larger follow-on.

Principal Participants and Their Tasks

This chapter is focused on Step 4—Model Development, but now that we have reached the heart of every data mining effort, it makes sense to step back for a panoramic view of the entire data mining process. This begins with a look at the single most important element: the team.

The data mining project team:

Our Acronym	Skills	Functions
DM/PM/DE	Data Miner Program Manager Domain Expert	Interview Domain Experts (usually the "end user" of business intelligence)
SE/DM/DO	Software Engineer Data Miner Data Owner	Interview Data Owners (usually MIS personnel charged with collection and maintenance)
SE	Software Engineer	Collect documentation (SOW, white papers, schemas, specs)
SE	Software Engineer	Select media and hosting mechanisms (how data will be transferred as stored)
SE/DM	Software Engineer Data Miner	Create the data mining environment (set up lab/workspace/intranet)
SE/DM	Software Engineer Data Miner	Co-locate tools (might include purchase, licensing and installation)

Task List/Levels of Effort

Task 1: Problem Definition (5%)

- Subtask 1A: DM/PM/DE   Interview Domain Experts
- Subtask 1B: SE/DM/DO   Interview Data Owners
- Subtask 1C: SE   Collect documentation
- Subtask 1D: SE   Select media and hosting mechanisms
- Subtask 1E: SE/DM   Create the analytic environment
- Subtask 1F: SE/DM   Co-locate tools

Task 2: Data Evaluation (20%)

- Subtask 2A: SE   Ingest data
- Subtask 2B: SE   Format data
- Subtask 2C: SE/DM   Validate ingest and format operations
- Subtask 2D: DM/SE   Randomize record order
- Subtask 2E: DM/SE   Sample data
- Subtask 2F: DM/SE   Partition data

Task 3: Feature Extraction and Enhancement (35%)

- Subtask 3A: DM/DE/SE   Data Evaluation, Cleansing, and Conditioning
- Subtask 3B: DM/SE   Autoclustering, Visualization, Statistical Regression, OLAP

Task 4A: Prototyping Plan (2%)

- Subtask 4A: DM/DE/PM   Formulate descriptive hypotheses, prepare prototyping plan

Task 4B: Prototyping/Model Development (20%)

- Subtask 4B: DM/SE/DE   Systematic Analytics, Model Construction

Task 5: Model Evaluation (3%)

- Subtask 5: DM/DE/PM   Model Evaluation, documentation of status

Task 6: Implementation (15%)

- Subtask 6: DM/DE/SE/PM Implementation and Delivery

Paradigm Selection

Paradigm selection is not a trivial undertaking, and cannot be reduced entirely to a mechanical process. But, a systematic approach such as the one presented here is very helpful in codifying the experience of expert practitioners, and can guide the general data mining practitioner.

Principal Participants and Their Tasks

DM/DE/PM Formulate descriptive hypotheses, prepare prototyping plan

6.3 Prototyping Plan Case Study

This case study describes a short sequence of experiments involving the use of special analytic tools to investigate the effect of feature winnowing (Chapter 4) on a high-dimensional data mining problem.

Likelihood Ratio Classifier Feature Winnowing Test

An empirical experiment was conducted to verify that the tool being considered for modeling, a particular Likelihood Ratio (LRAT) classifier tool, could be applied to relatively high-dimensional data (1,000 features, 48 megabytes) with reasonable results. Further, it was shown experimentally that naïve dimension reduction could be applied to the data with only modest loss of accuracy. To make sure that all tools were interoperable, and could handle the relatively large feature set, three scaling tests were conducted.

Scaling Test 1

Show that the classifier can solve the original high-dimensional problem. A 10,000-vector test set having 500 ground truth classes, and 1,000 features in each vector was synthesized using a data generator. LRAT was trained on half the data (5,000 vectors), achieving roughly 96% on the training set. Training time was 126 minutes.

On the blind test set (5,000 vectors), the trained LRAT machine got 95.2%. Execution time for all 5,000 vectors was 27 seconds (5.4 ms/classification), which includes file I/O time.

Scaling Test 2

Perform aggressive dimension reduction (1000D to 33D), and show that the resulting problem retains most of the class-discriminating information of the original. A proprietary feature winnowing application was then applied to intelligently merge the data into 33 features. Training on half of this lower-dimension file (5,000 vectors) resulted in LRAT performance of 86.86%. Training time was 4.6 minutes (30X faster than raw).

On the 33-dimensional blind test (5,000 vectors), LRAT performance was 86.74%. Execution time for all 5,000 vectors was about 1 second, which includes file I/O time. This is a modest loss of accuracy on a problem having 500 balanced ground truth classes.

Scaling Test 3

Perform hyper-dimension reduction (1,000D to 5D), and show that most of the class-discriminating information is still present. A proprietary feature winnowing method was then applied to merge the 1,000D data into only 5 features. Training on half this low-dimensional data (5,000 vectors) resulted in LRAT performance of 66.66%. Training time was 73 seconds (100X faster than raw).

On the 5-dimensional blind test (5,000 vectors), LRAT got 63.7%. Execution time for all 5,000 vectors was about 1 second, which includes file I/O time.

All of the tests were above done using the minimum parameter setting to obtain the simplest possible LRAT classifier. To see whether classification accuracy could be increased on the low-dimensional data set, retraining was performed with a higher setting.

At the higher setting LRAT got 82.02% on the 5-dimensional training set (5,000 vectors), and training time was 3.4 minutes (40X faster than raw). On the blind set (5,000 vectors), LRAT got 73.72%, and the execution time on all 5,000 vectors was 1 second.

Conclusions

LRAT could be applied to relatively high-dimensional (on the order of 1000 dimensions) data with reasonable results. Further, it was possible to perform hyper-dimension reduction and still retain most class-discriminating information: Approximately 73% of discriminating information was retained in the 5-dimensional case tested. Keep in mind that for a 500-class problem, random guessing will give a classification accuracy of only 0.2%.

Prototype Planning Checklist

Paradigm selection is driven by several factors, but primarily by the nature of the problem itself. The most important aspects of the problem for paradigm selection can be addressed in a formulaic way by running a checklist of questions like the following:

The Nature of the Problem

Question 1: How well is the problem understood?	
Why is this question important?	The less well understood a problem is the more reliance must be placed on black-box methods (described below).
What is this question seeking?	If no one really understands the problem intuitively, an expert system or other white-box solution is probably not the right approach.
Likely responses and their meanings	Domain experts will be able to tell you if anyone can solve instances of the problem manually.
Follow-up questions	What books and documents best describe the problem?
Special considerations	Domain intuition: low/medium/high (e.g. experts available, good documentation, etc.).

Question 2: How big is the problem?	
Why is this question important?	Scale is a cost and complexity driver.
What is this question seeking?	This is looking at whether your existing infrastructure and tool set are adequate to work on the problem.
Likely responses and their meanings	Domain experts can generally give very precise answers to this question.
Follow-up questions	Are there any documents available that describe the data?
Special considerations	<ul><li>Vector count: Number of exemplars (low/medium/high)</li><li>Feature count: Dimension of feature space (low/medium/high)</li><li>Class count: Number of ground-truth classes, values, categories (low/medium/high)</li><li>Cost/schedule/talent: Programmatic constraints on the effort (dollars, days, staff)</li><li>Applicable tools: Own/make/buy, familiarity, scope</li><li>Integration: Development vs. operational environment</li></ul>

Question 3: What kind of data do we have?	
Why is this question important?	Data mining tools usually work on either numeric data, or nominal data, but not both (there are exceptions). If the data are a mixture of nominal and numeric, this must be addressed in the data mining project plan.
What is this question seeking?	Are the data all of one type so that a single tool can be used in a single way?
Likely responses and their meanings	Usually a domain expert will be able to answer this question in detail.
Follow-up questions	Are there any documents available that describe the data?
Special considerations	• Feature type: Nominal/numeric/complex (bag of words, sequence, concept graph) • Feature mix: Homogeneous/heterogeneous by type • Feature tempo: Fresh/stale, periodic/sporadic, synchronous/asynchronous • Feature data quality: SNR (low/high), gaps (few/many), access (easy/hard), conformance • Feature information quality: Salience, correlation, localization, conditioning

Question 4: What question are we answering?	
Why is this question important?	You are attempting to get at the real, underlying purpose of the project, and how it should be approached.
What is this question seeking?	Is this a classification problem? An estimation problem? A planning problem? Properly categorizing the problem is essential to developing a principled approach to its solution.
Likely responses and their meanings	You will have to infer the answer from responses to probing questions you ask about how the product of your project will be used.
Follow-up questions	Do different users use the system in different ways? Do they have different goals, and therefore, different needs?
Special considerations	• Ground truth type: Nominal (e.g., class name), numeric (e.g., score), complex (e.g., plan) • Ground truth quality: SNR (low/high), gaps (few/many), accessibility (easy/hard)

Question 5: How deeply buried in the data is the answer?	
Why is this question important?	We are trying to determine how "hard" the problem is. Is there a lot of "low hanging fruit" that we can mine rapidly? Or will we have to wring value out in tiny, reluctant droplets?
What is this question seeking?	The difficulty of the problem is the major determiner in the kind of solution you will have to build, and the amount of data conditioning that will be required.
Likely responses and their meanings	Domain experts will have an intuitive notion of this, but it won't necessarily be a reliable predictor of what a data mining effort can accomplish.
Follow-up questions	Is there any "low hanging fruit"? What is it?
Special considerations	• Linearly separable; any two classes can be separated by hyperplane • Classes my encroach and interlock, are disjoint • Classes are unambiguous, but they overlap • Data contain class collisions (intractable/ambiguous)

Question 6: How must the answer be presented to the user?	
Why is this question important?	You want to present information in a form and manner that makes the user most effective. Data mining should be a *force multiplier* for the user.
What is this question seeking?	What is the most effective way to tell the data's story to the user? What should be included in that story, and what should be left out?
Likely responses and their meanings	Domain experts know what will help them, and will tell you.
Follow-up questions	Ask for documentation on the user interface.
Special considerations	• Forensics: GUI, reports, confidence factors, confidence intervals, conclusion justification • Integration: ASP/standalone/dll, shared library/fully integrated with user environment • Accuracy: Definition of success (e.g., % correct, confusion matrix, lift chart) • Performance: Throughput, ease of use, MTBF (mean time between failures) • Maintenance: Documentation/support, periodic retraining, new model generation capability

The Plausible Solutions

Once the problem has been described, the data miner must determine the plausible solutions.

First: A Notional List of Candidate Solutions

White box methods are those based upon a detailed understanding of the mechanisms underlying the domain. Black Box methods are those that model patterns, but have no understanding of the underlying mechanisms. These will be described in more detail below.

White Box Methods:

- OLAP (e.g., SQL reports, histograms, 2-dimensional plots)
- Conventional statistical inference (parametric statistics)
- Data-driven visualization (e.g., Excel)
- KBES (e.g., Fuzzy Logic, Petri nets, Bayesian Belief Networks)

Black Box Methods:

- Linear and logistic regression
- Abstract visualization (e.g., parallel coordinates)
- Autoclustering (e.g., K-Means, non-parametric statistics)
- Link analysis (recognizing things that "happen together")
- Rule induction (e.g., QUBIST, C5, grammatical methods for text)
- Neural networks (e.g., MLP)
- Decision trees (e.g., CART, C5)
- Belief nets (e.g., BBN)
- Numerical regression (e.g., RBF, SVM, ALN)

Second: The Characteristics of Various Solutions

Once the list of plausible solutions has been generated, the characteristics of each are enumerated in terms of their domain requirements. Some samples follow:

KBES (Knowledge-Based Expert System)

- Required intuition: high
- Vector count supported: high
- Feature count supported: medium
- Class count supported: medium
- Cost to develop: high
- Schedule to develop: high
- Talent to develop: medium, high

- Tools to develop: can be expensive to buy/make
- Feature types supported: nominal/numeric/complex
- Feature mix supported: homogeneous, heterogeneous
- Feature data quality needed: need not fill gaps
- Ground truth types supported: nominal, complex
- Relative representational power: low
- Relative performance: fast, intuitive, robust
- Relative weaknesses: ad hoc; must have relatively simple class boundaries
- Relative strengths: intuitive; easy to provide conclusion justification

MLP (Multi-Layer Perceptron)

- Required intuition: low
- Vector count supported: high
- Feature count supported: medium
- Class count supported: medium
- Cost to develop: low
- Schedule to develop: medium
- Talent to develop: medium
- Tools to develop: easy to obtain inexpensively
- Feature types supported: numeric
- Feature mix supported: homogeneous
- Feature data quality needed: must fill gaps
- Ground truth types supported: nominal, numeric
- Relative representational power: high
- Relative performance: moderately fast
- Relative weaknesses: inscrutable; subject to uncontrolled regression
- Relative strengths: easy to build

RBF (Radial Basis Function)

- Required intuition: low
- Vector count supported: high
- Feature count supported: medium
- Class count supported: high
- Cost to develop: low
- Schedule to develop: medium
- Talent to develop: medium
- Tools to develop: easy to obtain inexpensively
- Feature types supported: numeric
- Feature mix supported: homogeneous
- Feature data quality needed: need not fill gaps
- Ground truth types supported: nominal, numeric
- Relative representational power: high
- Relative performance: moderately fast

- Relative weaknesses: inscrutable; models tend to be large
- Relative strengths: uncontrolled regression can be mitigated

Decision Trees (e.g., CART)

- Required intuition: low
- Vector count supported: high
- Feature count supported: medium
- Class count supported: high
- Cost to develop: low
- Schedule to develop: medium
- Talent to develop: medium
- Tools to develop: easy to obtain inexpensively
- Feature types supported: nominal, numeric
- Feature mix supported: homogeneous, heterogeneous
- Feature data quality needed: need not fill gaps
- Ground truth types supported: nominal, numeric
- Relative representational power: high
- Relative performance: moderately fast
- Relative weaknesses: often produces many "low support" nodes or rules
- Relative strengths: can provide insight into the domain

SVM (Support Vector Machines)

- Required intuition: low
- Vector count supported: high
- Feature count supported: high
- Class count supported: two
- Cost to develop: medium
- Schedule to develop: medium
- Talent to develop: medium
- Tools to develop: easy to obtain inexpensively
- Feature types supported: numeric
- Feature mix supported: homogeneous
- Feature data quality needed: must fill gaps
- Ground truth types supported: nominal, numeric
- Relative representational power: high
- Relative performance: moderately fast
- Relative weaknesses: inscrutable; can be hard to train
- Relative strengths: minimizes need for expensive feature enhancement

Finally: Some Rough Paradigm Selection Heuristics

Finally, the problem description and the enumeration of paradigm characteristics are laid side-by-side. A simple set of heuristics can guide paradigm selection. A generic example of a paradigm selection heuristic follows:

IF

the ground truth is discrete;
there aren't too many classes;
the class boundaries are simple;
the number of features is medium;
the data are heterogeneous;
there is no comprehensive, representative data set with GT;
the population is unbalanced by class;
the domain is well-understood by available experts;
a conclusion justification is needed;
THEN consider a knowledge-based system (e.g., KBES)

ELSE IF

the ground truth is numeric;
there is a medium number of classes;
the class boundaries are complex;
the number of features is medium;
the data are numeric;
there is a comprehensive, representative data set tagged with GT;
the population is relatively balanced by class;
the domain is not well-understood by available experts;
a conclusion justification is not needed;
THEN consider a non-parametric regression (e.g., multi-layer perceptron)

ELSE IF

the ground truth is numeric or nominal;
there is a large number of classes;
the class boundaries are very complex;
the number of features is medium to large;
the data are numeric;
there is a representative data set tagged with GT;
the population is unbalanced by class;
the domain is not well-understood by available experts;
a conclusion justification is not needed;
THEN consider a kernel based regression (e.g., radial basis function)

ELSE IF

the ground truth is numeric or nominal;
there is a very small number of classes;
the class boundaries very complex;
the number of features is very large;
the data are numeric;
there is a comprehensive, representative data set tagged with GT;
the population is unbalanced by class;

the domain is not well-understood by available experts;
a conclusion justification is not needed;
THEN consider a margin optimizing regression (e.g., support vector machine)

ELSE IF

the ground truth is numeric or nominal;
there is a medium number of classes;
the class boundaries are very complex;
the number of features is medium to large;
the data are numeric, nominal, or complex;
there is a representative data set tagged with GT;
the population is unbalanced by class;
the domain is not well-understood by available experts;
a conclusion justification is needed;0
THEN consider a decision tree (C5, CART, BBN)

END IF

6.4 Step 4B: Prototyping/Model Development

Purpose:

- Develop Models (explanatory, predictive, or both)

Principal Participants and Their Tasks:

- DM/SE/PM Systematic Analytics, Model Construction

Step 4B is what is often referred to as *data modeling*. It's the step during which actionable patterns are exploited. This step uses the training set. If intermediate validation of a discovery or model is needed during this step, it's fair to use the *calibration set*. Using the *validation set* during this step, however, is an intolerable violation of methodology, because it invalidates later blind tests based upon the validation set.

White Box vs. Black Box Modeling

White box methods use comprehensive formal characterization of the system being modeled to emulate system processes. Since some methods assume a full knowledge of system internals, they are often referred to as *model-based* methods. A satellite motion model based upon kinematics and gravitation is an example.

Black box methods (also called *non-model-based*) use a stimulus/response approach (often probabilistic in nature) to emulate system processes. Since non-model-based methods do not assume knowledge of the actual system internals, they are sometimes referred to as *agnostic models*. A ground-vehicle motion model based upon a Kalman Filter[4] is an example.

Table 6.1 Black Box and White Box Characteristics

	Strengths	Weaknesses
White Box	• Understandable by humans, so easier to maintain • Naturally supports development of conclusion justification reports • Unlikely to give "ridiculous" answers • Easy to hold dynamic variables (e.g., labor rates) outside the model, making it insensitive to variation	• Tend to dramatically increase in complexity over time as ad hoc modifications are made • Inherently simplistic; doesn't naturally handle inscrutable cases, even when these are systematic • Often require the creation of multiple models or incorporation of ad hoc rules to handle special cases • Formulation of universal models is difficult and time consuming

	Strengths	Weaknesses
Black Box	• Trainable; can be developed without a complete understanding of the problem • Can handle arbitrary complexity without manual modification of the model • No need to subdivide problems into cases: one model can cover the entire universe of discourse • Can be retrained with new data to update for changing conditions	• Inscrutable • Very difficult to provide a conclusion justification capability • Uncontrolled regression and overtraining can lead to generation of "ridiculous" answers • Change in dynamic variables inside model (e.g., labor rates) will degrade model performance

Strengths and Weaknesses of Black and White Box Models

Black and white box approaches have characteristic strengths and weaknesses (see Table 6.1).

Training and Retraining a Model

An intelligent system once fielded will not be static, because the problem is not static. If the system is to survive increases in scope and scale, its pattern processing agents must be retrainable. This training might have to support the addition of new entities (e.g., entity types, entity behaviors) and incorporate automatic tuning and diagnosis. Machine learning technology is ideally suited to the construction of applications having these attributes. Applications that are not trainable are subject to a perpetual cycle of obsolescence and manual redesign.

The computational costs associated with cognitive systems are different during training and operation. During training, the greatest cost incurred for virtually all machine reasoning is based upon a single fundamental operation: compute a weighted distance between two symbols. The precise nature of this distance depends upon the nature of the symbols (e.g., text, numeric arrays, images).

During execution, the greatest computational cost for machine reasoning systems is in data conditioning and feature extraction. For this reason, it is important that efficient methods for these procedures be developed.

6.5 Model Development Case Study

Researchers[5] have investigated the application of predictive modeling to the problem of short-term electrical load forecasting for electric utilities. Short-term in this context typically means *next day*. These forecasts are based upon previous day actual loads and meteorological factors (e.g., max-min temperature, relative humidity).

This case study describes the application of a particular kind of classifier (radial basis functions, RBFs) to the long-term (next year) load forecasting problem. This work used 12 months of hourly meteorological data, and the corresponding hourly load data for both commercial and residential feeders. The RBF trained on 20% of the weather/load data (selected by simple linear sampling), and estimated the hourly load for an entire year (8,760 data points) with 9.1% error (RMS, relative to daily peak load). By comparison, monthly mean profiles perform at c. 12% error. The best short-term load forecasters operate in the 2% error range.

The Long-Term Load-Forecasting Problem

Long-term load forecasting is the prediction of load at some future time using estimates of conditions at that future time. Since no *previous day* actual load data is available to support such a forecast, long-term load prediction must be based exclusively on phenomenological factors (e.g., temporal and meteorological).

Data Collection

Actual load data was provided at two feeders: feeder1 served just commercial users, and feeder2 served just residential users. Load was expressed in amps at 11kv. Load data were collected every 30 minutes (on the half-hour), 24 hours/day during the entire period from November 1, 1993 to October 31, 1994. This is a total of 17,520 load values for each feeder. All load data were stamped with a date-time group.

Weather data were collected by a government meteorological station in the area. Weather data consisted of:

- Wet-bulb temperature (degrees Celsius)
- Dry-bulb temperature (degrees Celsius)
- Relative humidity (%)
- Wind direction (degrees of bearing)
- Wind speed (knots)
- Cloudiness factor (an integer: low = 1 to 10 = high)

Weather data were collected every hour (on the hour), 24 hours/day during the entire period from November 1, 1993 to October 31, 1994, a total of 8,760 sets of readings. (Exception: cloudiness factor was collected only every 3 hours, at 0200, 0500, 0800, 1100, 1400, 1700, 2000, and 2300 hours).

Commercial load forecasting and residential load forecasting were treated as completely separate problems. The commercial and residential data were not mixed or used jointly in any way for this study.

Selecting the Features

Because weather data was available only on the hour, the half hour load data was not used for this study. This left a pair of hourly load/weather data consisting of 8,760 data points for each of the commercial and residential sets. Cloudiness factor was not selected as a feature because it was available only for some hours.

For prototyping efficiency, it was desirable to keep the dimensionality of feature space as low as possible. The correlation coefficient of wind direction with load was very low, and the correlation coefficient of dry-bulb with wet-bulb temperature was very high (0.94). Therefore, wind direction and wet-bulb temperature were deemed irrelevant and redundant, and not selected as features. This left a set of meteorological features consisting of dry-bulb temperature, relative humidity, and wind speed.

Graphical display of the load data versus time showed consistent daily profiles. Three fundamental *day types* were observed: weekdays (Monday-Friday); weekend days (Saturday and Sunday); and holiday days (e.g., Christmas Day). Day type was selected as a feature. Month and hour of day were seen to be correlated with load, and were selected as features. This gave a set of temporal features consisting of month, day of week, and day type.

Thus, the selection process yielded a set of six temporal meteorological features: Month, day type, hour of day, dry-bulb temperature, relative humidity, and wind speed.

Coding the Feature Vectors

How should features be represented within the feature vector? A naive representation of time by hour number (0–23) would tell the RBF that 11 p.m., which has representation "23", is very far in feature space from midnight, which has representation "0". Similarly, for coding the month, December ("12") would be presented to the RBF as being very far in feature space from January ("1").

Also, relative humidity represented in percentage points attains much higher numeric values, and has greater dynamic range than any other feature. And, what should be the representation of day type?

A partial solution to the representation problem is offered by principle component analysis. This handles range and centering variations, but destroys the semantic identify of the features, which is needed for experimental work. Therefore, PCA was not applied in this study.

For this study, month and hour of day were coded by their corresponding average temperature. That is, the month January was represented in the feature vector as 20.4, the average temperature during January. Similarly, 8 a.m. was represented as 13.8, the average temperature (over the whole year) at that time. It would be preferable to code these variables by average load (the variable to be predicted), but using ground truth for feature coding is a perilous activity, and best avoided.

The humidity data were linearly rescaled to be in the range 0 to 20 (roughly commensurable with the temperature data). Wind speed data were not coded.

Day type was coded to show that holidays and weekends had similar average load levels, both of which were very different, and less than weekday levels: holiday = 1, weekend = 4, weekday = 12.

The Load-Forecasting Problem as a Classification Problem

Since load is a continuous random variable, a discrete RBF classifier might appear ill suited for load prediction. We posed the problem in terms of classification to exploit the RBF's controlled regression, and to guarantee the existence of a development path to an ultrahigh throughput hardware implementation.

Day Profiles and Quantized Correction Factors

For each of the seven days of the week, a load profile was computed. This profile was the entire year's arithmetic average of the 24 hourly loads for that day of the week. For example, the Monday profile consists of 24 loads: the hour 0 load is the average of the entire year's Monday at 12 a.m. loads, etc. Therefore, the Monday profile is the waveform of hourly loads for an "average Monday". A profile was also prepared for the average holiday, given a total of 8 day of week load profiles.

Because the day profiles were only gross averages, and do not take phenomenological features into account, they were weak predictors. For any particular date and time, the actual measured load was usually different from the profile load for that day of the week. The ratio F = *(actual load) / (profile load)* gives a correction factor for that date and time. If we could predict from temporal and meteorological features what correction factor to apply to the profile load, the profile could be corrected to a predicted load.

This is the approach taken under this study. In this way, by quantizing the range of correction factors observed (0.5–1.5, roughly), the load prediction problem was recast. It became the problem of selecting the correct one of (finitely many) quantization bins for the correction factor: it was now a classification problem rather than an estimation problem.

The approach may be stated:

- The interval from 0.5 to 1.5 was divided into a finite number of bins. The midpoint (for example) of each bin was its reconstruction value, F.
- For each of the feature vectors in the training set, the correction factor F was computed from profile load to actual load. The bin number containing this multiplier F became the desired output of the RBF for this feature vector. This output was an integer.
- The RBF was trained to produce the desired bin number as its output.

To use the RBF as a load predictor:

- Input a feature vector of temporal and meteorological features. Using these features as input, the RBF returned a bin number, which corresponded to a known correction factor, F.
- Multiply the profile value for the desired hour/day of week values by the correction factor F to obtain the load prediction.

The study RBF applied single point corrections to a template based upon phenomenological data. Notice that the RBF had to be run for each prediction desired, so prediction of an entire day's data required 24 runs.

The Training Set

Examination of the 365 days of available feature vectors revealed 14 days with corrupted data (typically, drop-outs resulting from sensors going off-line). These days were not considered during exemplar selection, leaving 351 days of data, having a total of 24 * 351 = 8,424 feature vectors.

Smoothing as a Post Process

The study prototype did not take into account the fact there is a behavior lag inherent in utility loads: consumers do not respond to weather conditions continuously and in real-time; rather, they tend to set their consumption based upon recent experience and perceived trends. It was found that this could be partially compensated for by spatial smoothing of the predicted load waveforms with an averaging filter. A 3 hour wide, centered-output window with uniform weights was used.

Results

Evaluation testing was against the whole 365 days of feature vectors (including bad days), and so constituted a test which was over 80% blind, and included nearly 4% real-world anomalous input.

The customary error measurement for load prediction in the literature is *RMS % of peak load* (RMS%pl). That is, an RMS error computed over the entire prediction period (usually 24 hours), divided by the period's peak load, and multiplied by 100%.

Short-term load predictors typically use previous day load data, and perform at a nominal 2% error (RMS%pl). Our stated error was the average of the 365 RMS%pl errors for the year.

Residential Feeder

The RBF was trained on the residential feeder data using six output quantization bins. The study RBF reconstructed the entire year's residential loads from the corresponding meteorological data and performed at 9.1% error.

Commercial Feeder

The same RBF was retrained on the commercial feeder data using six output quantization bins. The study RBF reconstructed the entire year's commercial loads from the corresponding meteorological data and performed at 6.9% error.

Note: Of the 1,685 feature vectors that were in the training set, the RBF returned the correct quantization bin 1,682 times, an accuracy of 99.8%.

Experiments were conducted at various quantization levels, using up to 120 bins. The results did not vary much with the number of quantization bins, although ambiguities in the training set did show up when using more bins (i.e., same weather data, different desired load).

Model Development Checklist

Question 7: Who should be involved in prototype reviews?	
Why this question is important?	You need to know whom to invite/accommodate for formal reviews, both on the customer side, and your side.
What is question seeking?	Who should you expect to be at reviews? Whom should you bring/send? What level of decision-making will occur at reviews?
Likely responses and their meanings	Attendees will vary from meeting to meeting.
Follow-up questions	Get contact information for likely attendees.
Special considerations	Be prepared for technical consultants retained by the customer to show up at reviews unannounced.

Question 8: What is a reasonable timing for prototype releases?	
Why this question is important?	The release schedule for prototypes should be kept somewhat loose, so that the benefits of RAD development can be fully realized. This is your chance to discuss this.
What is question seeking?	This information is helpful in creating a realistic project schedule, since, for example, you might want to have prototype releases somewhat synchronized with project reviews.
Likely responses and their meanings	Releases closer together than 30 to 60 days probably don't provide sufficient time for measurable progress. Releases more than 90 days apart will not get the full advantage of user feedback.
Follow-up questions	Be sure to determine in what form releases are to be made: documents or simulations only, Formal demos, etc.
Special considerations	A prototype delivery adds project overhead. You don't want too many.

Question 9: Where and how should prototype reviews be conducted?	
Why this question is important?	Face-to-face reviews are cost drivers (time, travel, lost work, etc.).
What is question seeking?	You are trying to determine the time and cost associated with these events so you can plan for it.
Likely responses and their meanings	It is customary to alternate locations between develop and customer; this provides some cost sharing.
Follow-up questions	Establish general dates for reviews, but make sure that everyone knows these are subject to change based upon project progress.
Special considerations	If you can get the customer to come to your location, it will save you time and money.

Question 10: What is the configuration management plan?	
Why this question is important?	For data mining projects, you will need to have some mechanism for source and version control for data and prototypes developed.
What is question seeking?	Do you have a configuration management plan?
Likely responses and their meanings	Sadly, this is often forgotten until some data loss disaster reminds everyone how important it is.
Follow-up questions	What will you tell your customer when 6 weeks of work is lost because of a versioning problem?
Special considerations	Lots of tools for versioning and configuration control exist. Some are freeware. There is no good reason for not having a robust and rigidly enforced configuration management system in place.

Question 11: Will I synthesize features?	
Why is this question important?	Because feature synthesis alters the view of the problem space, detection of problems is made more difficult. There are inherent risks; in particular, it is during synthesis that certain bad things (like Trojan Horsing) can happen, for example, by synthesizing the wrong data due to a software bug.
What is this question seeking?	Do we have a sound synthesis strategy? A sound strategy will include validation methods.
Likely responses and their meanings	The synthesis strategy should be included in the project final report.
Follow-up questions	Does the synthesis strategy violate any data policies for example, does it use any "forbidden fields" (e.g., race, gender, age, etc.)?
Special considerations	Feature synthesis algorithms should be automated.

6.6 Summary

Having read this chapter, you understand the practical aspects of planning and carrying out a data mining prototyping effort. You understand the process of paradigm selection along with the necessary trades, and you are familiar with the process of data mining model construction.

Coming up

The next chapter presents a treatment of model evaluation. It includes a detailed discussion of a wide range of model metrics, a model evaluation case study, and a model evaluation checklist.

6.6 Summary

Having read this chapter, you will be able to ...

Chapter 7

Model Evaluation (Step 5)

Purpose

The purpose of this chapter is to lay out the technical aspects of data mining model evaluation. This chapter also explains the meaning and use of a wide range of metrics commonly used to evaluate models created using data mining technology. An evaluation checklist is provided. A case study shows how model evaluation metrics can be used in a simulation to optimize a control system.

Goals

After you have read this chapter, you will be familiar with a wide range of quality metrics used for data mining model evaluation. You will know what these metrics measure, and how to compute them from a confusion matrix. You will see an example of how model metrics can be used in combination with simulation to perform sophisticated predictive analytics.

7.1 Introduction

The evaluation of a data mining project should be driven by the project technical goals and the project business case. For experimental/proof-of-concept projects, the expected deliverables are usually a report documenting data, methods, findings, suggestions for future work, and possibly a prototype demonstration.

Data mining efforts are often undertaken to improve some existing process, or answer a specific set of questions. Model evaluation in this scenario will involve looking at how the data mining project has or will improve processes, and whether it has provided usable answers to questions asked. Therefore, model evaluation for data mining projects usually means quantifying performance metrics, such as prediction accuracy, false alarm rates, speed of performance, and so on.

7.2 Evaluation Goals and Methods

During model evaluation, the data mining researcher and program manager take stock of the progress in discovery/exploitation, documenting successes and failures against the plan formalized in step 4A.

Evaluation of data mining applications can be complex, requiring the use of an array of metric and forensic techniques. The customary approach is to evaluate applications for performance versus project goals, and evaluate application stability.

7.2.1 Performance Evaluation Components

Performance evaluation has three components: metric, forensic, and functional.

Metric: Analysis of quantitative scores

- Validation methods and metrics (blind-testing, cross-validation, accuracy and confusion matrices)
- Speed of training, and speed of execution
- Consumption of machine resources (memory, bandwidth)
- Feature-space complexity (dimension, heterogeneity)

Forensic: Analysis of application feedback and self-awareness

- Confidences and belief vectors supplied by the application
- Conclusion Justification Report (CJR) generated by the application
- Sensitivity analysis (parameter sensitivity, adequacy of topology)
- Expert evaluation (Is the application getting the *right* answers for the right reasons?)

Functional: Analysis of system-level effects

- Impact on the user (error mitigation, reduced workload, increased cognitive bandwidth)

7.2.2 Stability Evaluation Components

Stability evaluation has two components: generalization, and self-assessment.

Generalization: Operates correctly and/or degrades predictably outside the region of feature space for which it was constructed.

Trainable applications base their processing upon examples from a training set. It is to be expected that such an application will correctly process inputs from its training set. But will it be able to handle inputs that it has not seen? The extrapolation of knowledge gleaned from a training set to the problem domain as a whole is called *generalization*. Generalization is an essential attribute for trainable applications operating in domains for which future inputs cannot be perfectly predicted.

During development, trainable applications extract and correlate information from examples of correct instances. These training examples consist of feature vectors with correct outcomes assigned (either by human experts, history, or by a classifier). There are several factors that drive model generalization:

- **Domain coverage.** Do the training data have examples of all phenomenology? Effective training requires that the training examples exhaust the *universe of discourse*; that is, examples must be included for all the input types that the finished system is required to handle. When a training set has examples of all of the input type the application must handle, we say that it provides domain coverage.
- **Feature salience.** Do the features selected have generalizable information content? Features are said to be *salient* when they are positively correlated with some correct outcomes. That is, they discriminate between different outcome decisions in a consistent way.
- **Representational power.** Is the application adequately parameterized for the problem? A trainable application's ability to generalize is limited by its power to parameterize boundaries in the feature space. Applications having few parameters typically have little representational power. An optimal application will have the minimum number of parameters required to represent the problem domain.
- **Avoidance of overtraining.** Has the classifier over-fit the training set? It is possible to *over train* a learning application. Knowledge that generalizes is usually learned in the early stages of training; if training is continued beyond a certain critical point, most applications will begin to memorize the training set. This is problematic, because an over trained application will use the idiosyncrasies of the training data in its processing, rather than general domain knowledge.
- **Blind testing.** Factory evaluation of data that has yet to be seen.
- **Avoidance of brittleness.** Use of maximum margins where appropriate to avoid brittleness (e.g., SVM, fuzzy rules)

Self-assessment: Is the model aware of its own limitations? Does it "know what it does not know"?

- **Domain drift.** Does the model consider whether the feature vectors being processed are within the range of the data used to train it?
- **Self-reports.** Can the model detect and compensate for degradation in its own performance?

Principal Participants and Their Tasks:

DM/PM   Model evaluation, documentation of status

If it is determined that prototyping work has been completed, the team proceeds to data mining Step 6, Implementation. If there are still discovery/exploitation tasks to execute and progress has been good, the team might go back to Step 4A for another pass. If progress is insufficient, the team might return to data mining Step 3, Feature Extraction and Enhancement, to consider selecting different/additional features so that data can be reworked. If negligible progress has been made, the team might need to return to data mining Step 2 or Step 1 to rethink the project goals.

7.3 What Does Accuracy Mean?

Every problem domain has a preferred method of measuring the correctness of results. Because the effects of different kinds of error vary from domain to domain, a variety of accuracy measures are used in practice. In some domains a false positive from a classifier is the most costly mistake, while in other domains a false negative is the most costly mistake. The cost of modeling error is problem dependent, making the best choice of accuracy measure problem dependent.

7.3.1 Confusion Matrix Example

A very general measure of correctness that provides sufficient information to compute many others is the confusion matrix. It is used to evaluate detectors and classifiers— data mining applications that detect/classify vectors into one of a number of ground truth classes.

Let the number of vectors classified be 100; suppose there are four ground truth classes; 1, 2, 3, and 4, each consisting of 25 vectors. A confusion matrix for the classifier shows performance for each class. Given the confusion matrix below, rows represent ground truth counts, and columns represent the classifier's decisions.

Table 7.1 Confusion Matrix Example 1

Confusion Matrix	Model Classification C1	Model Classification C2	Model Classification C3	Model Classification C4
Ground Truth C1	25	0	0	0
Ground Truth C2	0	1	19	5
Ground Truth C3	0	0	0	25
Ground Truth C4	0	0	1	24

The sum of the entries in row J will be the number of vectors in class J; and the sum of the entries in column K will be the number of vectors the classifier determined were in class K. For example, the last column of the second row indicates that the classifier has (incorrectly) assigned five of the class 2 vectors to class 4. A perfect classifier will produce a confusion matrix that is diagonal: only entries on the diagonal will be non-zero.

Many of the most commonly used performance measures are ratios drawn from the confusion matrix. We begin with four examples that show some of the very different things that "accuracy" can mean.

Classification Accuracy

Classification Accuracy answers the question: What proportion of the entire data set is being correctly classified? This is a single numeric value. It is the number of vectors correctly classified (without respect to class), divided by the total number of vectors. It is computed from the confusion matrix as:

Classification Accuracy = sum of diagonal values / sum of all values

Using the matrix above (Table 7.1), we have the following result:

Classification Accuracy = (25 + 1 + 0 + 24) / 100 = 50%

Recall

Recall answers the question: What proportion of the vectors in class J does the classifier decide are in class J? Note that sometimes the term *class accuracy* is used as a synonym for recall. There will be a recall value for each ground truth class. It is computed from the confusion matrix as:

Recall for Class J = value in row J and column J / sum of entries in row J

For the confusion matrix above (Table 7.1), we have the following class recalls:

Recall for class 1 = 25 / (25 + 0 + 0 + 0) = 100%
Recall for class 2 = 1 / (0 + 1 + 19 + 5) = 4%
Recall for class 3 = 0 / (0 + 0 + 0 + 25) = 0%
Recall for class 4 = 24 / (0 + 0 + 1 + 24) = 96%

Precision

Precision answers the question: When the machine says a vector is in class K, how likely is it to be correct? As with recall, there will be a precision value for each class. Precision measures the proportion of the vectors the machine classified as class K that actually are class K. It is computed from the confusion matrix as:

Precision for Class K = value in row K, column K / sum of entries in column K

For the matrix above (Table 7.1), we have the following precisions:

Precision for class 1 = 25 / (25 + 0 + 0 + 0) = 100%
Precision for class 2 = 1 / (0 + 1 + 0 + 0) = 100%
Precision for class 3 = 0 / (0 + 19 + 0 + 1) = 0%
Precision for class 4 = 24 / (0 + 5 + 25 + 24) = 44%

Geometric Accuracy

Geometric accuracy (not a standard industry term) answers the question: How accurate is the classifier when class imbalance is taken into account? This is a single numeric value represented by the geometric mean of the class precisions. Suppose that there are N classes. Then the geometric accuracy is computed as:

Geometric Accuracy = Nth root of the product of the class precisions

For the matrix above (Table 7.1), we have the following result:

Geometric Accuracy = fourth root of (1.0 * 1.0 * 0.0 * 0.44) = 0%

The value of geometric accuracy is non-zero only if the classifier has some level of success in every class. Using the geometric accuracy in the objective function for a classifier will prevent it from increasing its accuracy by ignoring small classes (which are often the classes of greatest interest.) Using geometric accuracy as part of the objective function makes it possible to train on sets that are not balanced by class.

How are Precision, Recall, and Overall Accuracies Related?

If either classification accuracy or geometric accuracy is 100%, the other will be 100% as well. The same is true for class recall and precision accuracies. However, in general the following is true:

- For a particular class, recall can be high *and* precision low (see class 4 above).
- For a particular class, recall can be low *and* precision high (see class 2 above).
- Having a class recall of 100%, in itself, doesn't mean much.
- Having a class precision of 100%, in itself, doesn't mean much.
- Classification accuracy can be greater than, equal to, or less than the geometric accuracy.

Other Accuracy Metrics

There are accuracy measures used in clinical research that correspond to precision and recall, but different terms are used to denote them. These terms map to their corresponding counterparts in data mining in a natural way.

Assume that a binary condition is either present or absent. Presence of the condition will result in a *positive* value, and absence of the condition will result in a *negative* value. Consider the confusion matrix in Table 7.2:

Table 7.2 Confusion Matrix Example 2

Confusion Matrix	Positive Test	Negative Test
Condition Present	TP = number of true positives	FN = number of false negatives
Condition Absent	FP = number of false positives	TN = number of true negatives

Warning—some authors (notably in clinical work) use the transpose of the matrix depicted here, which interchanges the rows and columns. They would have the confusion matrix in Table 7.3:

Table 7.3 Confusion Matrix Example 3

Confusion Matrix	Condition Present	Condition Absent
Positive Test	TP = number of true positives	FP = number of false positives
Negative Test	FN = number of false negatives	TN = number of true negatives

When you are interpreting a confusion matrix in the literature, make certain you understand how the authors have chosen to arrange rows and columns.

Legend:

TP = number of *condition present* instances for which application says condition present
FN = number of *condition present* instances for which application says condition absent
FP = number of *condition absent* instances for which application says condition present
TN = number of *condition absent* instances for which application says condition absent

Important—False positives, given by FP, are referred to as *Type I errors*. False Negatives, given by FN, are referred to as *Type II errors*. In classification and detection problems, these are linked in the sense that reducing one of them generally increases the other. Which type is most harmful is domain dependent. Table 7.4 provides definitions of some metric terms:

Table 7.4 Definitions of Metric Terms

Term	Definition	Formula
Sensitivity	Proportion of persons with condition who test positive	TP/(TP+FN)
Specificity	Proportion of persons without condition who test negative	TN/(FP+TN)
Positive Predictive Power	Proportion of persons with positive test who have condition	TP/(TP+FP)
Negative Predictive Power	Proportion of persons with negative test who do not have condition	TN/(FN+TN)

7.3.2 Other Metrics Derived from the Confusion Matrix

- **Precision.** The information-theoretic term for *Positive Predictive Power*. Precision is the term usually used in data mining.
- **Recall.** The information-theoretic term for sensitivity. Recall is the term usually used in data mining. Also referred to as PD, or *probability of detection*.
- **False Positive Rate.** The probability that the application indicates *condition present*, when it is actually absent. It is equal to 1 – specificity. Also denoted by α, or the significance level and by Probability of False Alarm (PFA).
- **False Negative Rate.** The probability that the application indicates *condition absent* when it is actually present. It is the probability of a missed detection, and is equal to 1 – sensitivity, and is also denoted by β.
- **Power of the Test.** $1 - \beta = 1 -$ False Negative Rate
- **Likelihood Ratio (positive).** Sensitivity / (1 – Specificity)
- **Likelihood Ratio (negative).** (1 – Sensitivity) / Specificity
- **F-Measure.** The harmonic mean of precision and recall. It is a single number that captures information about both of these complimentary error rates. It is given by:

$$F = 2(Precision)(Recall)/(Precision + Recall)$$

- **Equal Error Rate (EER).** The error rate when decisions thresholds are set so that the false positive and false negative rates are equal.
- **Receiver Operating Characteristic (ROC) curve.** The ROC is not derived from the confusion matrix. ROC curve refers to a plot of the number of false positives vs. the number of true positives as the decision threshold is varied from low to high. It was developed during the Second World War to calibrate early RADAR warning systems so they could be adjusted to favor one type of error over another. For example, a RADAR may be set to have a high probability of detection; but this also causes it to have a high PFA and low Specificity (lots of false alarms). The ROC curve shows how these two error rates are related.

If the decision being made has more than two possible outcomes, each of these metrics can be computed from the confusion matrix for each outcome versus all others. In this case, the confusion matrix will have a number of rows and columns equal to the number of ground truth classes. The same ratio definitions apply as in the 2-by-2 case.

7.3.3 Model Evaluation Case Study: Addressing Queuing Problems by Simulation

Can data mining techniques be used when there is no data? Analysis of systems for which no data are available can sometimes be carried out by using simulators. For this case study, we describe the analysis of a meter reading system for residential customers that was conducted *before it was built*.

A large municipality had a difficult operational problem they wanted to solve using automation:

1. The manual collection of readings from 50,000+ residential water meters every month required a standing army of meter readers and a fleet of vehicles.
2. Manual collection of readings was expensive, slow, and prone to error.

The customer's question: Could existing communication infrastructure be used to automate the collection of meter data? Supervisory Control and Data Acquisition (SCADA) technology existed to allow the meters themselves to autonomously *call-in* their readings to a collection center, and be assigned next month's call-in time. This was done over customers' existing phone lines, without interfering with their telephone service. But this theoretical solution was untested. Critical questions about scheduling and loading had to be answered to insure that this was also a practical solution. A simulation was constructed to address the fundamental questions:

1. Could over 50,000 autonomous meters be remotely scheduled for call-in so readings could be collected on schedule for a monthly billing cycle?
2. Could a call-in schedule be constructed to minimize collisions? A collision occurs when call-in attempts exceeded available phone lines at the collection center. When this happens, some of the meters would get busy signals, and have to call back later.

   This could be a system-killing problem, because the call-in hardware on the meters was battery powered. If meters had to call-in twice on average each month instead of once, 50,000 meter batteries would have to be replaced twice as often as planned.
3. How many telephone lines would be required to support optimized call-in, and how should they be managed?

The problem doesn't sound too difficult yet, until it is pointed out that the internal clock on a 50 cent SCADA device is not going to be very accurate because after a 30-day wait for its next call-in, these clocks could be off by several minutes. Further, these variations were not consistent for a clock, since they were affected by temperature and other factors. The scheduling problem actually came down to trying to remotely synchronize the behaviors of 50,000 randomly drifting clocks that cannot communicate with each other.

A simulator was constructed allowing the data miner to specify the number of meters, number of telephone lines into the collection center, time requirements, and scheduling methodologies. The simulator would then create and execute a dynamic queuing model which ran through the entire call-in schedule, maintaining relevant statistics for each scheduling model (service counts, collisions, number of redials, maximum queue depths, phone-line loading efficiency, etc.). The performance data for each simulation run were collected and analyzed (Figure 7.1).

Using this simulation, the data miner was able to *game* a collection of metrics across a wide spectrum of possible system configurations and scheduling strategies. The metrics collected included the number of meters being processed, the number of incoming phone in the collection center, the time required to service and reschedule an installed unit, the time required to service connection to a new unit, the maximum

```
NUMBER OF INPUT LINES (1<= ILINES <= 8):? 4
SECONDS ALLOCATED FOR A SCHEDULE SLOT (1<=SLOT<=120):? 10
MINIMUM SECONDS TO SERVICE INSTALLED UNIT (1<=MIN<=120):? 8
MAXIMUM SECONDS TO SERVICE INSTALLED UNIT (MIN<=MAX<=120):? 24
MAX NUMBER OF SECONDS TO BACKOFF ON COLLISION (1<= BK <= 99):? 90

IT IS ASSUMED THAT EACH UNIT WILL BE SCHEDULED FOR 1 SERVICE CYCLE.
THE NUMBER OF UNITS REQUESTING SERVICE SHOULD BE A MULTIPLE OF 4 .

NUMBER OF UNITS REQUIRING SERVICE (1<= UNITS <=8,000):? 8000

NUMBER OF UNSCHEDULED BUT AVAILABLE LINES ( 0 - 4 ):? 1

TIME:   01:42:39  ( 6159 )              QUEUEING TYPE:   VERTICAL
HAVE SERVICED 1143 UNITS OUT OF A TOTAL OF 8000 SCHEDULED UNITS.
MAXIMUM NUMBER OF TIMES ANY UNIT HAS BEEN BACKED OFF:   5

# BUSY LINES: 4          # UNITS QUEUED: 15          ASYNCH. CALL-INS: 13

LINE STATUS:  1149    1147    1146    1148

UTILIZATION EFFICIENCY:   74.20847 %          INSTALLED UNIT 177 AT 00:15:19

UNITS QUEUED:

( 91 , 10419 )( 213 , 10996 )( 678 , 6319 )( 869 , 7393 )( 1033 , 7014 )( 1042 ,
 7079 )( 1044 , 7003 )( 1082 , 7236 )( 1092 , 7365 )( 1108 , 7405 )
 
SIMULATION PARAMETERS:

TOTAL SERVICE TIME: 50299 SECONDS (13:58:19)
QUEUEING TYPE:   VERTICAL
SERVICED 8172 UNITS OUT OF A TOTAL OF 8000 SCHEDULED UNITS.
NUMBER OF UNSCHEDULED DIAL-INS: 176
NUMBER OF INPUT LINES:    4
NUMBER OF 'SPARE' INPUT LINES (AVAIL., BUT UNSCHED.): 1
NUMBER OF SECONDS ALLOCATED FOR A SCHEDULE SLOT: 10
AVE. NUMBER OF SECONDS REQUIRED TO SERVICE A UNIT:   16.02141
MAX NUMBER OF SECONDS TO BACKOFF ON COLLISION:   90

SIMULATION RESULTS:
TOTAL COLLISIONS (=REDIALS): 4282
MAXIMUM NUMBER OF UNITS SIMULTANEOUSLY QUEUED: 54
MAXIMUM NUMBER OF TIMES ANY UNIT WAS BACKED OFF:   7
NUMBER OF IDLE TICKS WAS 70265 OUT OF A TOTAL OF 201192 .
UTILIZATION EFFICIENCY:   65.07565 %
```

A Water-Meter Queuing Simulation Result

Figure 7.1 Queuing simulation results.

number of redials for any single unit, and the percentage utilization of the input phone lines. A Monte Carlo approach was utilized, in which system parameters were selected pseudo-randomly.

From these analyses, the data miner was able to specify the smallest number of telephone lines in the collection center to handle meter call-in, and a scheduling model that minimized meter redial.

7.3.4 Model Evaluation Checklist

Question 1: What is the model evaluation strategy?	
Why this question is important?	You cannot demonstrate success in a principled way without an evaluation strategy. In order for the strategy to be valid, you must get stakeholder buy-in.

(Coninuted on following page)

Question 1: What is the model evaluation strategy? (*Continued*)	
What is question seeking?	If you do not have an evaluation strategy, how will you know when you are done? How will you prove that you have achieved project goals?
Likely responses and their meanings	Write your strategy down; get others to agree to it. It should define success in unambiguous, quantitative terms.
Follow-up questions	Are evaluation methods and metrics incorporated that assess functionality, performance, and quality in the *customer's* terms?
Special considerations	In a business arrangement, only what is written down and agreed to by all is *real*.

Question 2: How does the user define quality?	
Why this question is important?	If you want customers to regard you as a provider of quality work, you'll need to know what *quality* means to them.
What is question seeking?	What attributes must our project product have, to be regarded as quality work by our customer?
Likely responses and their meanings	Most larger organizations have developed formal definitions of quality, and can provide them in writing.
Follow-up questions	If tradeoffs must be made between several components of quality, who in the customer organization should be asked to help make them?
Special considerations	*Quality* has become a buzzword. However, it is a buzzword that refers to something real and something important.

Question 3: How does the user define success?	
Why this question is important?	The default assessment of a data mining effort is failure. If you don't define success, failure is almost certain.
What is question seeking?	What must our project accomplish, in specific, numeric terms, to be regarded as a success by the customer?
Likely responses and their meanings	This will be tied in some way to the business case that was used to justify the project. This is probably a proprietary document (containing cost and strategy information). However, ask someone in the customer organization to tell you what they can about this business case.
Follow-up questions	Keep in mind that a project can be a technical success and a business failure. Business failure is always much worse.
Special considerations	Politics inside a customer organization can be an ally or an enemy. Sometimes programs will fail due to the actions of someone inside the customer organization for political reasons.

Question 4: If there is there an existing solution, what is the current level of performance?	
Why this question is important?	If there is an existing solution, you will probably have to outperform it according to some measure of performance.
What is question seeking?	If you don't know what the current capability is, you might not focus on the right work elements.
Likely responses and their meanings	Usually measures of performance for existing capabilities are well known and will be made available.
Follow-up questions	Ask for documentation on the performance of current systems.
Special considerations	This information is probably proprietary. Handle it carefully.

Question 5: What level of performance is needed to make additional work worthwhile?	
Why this question is important?	Just beating the current benchmark might not justify the work. It is likely that a specific margin of improvement has been suggested as part of making the business case for the data mining project.
What is question seeking?	You want to know what the real level of performance for success is. It might be higher or lower than what you have been told.
Likely responses and their meanings	Answers will vary, and are most likely just the personal opinions of those offering them.
Follow-up questions	Get a domain expert to show you exactly how the various performance measures they use are determined. Do not assume that you know what a user means by the terms "good, bad, fast, slow, correct, incorrect, accurate," etc., until these have been explained, documented, and agreed to.
Special considerations	When reporting performance measures, include information on the measurement context (system load, data size, etc.) so your results will not be misinterpreted.

Question 6: Is there a business case for this project?	
Why this question is important?	This is really getting at understanding how the project was justified to management.
What is question seeking?	The decision makers who approved the project have expectations of a return on their investment; you need to know these expectations, and be prepared to measure performance in these terms.

(Coninuted on following page)

Question 6: Is there a business case for this project? (*Continued*)	
Likely responses and their meanings	This information is usually known to customer technical staff, and readily provided.
Follow-up questions	Are there intangible expectations for the project? What are they?
Special considerations	Customer expectations are not always achievable. In this case, it is best to estimate what can be done, and allow the customer to suggest revised goals.

7.4 Summary

Having read this chapter, you are familiar with a wide-range of quality metrics used for data mining model evaluation. You know what these metrics measure, and how to compute them from a confusion matrix. You have reviewed an example describing how model metrics can be used in combination with simulation to perform sophisticated predictive analytics.

Coming up

The next chapter presents the implementation of the data mining spiral (Step 6). It describes the practical aspects of quantifying data mining model *business* evaluation (return on investment). Most importantly, it enumerates the most common project-killing mistakes that data miners make, and how to avoid them.

Chapter 8

Implementation (Step 6)

Purpose

The purpose of this chapter is to address the practical considerations involved in implementing a data mining project. This treatment includes many of the lessons learned by the author during 25 years of work in data analytics and trainable application development. It suggests not only steps to take for project success, but also mistakes to avoid. It presents a method for computing the return on investment for a data mining project. This chapter also introduces the reader to modern multi-paradigm and hierarchical data mining architectures.

Goals

After you have read this chapter, you will understand some of the complex technical and business trade-offs inherent in data mining project implementation. You will be aware of the subtle mistakes and oversights that trap data miners, which lead to project failure. You will understand how to produce a principled estimate of return on investment for a data mining project.

8.1 Introduction

Implementation requires packaging the final product for delivery. For an exploratory/proof-of-concept effort, this includes writing a technical document describing the project purpose, data, methods, and results. For a prototype development effort, this involves writing technical and user documentation, populating operational data structures, creating an installation set, and a prototype demonstration.

Principal Participants and Their Tasks:

DM/SE/PM   Implementation and Delivery

Running through the following checklist will help the data miner formulate a comprehensive implementation plan.

8.1.1 Implementation Checklist

Question 1: What is the CONOP of the current system/process?	
Why this question is important?	Your solution will not be accepted by end users if it disrupts their normal work process.
What is question seeking?	How will your solution interact with the system and user to be maximally helpful and minimally disruptive?
Likely responses and their meanings	These will vary from user to user; listen for common elements mentioned by multiple users.
Follow-up questions	What is the best way for the project solution to interact with the user?
Special considerations	It is possible that the data mining solution will not directly interact with the user at all, but instead will facilitate some internal system process.

Question 2: What is the legacy computing/processing/operational environment?	
Why this question is important?	There could be leftover software, hardware, and methods from earlier versions of the system. You might encounter some of these (e.g., as out of date dll's, data paths that don't appear to make sense, a mixture of old and new data formats, etc.)
What is question seeking?	What legacy considerations should the project take into account?
Likely responses and their meanings	This is just an *awareness* question to tuck away should inexplicable problems start popping up during implementation.
Follow-up questions	Is there documentation for earlier versions of the system if we want to refer to it? Are all OS versions, drivers, etc., current? If not, why not?
Special considerations	Familiarize yourself with the system's configuration management system. It can help you determine the dates that system and application software versions were installed, updates made, new third-party applications loaded, etc.

Question 3: What are the available interface mechanisms/processes?	
Why this question is important?	You will need this information to be able to communicate with the system and the user.
What is question seeking?	You are trying to obtain the necessary information to design your system interfaces.
Likely responses and their meanings	Usually these questions are answered in detail by the system specification. Often there will be a defined system API (Application Program Interface) that your software can use to interact with the system and the user.
Follow-up questions	Ask for copies of any system interface documentation that might be available and an API document if one exists.
Special considerations	If you have to communicate with the system and/or user by direct use of system services or I/O statements, be sure to coordinate this with the system developer to avoid conflicts. If there is a style guide of some sort for user communication, you will want to be consistent with it.

Question 4: At what points in the processing stream can data be tapped/injected?	
Why this question is important?	If you are creating an application that reads/writes/ updates/deletes data, you want to know at what times and places in the system architecture this is appropriate.
What is question seeking?	You must synchronize your actions with other system activities if you are processing during operational periods.
Likely responses and their meanings	This will require some detailed discussions with system developers.
Follow-up questions	Be prepared to ask for relevant documentation should it be needed.
Special considerations	Remember rule #1 for *helpful applications:* Do No Harm!

Question 5: What are the political/organizational considerations for interaction with the system?	
Why this question is important?	In systems that conduct operations that cross organizational boundaries, there are often organizational policies (or gentlemen's agreements) about what is allowed and when. You want to understand these policies so you do not violate them.

(Continued on following page)

Question 5: What are the political/organizational considerations for interaction with the system? (*Continued*)	
What is question seeking?	You want to practice proper etiquette and be a good citizen when running on a customer system.
Likely responses and their meanings	Answers will be vague; but there is often one or two big no-nos that everyone understands.
Follow-up questions	Ask for documentation of system policies.
Special considerations	This whole issue is very important. Nothing will get you eternally banned from an operational system faster than a policy violation.

8.2 Quantifying the Benefits of Data Mining

Every project funded by an enterprise has to justify its cost. A formal justification of this type is referred to as a *business case*. The business case describes and quantifies the costs and benefits of undertaking the project, describes the risks, and usually lays out a high-level plan for doing the work (i.e., rough staffing and schedule).

Because data mining projects are often experimental, they come under special scrutiny. A winning business case for a data mining effort usually boils down to a question like, "Does it make sense to spend $50K this year to reap a $30K savings every year for the next decade?" Expressed in this way, we see that using data mining to leverage information can make it a long-term value multiplier.

The business case question is sometimes made more complex by involving a trade between real dollars and hypothetical dollars, as in the following case study.

8.2.1 ROI Case Study

The most accurate model is not necessarily the best model. It is not necessary to use some direct measure of classification accuracy when training a classifier. In this case study, the objective function for training was changed from an *accuracy measurement* to a *model cost* measurement. The problem was to predict which credit applicants will be good (revenue generating) and which will be bad (non-revenue generating /default).

Because Type I and Type II errors have different costs, the highest *accuracy* model is not necessarily the best *profit* model. For this project, the customer estimated that accepting a bad customer costs three times as much (e.g., bad debt of $600/year, on average) as rejecting a good customer (e.g., lost opportunity of $200/year on average).

Once feature data was ready for modeling, the data mining team began to create supervised classifiers (ground truth was available for each vector) to predict which applicants would turn out to be good, called class 1 customers; and which applicants would turn out to be bad, called class 2 customers. The data mining project prototypes gave blind test results on a set of 22,639 vectors as in the following confusion matrix:

Confusion Matrix	Class 1 Customers Classified as Class 2	Class 2 Customers Classified as Class 2
Class 1 Customers Classified as Class 1	13,236	5,433
Class 2 Customers Classified as Class 1	1,273	2,697

Overall blind classification accuracy=70.4%

There are 5,433 Type I errors (potential good customers turned away) and 1,273 Type II errors (potential bad customers accepted). If the average annual loss for a bad customer is $600, and the average annual profit for a good customer is $200, we have a certain *model cost* for this classifier:

$$((5,433x\$200)+(1,273x\$600))/(13,236+5,433+1,273+2,697)=\$81.74$$

This is the total of Type I and Type II error costs divided by the number of customers, so it gives the model cost per customer-year. For benchmark purposes, the client's in-house model for this sample had a model cost in the high $90s.

We see that by assigning quantitative estimates of the average cost of the possible errors, the operational model cost can be estimated. This method allows the data miner to turn a technical accuracy metric into a principled business ROI. Further, this method can be reversed—it can be used to establish Type I and Type II error goals needed to meet a given ROI requirement.

Regularization Experiments

Next, a *regularizing* (smoothing) version of the good/bad customer regression engine was built to obtain regular decision regions, and address the overtraining problem. This was done by training five classifiers separately and arbitrating the results. The procedure was:

1. Divide the training data into disjoint sets
2. Train separate, totally independent classifiers on each set separately
3. Run all the classifiers on each input, determining the output by arbitration (e.g., averaging, voting, etc.)

Many experiments were run with various classifier settings. The best regularization results were obtained by training 5 RBF classifiers and allowing the underrepresented class to be selected if it was chosen by 2 of the 5 classifiers (a 40% sub-majority wins). The best run had the following blind results:

Confusion Matrix	Class 1 Customers Classified as Class 2	Class 2 Customers Classified as Class 2
Class 1 Customers Classified as Class 1	12,884	5,785
Class 2 Customers Classified as Class 1	1,264	2,706

Overall blind classification accuracy=68.9%
Model cost per customer-year=$80.61

The important fact to notice here is that even though this model has a lower overall accuracy than the previous model, it has a lower model cost: a less accurate model is leaving *more* money in the customer's pocket. This is a direct consequence of the fact that Type I and Type II errors have different costs.

Data Replication Experiment

After performing the regularization experiments, we learned that in the supplied data, the user had adjusted the population proportion of good and bad customers by replicating bad records. Since bad customer predictions have a higher error rate, this artificially inflated our model cost.

We removed the replicated records (which left 13,333 vectors), and reran the regularization experiments. The following confusion matrix was the best result:

Confusion Matrix	Class 1 Customers Classified as Class 2	Class 2 Customers Classified as Class 2
Class 1 Customers Classified as Class 1	10,239	1,608
Class 2 Customers Classified as Class 1	751	735

Overall blind classification accuracy=82.3%
Cost per customer=$57.92

This was a model cost improvement over the customer's in-house model of ~40%. In this particular domain, the best model was not the most accurate model. From a business standpoint, it was better to err slightly on the side of losing market share. In this business scenario, we can afford to turn away multiple good customers to avoid accepting one bad one.

8.2.2 ROI Checklist

Question 6: What are the cost elements within this domain?	
Why this question is important?	To compute an estimate of ROI, you want to know what components of cost to attack with your solution.
What is question seeking?	What functionality does our solution have to provide to produce a measurable return to the customer?
Likely responses and their meanings	Technical people will not have a good handle on this. But they will be able to quantify certain aspects, such as number of false alarms and time required to respond to a false alarm. A management representative can make an estimate of the associated labor cost, opportunity cost, etc.

(Continued on following page)

Question 6: What are the cost elements within this domain? (*Continued*)	
Follow-up questions	Make sure you have accurately understood and quantified the elements of cost your project could address.
Special considerations	Be sure to take into account the length of time the cost accrues. A cost of $10,000/year for 3 years is a $30,000 total cost.

Question 7: What are the benefit elements within this domain?	
Why this question is important?	You want to be able to estimate the possible payback from your project. This is its actual dollar value.
What is question seeking?	How much return can be expected?
Likely responses and their meanings	Technical people will not have a good handle on this. But they will be able to quantify certain aspects, such as number of false alarms and time required to respond to a false alarm. A management representative can make an estimate of the associated labor savings, customer goodwill from better service, etc.
Follow-up questions	Make sure you have accurately understood and quantified the elements of savings your project could provide.
Special considerations	Be sure to take into account the length of time your project's benefit accrues. A savings of $10,000/year for 3 years is a $30,000 total savings.

Question 8: How will this project affect the cost/benefit elements?	
Why this question is important?	You want to be aware of the potential positive and negative impacts of your project on the customer.
What is question seeking?	Providing a complete and accurate estimate of ROI requires a complete and accurate accounting of cost and benefit components.
Likely responses and their meanings	You will probably need information from both a technical person and a management representative to have what you need for a complete answer to this question.
Follow-up questions	Could the data mining project offer intangible costs/ benefits, such as improved service, reduced error rates, etc.?
Special considerations	Be prepared to accept the fact that some of the ROI estimation will be based upon best-available informed guesses.

8.3 Tutorial on Ensemble Methods

If two different data modeling techniques are used together, is it possible to produce a result superior to either one operating alone? Yes. It is often the case that intelligently combining the decisions of several individually weak engines can produce high quality results. These ensemble methods, techniques for optimally combining the results of multiple decision engines are sometimes referred to as *bagging methods* (described later).

Ensembling may be very desirable when two different algorithms for a process are available, each of which works well on cases where the other does not. Rather than choosing one algorithm, an effective ensembling approach would be to retain both, and adjudicate their outputs as a secondary process.

Adjudication refers to any process that accepts multiple preliminary decisions, and uses them to render a final decision. Many adjudication methods exist. For example, if the inputs are numeric estimates, they might be adjudicated by taking their weighted average. Or, if the inputs are classifications (nominal), counting the input decisions as votes for class assignments might be used.

The purpose of ensembling is to allow the strengths of one model to compensate for the weaknesses of others. Ensembles generally produce more accurate results than their individual constituents will, with less variation in the output. An important functional advantage of ensembles is their natural ability to fuse a variety of data types with a minimum amount of complexity. An excellent application is an application consisting of two sub-models: one that processes numeric inputs, and another that processes nominal inputs. Adjudicating the outputs of these two sub-models allows the application to perform feature level data fusion in a natural way (Figure 8.1).

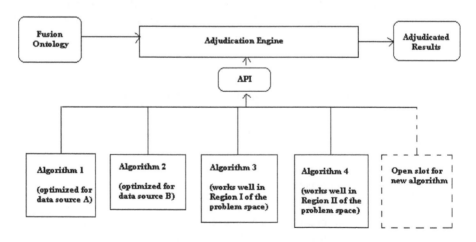

Ensemble Methods make "best-use" of all avaliable algorithms, and keep change in the R&D Environment at the API and above.

Figure 8.1   Ensembling of multiple decision engines.

The ensemble is a true *gestalt*. Properly implemented, it will be at least as good as the best single component and often better than either component individually. Ensembling can be performed and optimized automatically by using a trainable application as an adjudicator. After the sub-models are trained, they are used to generate training data for building the adjudicator. This is generally accomplished using regression methods, and can be done incrementally as part of system maintenance. Incremental updates by maintenance retraining enables an ensemble to adapt its decision logic as the problem space changes, without having to modify the underlying algorithms.

For example, kinematic Multi-Hypothesis Tracker (MHT) algorithms track entities based only upon motion, and feature-based MHT tracks entities based only upon entity characteristics. An ensemble approach would use both, passing two sets of tracking estimates to an adjudication engine where conflicts can be optimally resolved. In this way, neither one of the underlying MHT algorithms need to be modified because all changes to the ensemble are made in the adjudicator.

The use of ensembling can make a data mining architecture scalable:

- It is based upon structure of the problem space: inherently *divide and conquer*
- It implements efficient execution: only necessary processes are performed
- It is architecturally primitive: optimized sequence of simple operations
- It performs virtual time processing: the heavy lifting is done during training, not execution
- It is retrainable: doesn't start from scratch when the domain drifts
- It is parallelizable: different components of the ensemble can run in different places

8.3.1 Many Predictive Modeling Paradigms Are Available

Which modeling methods should be used for the construction of a predictive model? This question is domain dependent. In what follows, an architecture is presented that can be used to make many disparate methods interoperable, so the strengths of one cover the weaknesses of another. To make the best use of these sub-models, we intelligently segment the problem into regions in feature space, and optimize the models against each one region. These multiple engines feed their decisions to an adjudicator, which renders a final model prediction based upon the advice of the sub-models (see Figure 8.2).

Note: The author has constructed ensembling engines that automatically build, seamlessly integrate, and optimize 15,000 separate classifiers to address one decision problem!

The ensemble modeling process presented here can be automated so modeling applications having many separate internal models can be defined, implemented, and validated rapidly. This is done according to a principled data mining methodology (Chapter 2) to ensure best use of all data.

Some of the modeling paradigms that can be integrated into a multi-model ensemble in this way are:

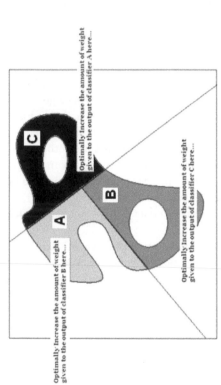

Optimally increase the amount of weight given to the output of classifier B here...

Optimally Increase the amount of weight given to the output of classifier A here...

Optimally increase the amount of weight given to the output of classifier C here...

Trained models can be ensembled into an optimized hybrid. Here, all three models are run, and more "credence" is given to models that are known to perform well on the current case. Ensembling is an automated optimization process that lets the strengths of each model compensate for the weaknesses of the others, making "best use" of data.

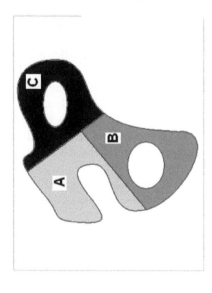

Classifier A Does Well. Classifiers B and C do less well.
Classifier B Does Well. Classifiers A and C do less well.
Classifier C Does Well. Classifiers A and B do less well.

Adjudicator is tuned
To optimally combine
Classifier outputs

Figure 8.2 Ensemble approach to predictive modeling.

- Neural networks (Perceptrons, Hopfield nets, recurrent nets, etc.)
- Conventional statistical inference
- Maximum likelihood classifiers
- Knowledge-based expert systems
- Radial basis functions
- Adaptive logic networks
- Nearest neighbor classifiers
- Support vector machines
- Decision trees, belief nets

Multi-Modeling

In multi-model systems, a collection of machine reasoners is used, each producing its own decision about the problem at hand. In order to obtain a final answer, a meta-scheme is used to adjudicate these results.

Bagging is a multi-modeling technique that adjudicates the decisions of multiple sub-models. It is a parallel approach. In this technique, all decision engine results are considered at once, and a final result is derived from them. It can be thought of as reasoning by committee. A natural way to implement bagging is to *divide and conquer.*

Sometimes performance on very difficult problems can be improved by breaking the feature space into separate regions and building separate model for each:

1. Segment the data into training, calibration, and validation sets. Notice that the regression value, y_j, is part of the vector.
2. Autocluster the training data with *many* centroids = "cluster center" (i.e., thousands).
3. Train a separate model on the points falling into each centroid.

To apply this multi-model to a feature vector, retrieve the centroid nearest the input feature vector using an appropriate distance measure. Apply the nearest centroid's classifier to the input feature vector. Consider using the distance of the input from the centroid as part of a confidence measure for the result.

Note: Having multiple models makes possible the generation of interval estimates, and enables the use of multi-model adjudication methods such as averaging and voting.

8.3.2 Adaptive Training

Machines cannot learn from experience unless they have experiences. To make this possible, a learning machine developer will typically program a learning machine *shell* having at least three components: an I/O interface, inferencing mechanism(s), and training algorithm(s). This novice system is much like a *tabula rasa*: a blank slate upon which experience writes. Having been endowed with these components, the shell can be apprenticed in the problem domain it is to master.

There are two types of machine learning: supervised, and unsupervised. The distinction has nothing to do with the presence or absence of an audience, but rather with the *a priori* provision of ground truth. In *supervised learning*, examples of the cases to be handled, along with the desired results, are provided. *Unsupervised learning* is based upon examples of cases for which no ground truth results are specified in advance.

Throughout the balance of this chapter, only supervised learning is addressed. Chapter 9 is provided as an extended treatment of supervised learning and chapter 10 as an extended treatment of unsupervised learning.

Most training algorithms for supervised learning work in about the same way. A collection of domain data (training data), along with the desired solutions (ground truth) is prepared by the developer. This training set is a set of problem/solution associations, which are examples of cases the machine is to learn. For example, a training set for voice identification might consist of several hundred digitized voice clips, and

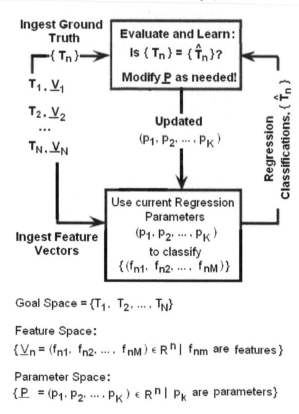

Supervised Learning by Feedback and Adaption

Goal Space = $\{T_1, T_2, ..., T_N\}$

Feature Space:
$\{\underline{V}_n = (f_{n1}, f_{n2}, ..., f_{nM}) \in R^n \mid f_{nm} \text{ are features}\}$

Parameter Space:
$\{\underline{P} = (p_1, p_2, ..., p_K) \in R^n \mid p_k \text{ are parameters}\}$

Figure 8.3   Supervised learning by feedback and adaptation.

the name of the speaker for each one. Each of these voice/name pairs is used to create a feature vector tagged with ground truth.

To train, the novice learning machine applies its ignorant inferencing mechanism to the feature vectors in the training set, producing an output for each one. Some of these outputs will be correct, and some incorrect. The training algorithm compares these outputs with the correct associations in the training set, and makes adjustments to the parameters used by the inferencing mechanism. The repetition of this process allows the learning machine to incrementally improve its performance in terms of scope, accuracy, and confidence (Figure 8.3).

How does the learning algorithm know what adjustments to make to the decision parameters to improve system performance? There are many approaches (training algorithms), including gradient techniques, regression methods, genetic algorithms, etc. Because each technique has its particular strengths and weaknesses, it is essential that comprehensive learning systems have a variety of interoperable learning paradigms available.

Once each of the models in the ensemble has been trained, a relatively simple two-tier architecture makes them interoperable (Figure 8.4).

The lower path from left-to-right streams data through an ensemble of classifiers. These are agnostic, in the sense that they process raw phenomenology (e.g., space-time patterns) using regression methods rather than heuristics (knowledge). They classify using pattern matching.

The upper path from left-to-right streams data through an ensemble of decision engines (typically a hierarchy of eclectic knowledge bases). These are trained rather than programmed, and apply domain knowledge to consider not just problem syntax (as does the lower path), but semantics. They accrue and evaluate evidence to render decisions based upon facts, constraints, and conditions in the problem space. They reason using knowledge.

If all of these pattern processors and machine reasoners had to be manually programmed, this architecture would be prohibitively expensive to build. Further, it would require tremendous effort to *tune* so the parts interoperate and function as a unified whole.

This problem can be solved by encapsulating the entire application in a *training harness* that adaptively trains all of the components in the context of their operational architecture using training data. This is accomplished by attaching a *learning loop* (Figure 8.3) to each engine. Once sub-model training is done, the adjudicator is trained to properly assess the stream of partial decisions produced by all of the sub-models acting in concert. Figure 8.5 shows the architecture in learning mode, with the training harness activated.

8.4 Getting It Wrong: Mistakes Every Data Miner Has Made

Eleven fundamental principles of data mining were introduced in chapter 2; they are the keys to *getting it right*. There are also some keys to *getting it wrong*, and it is very important to know about these, too.

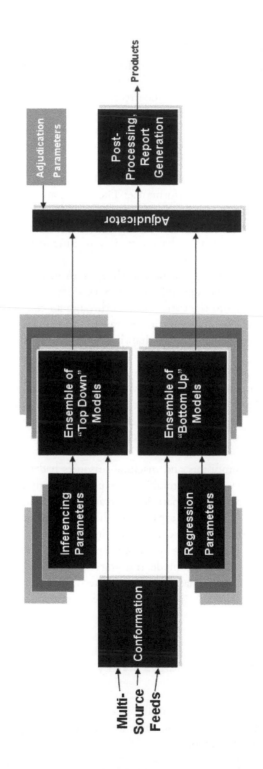

Figure 8.4 Two tier architecture for interoperability.

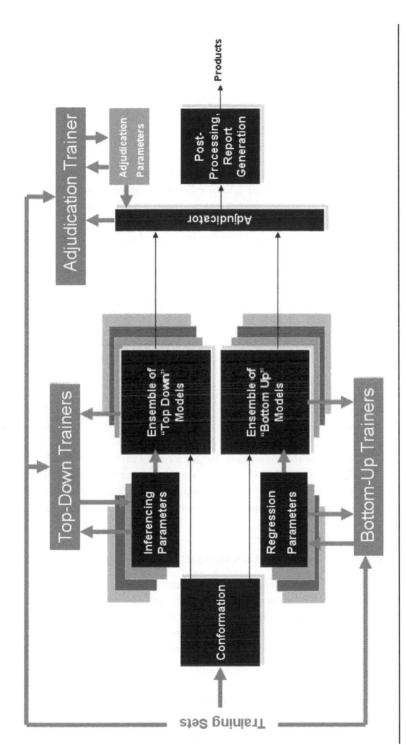

Figure 8.5 Learning mode architecture with "training harness."

A lot can be learned about what works by knowing what doesn't work, and why it doesn't work. This is particularly so in experimental and creative domains such as data mining. The following eleven short treatments describe the *worst of the worst*: mistakes that will doom your project or perhaps even get you fired. I know them all too well, because I have seen them all multiple times (usually as the perpetrator). If you are going to fail, try to find some less spectacular way than those contained in this list.

Mistake One: Bad Data Conditioning

This mistake covers everything from making arithmetic mistakes and formatting errors to selecting the wrong settings in a feature extractor. Sometimes it's even a stupid mistake: I once gave a file to an engineer to condition, and he finished his analytic process by rounding everything in the entire file down to zero.

A common instance of this mistake is to repair broken data in some way that makes things worse, for example by filling gaps in records with some valid data value. Next month you will be wondering whether the zero you see in field 17 is a *real* zero, or a *missing* zero and by that time, it's too late.

Visualization and reporting tools applied by an analyst familiar with the data are often effective in detecting information damage. Sanity checking by a domain expert is the best defense against this mistake.

Mistake Two: Failure to Validate

It is exciting when some data mining experiment produces a result that advances the effort. But you have to resist the temptation to trumpet your success until the results have been validated by a thorough process audit, and demonstration that you can replicate the results.

A common instance of this mistake is testing a model on the data used to create it. Of course it will give reasonable, even great, results on that set; but will it generalize? Before you trumpet your success, make certain it won't evaporate when the VP of Engineering hustles an ecstatic customer down to your office witness the miracle first-hand.

Mistake Three: GIGoO (Garbage In, Gold Out?)

Reality is a harsh critic; but it is a *fair* critic. Sometimes the data you are given just do not support the application you have been asked to build. The fact that you can't use a customer's shoe sizes to predict her hair color doesn't mean you have failed. Be prepared to admit the limitations of the data, and be ready to make thoughtful suggestions about less grandiose goals. What is *real* ought to be good enough—because that's all the good there is.

Mistake Four: Ignoring Population Imbalance

Real world data mining is often looking for the needle in the haystack that everyone would like to find. But the importance that derives from rarity has a side-effect: you probably won't have many examples to use for model development. In building fraud models, for example, keep in mind that the data you are given will probably not provide you with thousands of examples of fraud. This should be taken into account when you train.

For example, let's suppose that you are asked to create some kind of a recognizer for fraud for a business where only 1 out of every 100 cases is fraudulent. If you just call every case you see *non-fraudulent*, you will be right 99% of the time. But what have you actually accomplished? Nothing.

Many adaptive algorithms train by maximizing or minimizing some performance score. Unless they are carefully designed, they might be able to push their score up by doing exactly what the non-fraudulent example above does.

Classes for which only a few instances are available (residual classes) are sometimes lost in the information glare of an overwhelming majority of common (and therefore, uninteresting) cases. Techniques to overcome this include boosting; enriching the residual class by including multiple copies of each instance (replication); by removing members of other classes (decimating); or by adjusting the objective score used to train the algorithm using the geometric accuracy method described in chapter 7.

Populations to be used for mining activities can be balanced using techniques such as replication and decimation (chapter 4). Sampling, segmentation, coding, quantization, and statistical normalization may also be used to address imbalance. Imbalance can be a difficult problem whose solution may require special expertise.

Mistake Five: Trojan-Horsing Ground-Truth

This is one of the easiest mistakes to make—and one of the most dangerous. Fortunately, it is usually easy to detect, if you are looking for it.

Let's suppose you are trying to construct a classifier that recognizes when a picture contains one or more cats. You have been provided with an assortment of pictures, some containing cats, and some not. Each photograph has a date stamp added to the image by the camera. You carefully digitize these, and extract various kinds of shape descriptors, texture measures, etc. from the pictures. You train up and get good results.

What you didn't notice is that all the pictures that contained cats were taken on the same day. What your detector has actually done is learn that a particular squiggly shape in the corner of the picture (the date) is perfectly correlated with the desired answer. Further, learning to recognize that specific letter date is not all that hard. You have unwittingly Trojan-Horsed the ground truth into the data.

There are lots of ways this happens. Suppose you are working on financial spreadsheet data, trying to estimate next month's revenue in dollars. What you might not know is that someone in the European branch office needed the revenue in Euros per week, and put that in column 47 of the spreadsheet with a helpful name—written in Swedish. You have Trojan-Horsed the ground truth.

Trojan Horsing can often be detected by computing the correlation coefficient of each feature with the ground truth. If any have an absolute value very close to 1, they could be ground truth masquerading as usable features, and should be checked manually as possible Trojan Horses.

Mistake Six: Temporal Infeasibility

This mistake is easy to make unless you are watching out for it. It arises because data mining researchers are generally given data that contains all the fields and records that might be useful in understanding the problem. This does not mean, though, they can all necessarily be used for modeling.

When looking at a record in a data file, don't assume this is how it exists in the database your model will use operationally: clean and complete all fields arriving at the same time along the same data paths, and so on.

If there are multiple data sources, it is quite possible that the fields in the records you were given for data mining are never brought together in the operational system. Even if they are, they might have arrived hour, days, or months apart. Particularly if some came from correcting records, audits, roll-ups from later analyses, and so on. At the time your application has to be executed, will all of the fields be here, in this format? Unless you have asked, why would you think so?

Building a model that works in theory but can't be used because the data are not available when the model must run is the temporal infeasibility trap. Avoiding temporal infeasibility is best accomplished by having a domain expert fully conversant with the business process review the feature set for consistency with the business cycle.

Mistake Seven: Being a "One-Widget Wonder"

They say that if all you have is a hammer, everything looks like a nail. This is true in data mining, but the truth of this doesn't always sink in. The obvious facts are that every analysis tool is an implementation of some process; processes are formalizations of specific algorithms; and thinkers with some particular idea in mind devise algorithms. It is silly to believe that there was one idea back there that is the solution to every problem you will ever work on.

Even wonderful tools work well on some problems, and poorly on others. This is the reason ensemble methods were invented, and even these must be tweaked out in challenging situations. If all you have is one tool/method, there might be only one problem you can address properly.

Remember: the solution must be applied to the problem, and not the other way around. The successful data miner will not only employ an eclectic set of tools; they will know when and how to use each tool.

Mistake Eight: Poor Configuration/Audit/Version Control

This is one of the hardest lessons I have ever had to learn. I was into day two of a five-week predictive modeling task for a tricky problem. During a calibration test, I stumbled across an unusual collection of settings that created a machine with remarkable performance on the problem.

Rather than immediately capturing the context and settings for this architecture, I tried to make it a little better by applying some small adjustments. That resulted in a small change, so I did it again. Two hours later, with hundreds of output files from failed *tweaks* scattered across the working directory, I realized that I didn't know how to reproduce the original great result.

Five weeks later, at around 11 PM on the day before the results were due, I managed to recreate the miracle. It had taken days and nights and weekends of work to arduously track down what had been a gift of providence.

As with every principled experimental process, everything needed for repeatability of the results must be documented. The best way to do this is to create scripts of some sort to automate data transformation, feature extraction, and model construction/ testing. These scripts can be saved, rerun, shared with others—or even delivered to customers or embedded in applications. If that isn't practical (e.g., automation doesn't yet exist for some new process), keep a little text window open on your desktop and log steps/settings as you work. At the end of an experiment, append a line or two describing the results, and save this log entry to a directory with the date embedded in its name.

Mistake Nine: Neglecting to Define Success

Enterprises with deep pockets sometimes undertake data mining projects as purely speculative research and development efforts with the full understanding that they might or might not yield a return. Some great things have come about in exactly this way. The definition of success for these efforts is, *Spend this money doing the best you can, and tell us what you get.*

For most customers, an outcome like this doesn't smell like success. They funded the project with the expectation of a tangible return. In such cases, it behooves the data miner to work with the customer to get a description of success" committed to writing. This is a project manifesto, not a project plan, and should not unduly constrain the effort. At the very least, it needs to state some measurable goals for the effort. (Note again: *measureable*). I have found that a list of goals with performance targets (accuracy improvements, labor savings, etc.) works best.

Even R&D projects are at risk of merely wandering through *technology land* if they are not focused on a goal statement of some kind. For R&D projects, it is usually best not to put performance numbers in a goal statement. These numbers will end up becoming project drivers that discourage the principled risk taking that should be part of a research effort.

Realize, too, that goals that are not written down and agreed to early on will morph in peoples' minds over the course of time, and can become unrecognizable. This results in lots of unpleasant confusion and surprise when the final report is inconsistent with *what people think they thought you meant.*

Mistake Ten: Ignoring Legacy Protocols

Data mining applications are often developed to enhance the operational performance or utility of existing computing systems (i.e., legacy systems). If these systems have been in use for a while, users will have developed work styles that mesh with their system concept of operation (CONOP). These work styles will even include exploitation of system quirks and bugs, should this prove to be useful.

New applications integrated into legacy environments change things. From the perspective of power users who have streamlined their processes, change is bad unless it is helpful, in which case it is merely *tolerable.*

Applications that make legacy users alter their work style will be resisted, even if they are useful. Applications that actually disrupt establish patterns of work will not be used. It is a strange catch 22 scenario: overburdened users are not willing to risk the learning-curve downtime required to try an application that *might* save them time.

No matter how good a technical solution is, if it disrupts legacy protocols, it will be an operational failure. It is critically important that data mining applications fielded into a legacy system mesh with the work styles of system users. You can only understand these styles by spending time with users.

Mistake Eleven: Not Considering the Reason the Data Were Originally Gathered

In the real world, data are always collected for some reason. The collection methods, data formats, and storage architectures were specified with these reasons in mind. The data were probably not collected to provide a sandbox for your data mining project.

This means that data miners are usually working with material presenting an odd mix of deficiencies from a data mining perspective. For example, if an address is missing from a record, the original application might not have cared; but the address might be an element of information that is critically needed for a mining problem.

More importantly, the original purpose for which the data were collected determines its information content. This happens in many ways such as selecting a precision that was originally adequate, but ill serves the data mining application. An important and dangerous challenge to data reuse has to do with how data were originally coded.

This challenge can be caused by wrongly imputing units (meters/feet, pounds/pesos), which can crash you into another planet (Mars Global Explorer). It can also be caused by wrongly imputing meaning to the data. For example, suppose data were originally collected to document insurance claims, and now these data are being used to detect instances of insurance fraud. Originally, information in claim field 47 was coded into 3 categories, "Low, Medium, High." But you don't know things like:

1. The definitions of these terms has changed since the data was collected, and what was *high* three years ago is now being entered into the data base as medium.
2. Non-responses in the input data are lumped in with *low*.

There are other subtle ways this phenomenon presents, but you get the idea. The point is that even though the data were entered correctly and validated, they misrepresent the facts. If at all possible, the history or *pedigree* of the data should be investigated. This is particularly important for older repositories, and repositories accessed by many users.

8.5 Summary

Having read this chapter, you understand some of the complex technical and business trade-offs inherent in data mining project implementation. You are aware of common data mining mistakes that lead to project failure. You understand how to produce a principled estimate of ROI for a data mining project, enabling you to express the project outcome in terms of its business implications.

Coming up

The chapter you have just read is the last of the groundwork chapters of the book, which together constitute a treatment of the major components of data mining technology.

Each of the following chapters is devoted entirely to a specific data mining problem class, or *genre*. The genre chapters address the three broad application areas of data mining as a scientific and engineering discipline: supervised learning, unsupervised learning, and the automation of heuristic reasoning to build decision support applications.

Chapter 9
(Supervised Learning)

Genre Section 1—Detecting and Characterizing Known Patterns

Purpose

The purpose of this chapter is to address supervised learning, the most common application of data mining technology for producing operational applications. It concerns the use of data mining methods to create detectors, classifiers, estimators, and other decision support tools for users operating in complicated environments.

The aspect that distinguishes this genre from the others is that here we are looking through data for instances of *known* patterns: patterns that have been seen before. A representative sample of the patterns of each type to be classified is available or can be generated.

Goals

This genre section will address supervised learning, the most common application of data mining technology for producing operational applications. This type of development uses data mining methods to create detectors, classifiers, estimators, and other decision support tools for users operating in complicated environments. Many of the concepts and methods described in Chapters 1–8 come together in this section, making this work possible.

Examples:

- Biometric identification (known fingerprint, known face, known voice, etc.)
- Object recognition (vehicle model classification from imagery/sound)
- Pattern matching (signal classification, e.g., AM vs. FM)
- Optical Character Recognition (OCR)
- Detection of known computer viruses

9.1 Introduction

This genre addresses problems whose solutions are instances of *supervised learning*. Supervised learning is probably the most mature application of data mining technology, with fundamental techniques that substantially predate the advent of automated computing.

The term *supervised* refers to the fact that when conducting supervised learning, we have been given ground truth assignments (the correct answer) for each of the entities being learned. The inputs to the training process consist of pairs: a feature vector containing attributes of the entity to be classified, and the answer that is to be associated with it (the ground truth). Ground truth can be obtained in a number of ways and often it is the stored outcomes for previously collected historical data. Sometimes ground truth is generated by an "oracle." The term *oracle* refers to any mechanism, manual or automated, for determining the ground truth associated with inputs to be classified. Usually it is either a human expert who manually tags feature vectors with ground truth, or an existing classifier.

To perform supervised learning we create a training set that contains feature vectors representing objects or entities to be classified, along with ground truth assignments for each. The goal of the learning process is the creation of an automated application that can accurately classify or infer the ground-truth of entities based upon their features.

9.2 Representative Example of Supervised Learning: Building a Classifier

The following is an extended, detailed example that goes through the various stages of building a classifier for a supervised learning problem. The problem is a real, well-known problem (Fisher Iris Problem) that is small enough to dig into. Everything done here is real, and is typical of how an experienced data mining expert might proceed.

9.2.1 Problem Description

The problem description begins with an initial discussion with the customer and domain experts as follows:

The customer says: The problem is to build a predictive model that ingests size measurements taken from a particular type of flower, and determine to which specific variety the flower belongs.

The data miner notes: This problem is the assignment of an entity to one of a fixed number of known categories based upon entity attributes. Therefore, this is a classification problem. The solution will be a classifier. Additionally:

- The attributes are sizes, so they provide continuous numeric features.
- Visualization is often very informative when features are numeric.

9.2.2 Data Description: Background Research/Planning

This activity includes discussions with domain experts, research before any data has been seen.

The customer says: We will use a very famous, real data set: the Fisher Iris Data Set. The Fisher Iris Data Set consists of four measurements taken from each of 150 iris flowers. These data were used by Ronald Aylmer Fisher in 1936 to develop what is now called the Fisher Discriminant, a linear classification technique. The Fisher data set is balanced by class, having 50 samples of each of 3 iris varieties: 50 iris *setosa*, 50 iris *versicolor*, and 50 iris *virginica*.

From each flower, four measurements were taken (in centimeters): sepal length, sepal width, petal length, and petal width. The entire data set is given in tabular form in Figure 9.16 at the end of this chapter.

The data miner notes:

- The problem is very low-dimensional (at most four raw features). It might make sense to consider synthesizing some additional features.
- The number of ground truth classes is very small (only three). This eliminates a major source of computational complexity.
- There are not very many feature vectors. Partitioning the data into more than two or three parts is probably not a good idea. Also, with few examples, the developed model might not generalize well.
- The problem is balanced by class (same number of instances of each class), so it will not initially be necessary to replicate instances, decimate instances, or modify the classifier objective function.
- It might be helpful to do some general background reading about irises to be able to get maximum benefit from future discussions with domain experts.
- Do a literature search: get Fisher's 1936 paper and his 1950 book. Check out a copy of Duda and Hart,[6] a book that describes an analysis of this data set.
- Given the size and apparent low complexity of this problem, existing tools and infrastructure should be adequate.
- Ask the customer for access to existing document on the problem, and the data.
- Ask the customer how your classifier will be deployed. If it must be integrated with a legacy system, ask for access to system documentation and CONOP. Ask to see the legacy system in operation, and to talk with users.

9.2.3 Descriptive Modeling of Data: Preprocessing and Data Conditioning

This activity begins once data are received.

- **Audit the data for quality.** The preconditioning activity begins with an assessment of the syntactic quality of the data. This involves checking for formatting and alignment problems, missing data, repeated data, improper rounding (which can lead to loss of precision), and consistency with available data documentation. This process should be at least partially manual, for two reasons: there are some things you can only see by actually putting eyes on the data; does it "look" right? Secondly, this will help you develop some familiarity with and intuition for the problem space. However, for large data sets, most of an auditing process will have to be automated. At the very least, every datum should be range-checked, and all gaps noted.
- **Format/conform data if required.** It will probably be necessary to reformat some of the data for ingestion by the analysis tools to be used. This process should be automated to insure efficiency and repeatability. This can be a time-consuming process, and will probably require the generation of some ad hoc software.
- **Compile descriptive statistics on entire data set.** This is the first authentic analytic activity. It is here that the miner will get the first real look at the data set as a distribution. Many databases and spreadsheets have integrated tools for computing descriptive statistics. Figure 9.1 shows a sample descriptive statistics report for the four features in the Fisher data set.

    Carry out any necessary corrections and automate if possible (gap filling, outlier detection, and processing, etc.). This process should elevate the data to analysis ready quality.
- **Randomize order of records to avoid co-location bias.** This step is not necessarily required, but should be performed if data are provided in a flat file. Data

(units: centimeters)	sepal length	sepal width	petal length	petal width
Mean	5.843333333	3.057333333	3.758	1.199333333
Standard Error	0.067611316	0.035588333	0.144135997	0.062236445
Median	5.8	3	4.35	1.3
Mode	5	3	1.4	0.2
Standard Deviation	0.828066128	0.435866285	1.765298233	0.762237669
Sample Variance	0.685693512	0.189979418	3.116277852	0.581006264
Kurtosis	-0.552064041	0.228249042	-1.402103416	-1.340603997
Skewness	0.314910957	0.318965665	-0.27488418	-0.102966748
Range	3.6	2.4	5.9	2.4
Minimum	4.3	2	1	0.1
Maximum	7.9	4.4	6.9	2.5
Sum	876.5	458.6	563.7	179.9
Count	150	150	150	150

Figure 9.1   Descriptive statistics for the Fisher Iris Data Set.

1	5.1	3.5	1.4	0.2	1	0.856826
2	4.9	3	1.4	0.2	1	0.200967
3	4.7	3.2	1.3	0.2	1	0.940021
4	4.6	3.1	1.5	0.2	1	0.754746
5	5	3.6	1.4	0.2	1	0.559449
6	5.4	3.9	1.7	0.4	1	0.75296
7	4.6	3.4	1.4	0.3	1	0.669683
8	5	3.4	1.5	0.2	1	0.798224
9	4.4	2.9	1.4	0.2	1	0.74738
10	4.9	3.1	1.5	0.1	1	0.912014
11	5.4	3.7	1.5	0.2	1	0.394846
12	4.8	3.4	1.6	0.2	1	0.576837
13	4.8	3	1.4	0.1	1	0.0615
14	4.3	3	1.1	0.1	1	0.874126
15	5.8	4	1.2	0.2	1	0.256284
16	5.7	4.4	1.5	0.4	1	0.156229
17	5.4	3.9	1.3	0.4	1	0.560522
18	5.1	3.5	1.4	0.3	1	0.866003
19	5.7	3.8	1.7	0.3	1	0.184352
20	5.1	3.8	1.5	0.3	1	0.206943

Appended a column of random numbers

128	6.1	3	4.9	1.8	3	0.000105
42	4.5	2.3	1.3	0.3	1	0.006435
21	5.4	3.4	1.7	0.2	1	0.007661
30	4.7	3.2	1.6	0.2	1	0.018055
111	6.5	3.2	5.1	2	3	0.03157
115	5.8	2.8	5.1	2.4	3	0.05138
5	5	3.6	1.4	0.2	1	0.053255
56	5.7	2.8	4.5	1.3	2	0.06577
109	6.7	2.5	5.8	1.8	3	0.069724
87	6.7	3.1	4.7	1.5	2	0.075649
131	7.4	2.8	6.1	1.9	3	0.077536
69	6.2	2.2	4.5	1.5	2	0.104858
84	6	2.7	5.1	1.6	2	0.106428
32	5.4	3.4	1.5	0.4	1	0.109537
112	6.4	2.7	5.3	1.9	3	0.118933
41	5	3.5	1.3	0.3	1	0.121458
51	7	3.2	4.7	1.4	2	0.127169
113	6.8	3	5.5	2.1	3	0.132538
34	5.5	4.2	1.4	0.2	1	0.134935
100	5.7	2.8	4.1	1.3	2	0.143358

Sorted all columns using random column

Figure 9.2 Avoidance of co-location bias.

in a flat file are in a certain order for some reason, and you don't want that unknown reason biasing your partitioning operation. A simple way to order-randomize a flat file is to append a column of random numbers. By sorting the entire record on this random column, the order of the records is randomized (Figure 9.2).

- **Partition the data.** Once the data are order-randomized, they can be partitioned by just grabbing blocks of sequential records. This will give a representative sample in the sense that the relative frequencies of occurrence of each class will be reflected in the resulting partitions. The Fisher data are already balanced by class, so no special processing is required.

  In the case that certain classes have very few representatives, you might have to replicate instances of residual classes to guarantee they occur in each partition. Be careful, though, that the test file examples are not present in other partitions. This would invalidate your blind test results. For this activity, the data were divided into two, equal sized, 75-vector partitions: TRAIN.CSV, and BLIND.CSV.

- **Compute pair-wise correlations.** Using only the calibration (or training) data, compute the Pearson Correlation Coefficients of each pair of features, and for each feature with the ground truth. The feature-to-feature correlations will tell you whether the features are independent, and the feature to ground truth correlations will provide information on the accessible information content of each feature individually. The correlations for the Fisher data are in Figure 9.3.

  Notice that petal length and petal width are highly correlated with the ground truth class (rho of 0.95 and 0.96, respectively). This indicates these features are probably very information rich. However, they are highly correlated with each other (0.96), so they are not independent information sources. It might make sense to use only one of them.

- **Visualize data.** Visualization allows the user to interact at an intuitive level with the data. Figure 9.4 provides some scatter plots depicting the entire data set as one feature plotted against another. In the plot, two coherent aggregations can be seen visually. Keep in mind there is no reason to believe that the two aggregations seen in each plot are the same aggregations in each plot.

  There is also no reason to believe the two aggregations seen in any particular scatter plot are in any way related to the ground truth classes for our problem. If this happens to be the case, that is great; but it need not be. Scatter plots are helpful, but features can be correlated pair-wise without being jointly correlated. Therefore, we need to look at the data in it native four-dimensional feature space. One way to do this is to use an Inselberg plot (Figure 9.5).

  Full spatial visualization (Figure 9.6) reveals that two aggregations actually exist in the higher-dimensional feature space.

Correlation	sepal length	sepal width	petal length	petal width	class
sepal length	1.00				
sepal width	-0.12	1.00			
petal length	0.87	-0.43	1.00		
petal width	0.82	-0.37	0.96	1.00	
class	0.78	-0.43	0.95	0.96	1.00

Pairwise Pearson Correlation Ceofficients for features and ground truth

Figure 9.3   Pearson correlation coefficients.

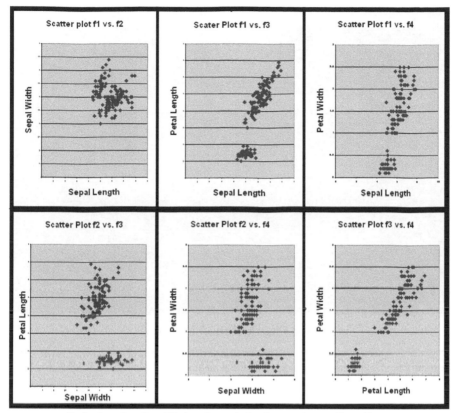

Pairwise Scatter Plots of each feature versus the others

Figure 9.4   Visualization of feature comparisons.

- **Decide whether some sort of registration/normalization is needed.** For example, it might be reasonable to synchronize or z-score the data. If some correction process is to be performed, compute the correction parameters from the calibration set, not the blind set. Apply the parameters to all sets to *calibrate*. Calibration must eventually be automated since this same calibration must be applied to any data to be processed by the fielded classifier. The calibration parameters derived from the calibration set will also be used to condition blind data for processing. Perform a preprocessing data audit to minimize the chances that the data have not been inadvertently biased or degraded.

9.2.4 Data Exploitation: Feature Extraction and Enhancement

- **Code/quantize/transform features (if necessary).** This is usually done early on because of limitations in available tools, but is also done during later spirals in anticipation of improved classifier performance.

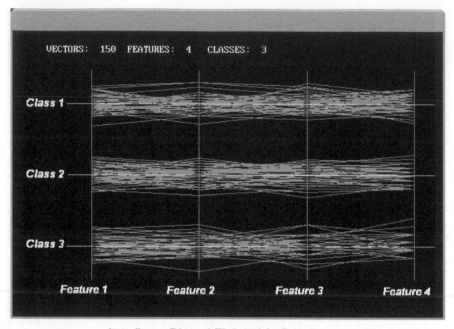

Inselberg Plot of Fisher Iris Data

Figure 9.5   Visualization of native feature space.

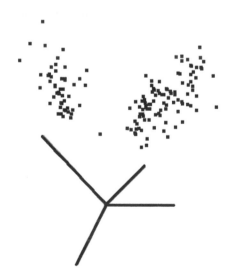

Fisher data set in its "native" four-dimensional space

Figure 9.6   Spatial visualization in high dimensional space.

Correlation	Sepal Length	Sepal Width	Petal Length	Petal Width	Synthesized	Class
Sepal Length	1.00					
Sepal Width	-0.12	1.00				
Petal Length	0.87	-0.43	1.00			
Petal Width	0.82	-0.37	0.96	1.00		
Synthesized	-0.32	0.31	-0.42	-0.38	1.00	
Class	0.78	-0.43	0.95	0.96	-0.31	1.00

Feature-to-feature and feature to Ground Truth correlation after Z-Score Normalization

Figure 9.7 Feature correlation after z-score normalization.

- **Compute feature correlations.** You are simply redoing the correlation computation. This is necessary because transformations and corrections that have been applied to the data will change their correlations with each other, and with the ground truth.
- **Synthesize/winnow features.** This is an opportunity to combine existing features in a nonlinear way with the hope of improving performance. This can be done in a principled way by analysis of scatter plots; this is an esoteric topic that will not be addressed here. We will synthesize a new feature for the Fisher data using the following nonlinear combination method:

$$f5 = \sqrt{(|(f1-f3)| \, |(f2-f4)|)}$$

This is an ad hoc nonlinear transform. It is the product of the difference of the lengths and the difference of the widths. The intent is to form a nonlinear mixture of strong features (f3 & f4) and weak features (f1 & f2). Hopefully, this will expose some information about the ground truth, while being independent of the other features.

We then z-score each column of data to statistically normalize the features. The new correlation matrix after normalization is in Figure 9.7.

Notice the synthesized feature is not strongly correlated with the ground truth (-0.31), so it isn't a strong feature; but neither is it strongly correlated with the other features, so perhaps it reveals some new information. Experimentation will tell whether the synthesized feature should be retained or not.

9.2.5 Model Selection and Development

The data are now five-dimensional, having the original four raw features and the synthesized feature. There are three ground truth classes. All indications are that this is not a difficult problem, so a very simple two-layer neural network is probably sufficient (tests show this is true), but for our illustration we choose a more powerful three-layer architecture. I typically use a few more neurons in the input layer than there are features, and about twice that amount in the hidden layer (cf. the Kolmogorov Neural Network Mapping Existence Theorem[7]). The output layer for this neural network has

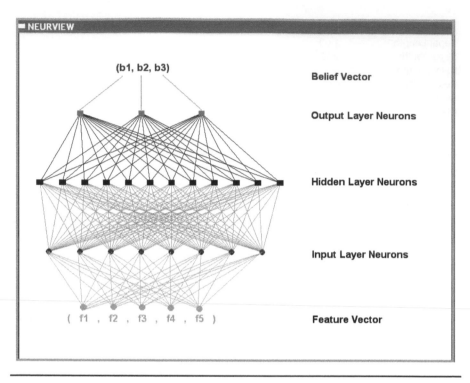

Figure 9.8   Multi-layer perceptron neural network.

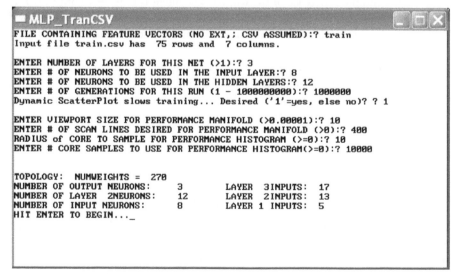

Figure 9.9   Neural network training example.

one neuron for each ground truth class, since these outputs are generating *beliefs* that the input is in their class. The output neuron that produces the greatest belief value determines the classification decision of the neural network.

The architecture of this neural network is depicted in Figure 9.8. There are many neural network architectures; this one is called a Multi-Layer Perceptron (MLP), since the neurons that perform the transforms are arranged in layers. This neural network has three layers. Numeric data comes into each box at the bottom, is transformed, and is fed-forward to the next layer out of the top. For this reason, these neural networks are sometimes referred to as feed-forward neural networks.

9.2.6 Model Training

A MLP trainer was used to implement the architecture in the figure above. It used a gradient-assisted Monte Carlo method to adjust the interconnect weights to maximize an accuracy score. Total training time was less than 60 seconds. The main input display page for the trainer is shown in Figure 9.9. It shows the parameters selected by the user, and states the number of neurons chosen for each layer.

9.2.7 Model Evaluation

The neural network trainer produces certain diagnostic and performance metrics as it learns, and displays these to the user. For this training experiment, the neural network rapidly trained to 100% accuracy and very high certainty. This is not always a good thing, since overtraining might have occurred. Blind testing should tell us whether the neural network generalizes or not. The performance metrics for the neural network on the training set are in Figure 9.10.

```
TIME OUTPUT GENERATED:    22:57:03
DATA FILE CONTAINING SIGNATURES:
NUMBER OF SIGNATURES PROCESSED:   75
TOPOLOGY: |5|8|12|3|   NUMWEIGHTS:   270
NUMBER OF TRAINING PASSES: 1000000|
NETWORK SATURATION: 65.6872
GEOMETRIC MEAN OF CLASS PRECISIONS:   100%
PERCENTAGE OF SIGNATURES CORRECTLY CLASSIFIED:   100%
AGGREGATE NETWORK CERTAINTY OF CLASSIFICATION:   99.99986


CONFUSION MATRIX:

 1|        24      0       0
 2|         0     27       0
 3|         0      0      24
```

Figure 9.10 Confusion matrix of training data.

```
GEOMETRIC MEAN OF CLASS PRECISIONS:   91.35967%
PERCENTAGE OF SIGNATURES CORRECTLY CLASSIFIED:   92%
AGGREGATE NETWORK CERTAINTY OF CLASSIFICATION:   85.01221%

CONFUSION MATRIX:

    1|        26      0      0
    2|         0     19      4
    3|         0      2     24
```

Results for Blind Test set: 92% of the test vectors were correctly classified

Figure 9.11   Blind set classification of trained neural network.

The trained neural network was then used to classify the vectors in the blind set, with the results shown in Figure 9.11.

This result (92%) is probably not a bad result for a first experiment. The confusion matrix shows we are misclassifying four class 2 vectors as class 3's, and two class 3 vectors as class 2's. This is not surprising, since it is classes 2 and 3 that are encroaching on each other.

It appears that the classification ability of the neural network generalizes fairly well to data the machine has not seen before. If we are satisfied with the confusion matrix and speed of the neural network, we can deploy it. If not, we can perform some additional training experiments, and/or go back for another development spiral to enhance features, or try other types of neural architectures and classifiers.

9.3 Specific Challenges, Problems, and Pitfalls of Supervised Learning

This section describes the inherent challenges of problems in this genre, and suggests appropriate methods for addressing them.

9.3.1 High-Dimensional Feature Vectors (PCA, Winnowing)

The amount of time and storage required to train a classifier is a function of how difficult the problem is, how complex the classifier is, and how large the training set is. The most important factor in training set size is not the number of vectors, since the training effort is usually directly proportional to this. The real data complexity issue is the number of features in each vector.

A trainable machine is attempting to learn some relationship among the features in a training vector that determine the class to which it should be assigned. The number of possible groupings of features grows exponentially with the number of features. If training is taking too long, you will usually reduce computation time by removing a few features, rather than by reducing the number of vectors.

This super-linear growth in complexity with increasing dimension is often referred to as *the curse of dimensionality*. It presents the data miner with a difficult decision: Is the information gained by adding more features worth the performance cost? This question becomes particularly vexing when the information gain can't even be measured because training with the additional features is too time-consuming an experiment.

For reasons of efficiency in space and time, elimination of unnecessary complexity, and avoidance of numerical problems (overtraining and multi-colinearity), the *best* model is usually the simplest one that gives acceptable performance (time, size, accuracy, understandability). Such a model is called *parsimonious*.

The practical value of parsimonious models makes effective feature winnowing an essential capability. One dimension reduction, Principal Component Analysis (PCA), has been addressed earlier. We now present an example of another automated feature winnowing method, the Encoder-Decoder Network as an illustration. Many other methods can be found in the research literature.

An Encoder-Decoder Network is a neural network that has an *hourglass* architecture. The idea is simple: The neural network is trained to produce input feature vectors from a data set (these enter at the bottom) as its outputs (these appear at the top). If this is possible, it means that all or most of the information in the original vector has to be present in the output of the *bottleneck* at the middle layer. We throw away the top layer, and use the bottom two layers as a winnowing engine for this problem; in this case, reducing the dimension from 7 to 4 (Figure 9.12).

9.3.2 Not Enough Data

Sometimes usable data is in short supply. Perhaps there are few instances available with ground truth, or some important class is underrepresented. In such a case, it might not be possible to divide the data into separate segments for training, calibration, and validation. How should we proceed?

If the data were produced by some process for which parameters are known, it might be possible to construct a simulation that can be used to generate data. This is often the case for queuing problems, such as creating a plan for scheduling elevators in a tall building, sequencing things for processing by a server bank, vehicle traffic models, etc.

If this is not possible, sometimes a replication strategy can be used: include copies or slight variants of existing data to increase the vector count (usually in an unprincipled manner). If possible, this should be done without making significant changes to the data distribution or relative proportion of ground truth classes.

Finally, a commonly used strategy is called. This strategy partitions the data into N segments, numbered 1 though N. A model is trained on all the data but that in segment 1, and blind tested on segment 1. This model is then discarded. A model is then trained on all the data but that in segment two, and blind tested on segment two. In this way, N separate models are trained and blind tested on a small holdback set. The model to

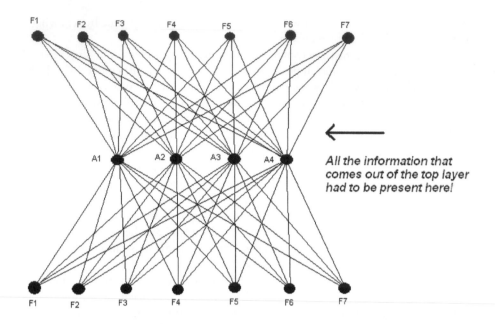

A Neural Network with a "bottleneck" compresses data

Figure 9.12   Neural network bottleneck.

be deployed is trained on all the data and the average of the results of the N blind tests provides an estimate of this models blind performance. In the research literature, a frequently used value for N is 10.

9.3.3 Too Much Data

Having too much data is more of a storage problem than a data mining problem. It is usually not too difficult to select representative samples from a large corpus to obtain sets that are of manageable size. If there is a large amount of data available for modeling, it probably makes sense to escrow some data to cover contingencies that might arise (e.g., additional blind test sets are needed).

9.3.4 Unbalanced Data

When building classifiers using supervised learning methods, an important but oft overlooked problem is class *imbalance*. This occurs when the ground truth classes are not represented in the same proportions. In this case, some classes occur much more frequently than others do. This causes problems because classes that are more abundant will tend to have a disproportionate effect on the training process. This can be a serious concern because it is usually the rarer, underrepresented classes that are of the most interest in data mining applications.

There are several balancing strategies. Replication (including multiple copies) of underrepresented data, and decimation (removing copies) of overrepresented data is one approach. Another is to use a simulator or some other synthesis mechanism to generate additional vectors of the underrepresented classes. Replication, decimation, and synthesis are easy to employ, but because they change the class proportions, they can bias the training data if not performed carefully.

Algorithmic methods can also be used to compensate for class imbalance. These adjust the learning algorithm so that rare classes are allowed to have greater impact in the training process. For example, if there are twice as many class A's as class B's, the effect of class B's in the training algorithm can be doubled. This doesn't always produce good results, but works often enough that it is worth trying.

A related method is classical *boosting*. In boosting, vectors in the training set that are misclassified are presented for learning more frequently in subsequent epochs, giving the learning machine extra practice on vectors it is missing. Boosting also addressed the imbalance problem, since underrepresented classes are more likely to be misclassified.

9.3.5 Overtraining

Suppose that during training, the classifier is allowed to process a semi-blind data set (vectors that are not part of the training set, but are used for diagnostics during training). A sample taken from the calibration set is often used for this purpose. As long as performance on this semi-blind set continues to improve, the training process is still learning facts about the problem that will generalize to new data.

However, as training continues, a point is usually reached where performance on the semi-blind set decreases, even though performance on the training data is continuing to improve (Figure 9.13). What is going on here?

This is a phenomenon called *overtraining*. The machine is beginning to learn the idiosyncrasies of the training data; coincidences that will not generalize to other data. The machine is *over fitting* the training data, and continuing beyond this point amounts to memorizing the training set. If that's what you want to do, you should be building a database, not a classifier.

Interleaving training epochs with tests using a semi-blind set provides a practical, problem-specific means of determining when supervised training should be stopped. A typical schedule is 1 test epoch for every 100 training epochs; clearly, this is problem dependent.

9.3.6 Noncommensurable Data: Outliers

When processing numeric data, it often happens that different features have different ranges because of the units used to represent them. One feature might be age in

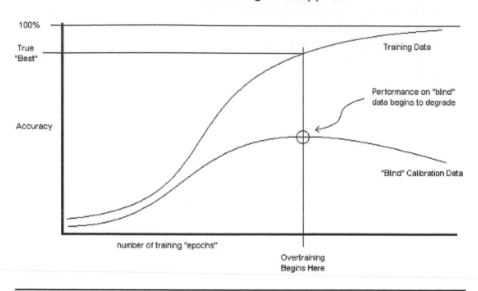

Figure 9.13   Over fitting the training data.

years, and another feature might be annual salary in dollars. Here the age feature has a range of around 100, while the salary feature could have a range in the millions. This variability can cause numerical problems when building a trainable model and most notably, loss of precision. It also makes the data impossible to plot on a scale having uniform axes.

These numeric and plotting problems can be eliminated by normalizing the features into a common range. There are several ways to do this, but some introduce ad hoc nonlinear effects (e.g., applying a log of sigmoid transform to the data).

Another approach is *amplitude normalization*, in which the values for each feature are divided by the largest value assumed by that feature. However, this becomes a problem when there are a small number of values that are much larger in absolute value than most others (e.g., a big outlier). Nearly all the data end up close to 0, with a few instances close in absolute value to 1.

A much better approach is to replace each feature value by the z-score for that feature. Using the calibration set, this is done as follows:

1. Compute the mean value, μ, for the feature.
2. Computer the standard deviation, σ, for the feature.
3. Replace each feature value with its distance above or below the mean in standard deviations:

$$Z_i = \frac{x_i - \mu}{\sigma}$$

If $\sigma = 0$, set $Z_i = 0$

Z-score normalization has very nice properties. One outlier generally has little effect on the scoring, and for many data sets (after z-scoring), almost all data will fall somewhere in the range [−6, 6]. An additional benefit is that, since few features should have large z-scores (say, $|z|>6$), z-scoring provides an objective numeric test for detecting outliers. A rejection threshold can be established early in a data mining project and applied automatically; data exceeding the threshold can be *clipped* to the maximum or minimum values.

It is very important that data to be processed by a model trained on normalized data be normalized in exactly the same way. For example, the mean and standard deviation used for z-scoring each feature must be saved so it can be used to preprocess data for the fielded model.

9.3.7 Missing Features

The standard imputation techniques described earlier can be applied for filling in missing data for use in supervised learning. However, it is important to determine *why* data are missing. Getting the answer to this question reveals a lot about the domain, and the integrity of its data.

9.3.8 Missing Ground Truth

When ground truth is missing for some vectors, it can sometimes be filled in by reference to historical data, the use of a legacy system, or advice from an expert. A completely automated technique is to mix the untagged data with the Calibration Set, and apply a clustering algorithm. The data with missing ground truth is assigned the same ground truth as the tagged vectors with which it naturally clusters. This last method is preferred, since it is automated and repeatable.

9.4 Recommended Data Mining Architectures for Supervised Learning

Each problem domain has its own unique aspects, some of which might require adjustments to the generic data mining process. This section addresses data mining process adjustments for this supervised learning.

Supervised learning applications ingest data tagged with ground truth and infer models capable of reproducing this tagging in unseen data. Therefore, most instances of supervised learning are *regressions*: mathematical models that fit a curve to the training data. The term *curve* here is used in a very general sense, since regressions need not have simple, one-dimensional numeric outputs that could be plotted on graph paper. A regression is much more likely to be a fit of some N-dimensional hyperplane to a

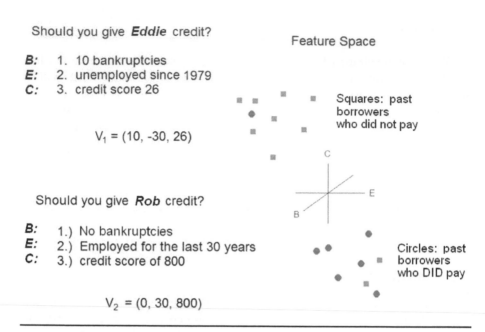

Should you give **Eddie** credit?

B: 1. 10 bankruptcies
E: 2. unemployed since 1979
C: 3. credit score 26

$$V_1 = (10, -30, 26)$$

Feature Space

Squares: past
borrowers
who did not pay

Should you give **Rob** credit?

B: 1.) No bankruptcies
E: 2.) Employed for the last 30 years
C: 3.) credit score of 800

$$V_2 = (0, 30, 800)$$

Circles: past
borrowers
who DID pay

Figure 9.14   A decision problem in 3D space.

complicated scatter plot (giving an estimator), or a twisted surface that winds its way between various clusters of points (giving a classifier).

Figure 9.14 depicts a classification problem using three features. The scatter plot shows outcomes from past instances of this decision problem.

Figure 9.14 shows that in the past, paying and nonpaying customers tend to form separate clusters in the feature space of bankruptcies, employment history, and credit score.

In Figure 9.15, a two-dimensional plane serves as a decision surface; problem instances are classified based upon the side of the surface on which they fall.

Training the decision model in Figure 9.15 was a regression problem; find an equation for some decision surface that separates the ground truth classes. With this illustration in mind, numerous paradigms are seen to be candidates as the model for building supervised classifiers and supervised estimators.

Classifiers:

- Linear Discriminant (e.g., as in the credit example above)
- Neural Networks (discrete outputs: MLP's, Boltzmann Machines)
- Support Vector Machines (SVM's: variants based upon kernel choice)
- Likelihood Methods, Bayesian Networks (i.e., probabilistic methods)
- Random Forests (hierarchical decomposition of feature space)
- Decision Trees (many variants based upon "splitting rules")
- Nearest Neighbor Classifiers (many variants such as KNN, RCE)

Estimators:

- Linear Approximators
- Series (polynomials, Taylor Series, Fourier Series, Bezier curves, splines)
- Radial Basis Functions
- Adaptive Logic Networks
- Neural Networks (continuous outputs: MLPs)

There are many others, but these are among the most mature and commonly used. Their theories are well-developed, and multiple books and papers have been written about each. The common element is that all are based upon some mathematical function that interpolates, approximates, or discriminates a set of *a priori* examples.

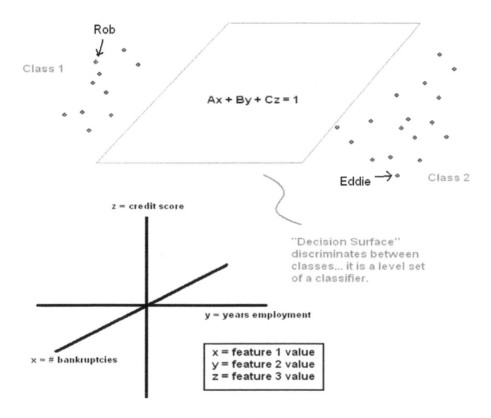

If the training set is representative of the actual problem domain, new data points should follow the learned patterns.

Figure 9.15   Training of the decision model.

9.5 Descriptive Analysis

This section provides a summary of descriptive modeling methods and objectives for supervised learning. Recall that descriptive modeling is a preliminary analysis during which data attributes are characterized formally. This is generally done using simple analytic tools such a histograms, scatter plots, graphs/charts, and basic statistical techniques to obtain means, variances, ranges, simple correlations, and demographic/metadata.

Collectively, these constitute a characterization of the data called a *descriptive model*. There are many software applications that support descriptive analysis (e.g., Excel, SAS, Oracle database products). The choice of descriptive modeling tool is often determined by data type and how the data are stored (e.g., nominal/numeric, whether it is in a database vs. flat file).

Descriptive modeling methods are of four types. For supervised methods, their greatest value lies in the depiction of relationships between ground truth and subsets of the features.

- **Meta-data model.** These provide data externals such as storage size, number of records, number of fields, data format types, pedigree (source, age, accuracy).
- **Distributional models.** These consist of descriptive statistics such as data ranges, means/medians/modes, variances, demographics (e.g., number of items in each ground truth class), prior probabilities, tables, and charts giving summary statistics.
- **Association models.** These depict relationships among the data, such as correlation tables, association rules, network models, and relationship trees.
- **Visualizations.** These are visual depictions of the data in some feature space, such as scatter plots, histograms, graphical charts, animations.

9.5.1 Technical Component: Problem Definition

These are the items that must be addressed to ensure that the data mining problem has been properly characterized. For supervised learning, it is particularly important to express these issues in terms of the ground truth.

User Problems and Needs Being Addressed:

- What type of supervised learning problem is being addressed? The most common types are the classifier, and estimator.

Functional Project and Performance Goals:

- A specific functional goal (what must be done) for the effort must be specified in written form and agreed to by all parties. This should include a description of the data set used for model development, and an enumeration of the ground truth categories.

- A characterization and quantitative description of target performance levels should be in written form and agreed to by all parties. This generally includes accuracy and error rate estimates. Performance levels need not be specified numerically for proof-of-concept or experimental efforts, but should be understood by all.

Enterprise Requirements:

- Keep in mind there are two kinds of success in data mining efforts; technical success, and business success. Technical success (e.g., meeting reasonable accuracy goals) is often easier to achieve, since good technical results do not necessarily have operational value to the enterprise.

    What requirements must be met for a data mining effort to have operational value, that is, is there a business case for the project? This involves consideration of operational impact, implementation cost, user training, and performance issues traded against expected benefits.

Resources:

- Project Staffing
- Cost and Schedule

In simple scenarios where modeling is done from flat files (rather than a structured repository like a database), it generally takes about 1 or two weeks to condition the data for modeling, and another 4 to 6 weeks to reach the first substantial prototype. A substantial prototype is one that implements all the desired elements of processing to a level sufficient such that the level of performance of the final, delivered model can be estimated. Once the first prototype has been evaluated, successive prototypes can often be produced in 1 or 2 week cycles.

If the data to be mined are in a relational database or data warehouse, special skill and additional work are usually needed to prepare them for modeling. This is because the database schema (organizational system) is almost always designed around the data input model (how the data arrive) and/or the data output model (how the data are accessed) rather than around an information model relevant to the data mining task. Significant elements of information will be implicit (in the relations) rather than explicit (in the "bits"), and most of these will vanish if data are extracted without a thorough understanding of the database schema.

Characterizing the Operational Environment (locations/software/hardware/tools/legacy integration):

- The development and operational environments should be specified.
- Any special tools and development applications should be specified.
- An integration strategy for deploying data mining applications should be developed.

Structured Interviews (methodology, question lists):

- Secure a list of available, user-approved domain experts.
- Make initial contacts with experts to secure their cooperation.
- Put together a Knowledge Acquisition Plan (KAP), which includes a chief domain expert (to definitively resolve issues), a list of domain questions, and an interview schedule for discussions with domain experts.

Configuration Management

Management of the data and process configuration is particularly important when using a spiral development methodology against a floating baseline and changing requirements. Two essentials are:

- Nomenclature and naming conventions for data, processes, baselines
- Documenting the workflow for reproducibility (requires automation)

9.5.2 Technical Component: Data Selection and Preparation

This includes common data problems (outliers, gaps, consistency, collisions, imbalance, etc.). Have a plan to detect and address the following:

- Identifying/handling outliers (statistical methods)
- Handling missing fields (weak fill values, de-gapping, gap masking)
- Handling temporal problems (aging, cycling, trends, nonstationarity, etc.)
- Checking consistency (semantic filtering)
- Handling class collisions
- Handling class imbalance (replication, decimation)

9.5.3 Technical Component: Data Representation

The following areas must be addressed in the project plan and some empirical experiments will be necessary. The results of this investigation will determine the nature and amount of data conditioning needed for the project. Expect changes to the project plan as these areas are addressed.

Data Representation Solution Checklist:

- Nominal vs. numeric trades
- Coding (converting nominal to numeric data)
- Quantization (converting numeric to nominal data)

Feature Extraction and Transformation:

- Data registration

- Data normalization
- Feature synthesis

Feature Enhancement:

- Feature salience (discriminating power of a feature)
- Feature independence (information contribution of a feature)
- Information-theoretic transforms (making information more accessible)

Data Division:

- Sampling
- Stratifying
- Segmenting (creating training, calibration, validation, and holdback sets)

9.6 Predictive Modeling

This section is a summary of predictive modeling methods and objectives for supervised learning. Predictive modeling is a generic cover term that can refer to just about any sort of supervised learning application (the term *predictive* does not imply prognostication.). Recall that predictive modeling uses the results of descriptive modeling to construct applications (models) that solve enterprise problems. Predictive models are generally classifiers or estimators.

Predictive modeling (e.g., the development of a classifier or estimator) is generally done using relatively sophisticated modeling tools such learning engines and adaptive algorithms to create models that detect/classify patterns of interest in data. The resulting applications are called *predictive models*. There are a wide range of software tools that support aspects of predictive modeling. These range in power and complexity from relatively simple regression modelers (e.g., Excel) to very sophisticated predictive modelers (e.g., SAS). The choice of predictive modeling tool is largely driven by user performance requirements and the data distribution (e.g., required levels of accuracy, nature of the available training data).

9.6.1 Technical Component: Paradigm Selection

A notional decision tree for this process can be found in groundwork chapters of the text. There are really only two salient issues to address here:

- What type and complexity of feature inputs are available?
- What type of decision is being made (classifier, estimator, planner, etc.)?

The paradigm is merely an algorithmic bridge that carries the user from feature space to goal space; it has to be of a type that can span the gap presented by the problem to be solved. For example, it makes no sense to use a neural network if the features are non-numeric, and it makes no sense to use a polynomial as a classifier.

9.6.2 Technical Component: Model Construction and Validation

Once the paradigm has been selected, the problem of its specific architecture must be addressed. Problems that are more complicated usually require the most elaborate architectures (e.g., more layers and neurons in an MLP, higher degree in a polynomial regression, etc.). For supervised learning systems, this usually means:

Construction:

- Will special tools be required (e.g., third party applications)?
- How will the models be "trained"?

Meta-Scheme Development:

- Will several models be built and then "bagged"?
- Will a "boosting" model be run on the results of the main model?

9.6.3 Technical Component: Model Evaluation (Functional and Performance Metrics)

It is important to establish the metrics for a technical project up front in writing, and get agreement. If this is not done, trouble is inevitable. For supervised learning applications, this usually includes:

- Accuracy: %, Type I/II errors, confusion matrices, ROC curves, etc.
- Timeliness, utility, cost, ROI

9.6.4 Technical Component: Model Deployment

Deployment mechanisms should be considered at the beginning of a data mining effort, since design decisions made during the mining process could preclude some. Will an application developed be deployed using an API, as a plug-in, using a file interface, on a menu bar, as a stand-alone process, etc.?

9.6.5 Technical Component: Model Maintenance

Every application deployed to an operational environment must have a maintenance plan, since normal system maintenance and version upgrades will cause the application to require adjustment and testing.

For supervised learning systems, this often means incorporating a retraining capability, automating regression testing, adding/removing features and ground truth classes, and having embedded diagnostics.

	Sepal		Petal				Sepal		Petal				Sepal		Petal		
VID	Len	Wid	Len	Wid	Var	VID	Len	Wid	Len	Wid	Var	VID	Len	Wid	Len	Wid	Var
1	5.1	3.5	1.4	0.2	set.	51	7	3.2	4.7	1.4	vers.	101	6.3	3.3	6	2.5	virg.
2	4.9	3	1.4	0.2	set.	52	6.4	3.2	4.5	1.5	vers.	102	5.8	2.7	5.1	1.9	virg.
3	4.7	3.2	1.3	0.2	set.	53	6.9	3.1	4.9	1.5	vers.	103	7.1	3	5.9	2.1	virg.
4	4.6	3.1	1.5	0.2	set.	54	5.5	2.3	4	1.3	vers.	104	6.3	2.9	5.6	1.8	virg.
5	5	3.6	1.4	0.2	set.	55	6.5	2.8	4.6	1.5	vers.	105	6.5	3	5.8	2.2	virg.
6	5.4	3.9	1.7	0.4	set.	56	5.7	2.8	4.5	1.3	vers.	106	7.6	3	6.6	2.1	virg.
7	4.6	3.4	1.4	0.3	set.	57	6.3	3.3	4.7	1.6	vers.	107	4.9	2.5	4.5	1.7	virg.
8	5	3.4	1.5	0.2	set.	58	4.9	2.4	3.3	1	vers.	108	7.3	2.9	6.3	1.8	virg.
9	4.4	2.9	1.4	0.2	set.	59	6.6	2.9	4.6	1.3	vers.	109	6.7	2.5	5.8	1.8	virg.
10	4.9	3.1	1.5	0.1	set.	60	5.2	2.7	3.9	1.4	vers.	110	7.2	3.6	6.1	2.5	virg.
11	5.4	3.7	1.5	0.2	set.	61	5	2	3.5	1	vers.	111	6.5	3.2	5.1	2	virg.
12	4.8	3.4	1.6	0.2	set.	62	5.9	3	4.2	1.5	vers.	112	6.4	2.7	5.3	1.9	virg.
13	4.8	3	1.4	0.1	set.	63	6	2.2	4	1	vers.	113	6.8	3	5.5	2.1	virg.
14	4.3	3	1.1	0.1	set.	64	6.1	2.9	4.7	1.4	vers.	114	5.7	2.5	5	2	virg.
15	5.8	4	1.2	0.2	set.	65	5.6	2.9	3.6	1.3	vers.	115	5.8	2.8	5.1	2.4	virg.
16	5.7	4.4	1.5	0.4	set.	66	6.7	3.1	4.4	1.4	vers.	116	6.4	3.2	5.3	2.3	virg.
17	5.4	3.9	1.3	0.4	set.	67	5.6	3	4.5	1.5	vers.	117	6.5	3	5.5	1.8	virg.
18	5.1	3.5	1.4	0.3	set.	68	5.8	2.7	4.1	1	vers.	118	7.7	3.8	6.7	2.2	virg.
19	5.7	3.8	1.7	0.3	set.	69	6.2	2.2	4.5	1.5	vers.	119	7.7	2.6	6.9	2.3	virg.
20	5.1	3.8	1.5	0.3	set.	70	5.6	2.5	3.9	1.1	vers.	120	6	2.2	5	1.5	virg.
21	5.4	3.4	1.7	0.2	set.	71	5.9	3.2	4.8	1.8	vers.	121	6.9	3.2	5.7	2.3	virg.
22	5.1	3.7	1.5	0.4	set.	72	6.1	2.8	4	1.3	vers.	122	5.6	2.8	4.9	2	virg.
23	4.6	3.6	1	0.2	set.	73	6.3	2.5	4.9	1.5	vers.	123	7.7	2.8	6.7	2	virg.
24	5.1	3.3	1.7	0.5	set.	74	6.1	2.8	4.7	1.2	vers.	124	6.3	2.7	4.9	1.8	virg.
25	4.8	3.4	1.9	0.2	set.	75	6.4	2.9	4.3	1.3	vers.	125	6.7	3.3	5.7	2.1	virg.
26	5	3	1.6	0.2	set.	76	6.6	3	4.4	1.4	vers.	126	7.2	3.2	6	1.8	virg.
27	5	3.4	1.6	0.4	set.	77	6.8	2.8	4.8	1.4	vers.	127	6.2	2.8	4.0	1.0	virg.
28	5.2	3.5	1.5	0.2	set.	78	6.7	3	5	1.7	vers.	128	6.1	3	4.9	1.8	virg.
29	5.2	3.4	1.4	0.2	set.	79	6	2.9	4.5	1.5	vers.	129	6.4	2.8	5.6	2.1	virg.
30	4.7	3.2	1.6	0.2	set.	80	5.7	2.6	3.5	1	vers.	130	7.2	3	5.8	1.6	virg.
31	4.8	3.1	1.6	0.2	set.	81	5.5	2.4	3.8	1.1	vers.	131	7.4	2.8	6.1	1.9	virg.
32	5.4	3.4	1.5	0.4	set.	82	5.5	2.4	3.7	1	vers.	132	7.9	3.8	6.4	2	virg.
33	5.2	4.1	1.5	0.1	set.	83	5.8	2.7	3.9	1.2	vers.	133	6.4	2.8	5.6	2.2	virg.
34	5.5	4.2	1.4	0.2	set.	84	6	2.7	5.1	1.6	vers.	134	6.3	2.8	5.1	1.5	virg.
35	4.9	3.1	1.5	0.2	set.	85	5.4	3	4.5	1.5	vers.	135	6.1	2.6	5.6	1.4	virg.
36	5	3.2	1.2	0.2	set.	86	6	3.4	4.5	1.6	vers.	136	7.7	3	6.1	2.3	virg.
37	5.5	3.5	1.3	0.2	set.	87	6.7	3.1	4.7	1.5	vers.	137	6.3	3.4	5.6	2.4	virg.
38	4.9	3.6	1.4	0.1	set.	88	6.3	2.3	4.4	1.3	vers.	138	6.4	3.1	5.5	1.8	virg.
39	4.4	3	1.3	0.2	set.	89	5.6	3	4.1	1.3	vers.	139	6	3	4.8	1.8	virg.
40	5.1	3.4	1.5	0.2	set.	90	5.5	2.5	4	1.3	vers.	140	6.9	3.1	5.4	2.1	virg.
41	5	3.5	1.3	0.3	set.	91	5.5	2.6	4.4	1.2	vers.	141	6.7	3.1	5.6	2.4	virg.
42	4.5	2.3	1.3	0.3	set.	92	6.1	3	4.6	1.4	vers.	142	6.9	3.1	5.1	2.3	virg.
43	4.4	3.2	1.3	0.2	set.	93	5.8	2.6	4	1.2	vers.	143	5.8	2.7	5.1	1.9	virg.
44	5	3.5	1.6	0.6	set.	94	5	2.3	3.3	1	vers.	144	6.8	3.2	5.9	2.3	virg.
45	5.1	3.8	1.9	0.4	set.	95	5.6	2.7	4.2	1.3	vers.	145	6.7	3.3	5.7	2.5	virg.
46	4.8	3	1.4	0.3	set.	96	5.7	3	4.2	1.2	vers.	146	6.7	3	5.2	2.3	virg.
47	5.1	3.8	1.6	0.2	set.	97	5.7	2.9	4.2	1.3	vers.	147	6.3	2.5	5	1.9	virg.
48	4.6	3.2	1.4	0.2	set.	98	6.2	2.9	4.3	1.3	vers.	148	6.5	3	5.2	2	virg.
49	5.3	3.7	1.5	0.2	set.	99	5.1	2.5	3	1.1	vers.	149	6.2	3.4	5.4	2.3	virg.
50	5	3.3	1.4	0.2	set.	100	5.7	2.8	4.1	1.3	vers.	150	5.9	3	5.1	1.8	virg.

Figure 9.16 Fisher data set.[8,9] *Note:* Measurements are in centimeters. The abbreviations used are: VID=Vector ID (merely a one-up count), Len=Length, Wid=Width, Var=Variety (Species), set.=*setosa*, vers.=*versicolor*, virg.=*virginica*.

9.7 Summary

This genre section has addressed supervised learning, the most common application of data mining technology for producing operational applications. It has described the use of data mining methods to create detectors, classifiers, estimators, and other decision support tools for users operating in complicated environments.

Chapter 10 (Forensic Analysis)

Genre Section 2— Detecting, Characterizing, and Exploiting Hidden Patterns

Purpose

The practical purpose of this chapter is to characterize the information to be collected and organized during the Data Evaluation Step (Chapter 4) of a data mining spiral. Rather than developing these ideas in prose from which the reader must extract actionable chunks, the material is presented as a topically organized checklist of questions to be addressed. This chapter also describes some techniques for conducting the preliminary analysis of domain data. That is, analysis that is done before the Feature Extraction Step (Chapter 5).

The aspect that distinguishes this genre from others is that here we are searching data for instances of *unknown* patterns; patterns that are not well characterized, and for which representative examples are not available.

Goals

After you have read this chapter, you will understand supervised and unsupervised data mining methods as they relate to each other. You will understand how data clustering is an unsupervised data mining process. You will have seen examples of the formulation of objective functions, and a hierarchical architecture for unsupervised processing. You will be familiar with the fundamentals of multilayer perceptron neural networks. You will have seen how text mining can be used to build sensitive and specific search applications.

Examples:

- Motion Pattern Analysis
  - o Vehicle traffic (Kirchhoff applies, because matter is conserved.)
  - o Network traffic (Kirchhoff does not apply, because information is not conserved.)
- Data Clustering
- Document Analysis
  - o Steganography
- Clique detection
  - o Network analysis
  - o Collaborative filtering
- Fraud and Abuse
  - o Money laundering
  - o Network intrusion detection
- Time Series Analysis
  - o Forecasting
  - o Market prediction
  - o Customer acquisition/attrition prediction
- Finite State Modeling
  - o Processes with random elements (Hidden Markov Model)
  - o Behavior modeling
- Process Optimization, Scheduling, and Planning
  - o Constrained optimization
  - o Resource management
- Change Detection/Anomaly Processing

10.1 Introduction

The approach taken in this chapter is more descriptive than pedagogical. While supervised learning can be treated as a special case of the regression problem, unsupervised learning covers an application space much too broad to be covered by any single theory. However, we will establish a metaphor for unsupervised architectures that casts them as realizations of supervised learning, where training examples have been replaced by working hypotheses captured in an *objective function*.

With this metaphor in view, we will describe the fundamentals of unsupervised learning though carefully chosen case studies and examples that highlight the various design and development considerations for this genre.

10.2 Genre Overview

This genre consists of problems whose solutions are instances of unsupervised learning. Techniques discussed in Chapter 9 (supervised learning) rely on having labeled examples of target patterns. For unsupervised learning, the data input is a set of unlabeled feature vectors (no ground truth).

The goal of unsupervised learning is fundamentally the same as the goal of supervised learning: the detection, characterization, and exploitation of actionable patterns in data.

Is it even possible to construct an application to search for unknown patterns? The answer to this depends upon what *unknown* means in the problem domain. Supervised learning *knows* target patterns in the sense that it has examples that can be used for modeling. These are *known unknowns*: we are certain they really exist, and we can more or less precisely characterize them.

But supervised learning is not designed to address the problem of *unknown unknowns*: phenomena of uncertain existence and nature, not heretofore observed, characterized, or necessarily even hypothesized.

Fortunately, saying that we don't have specific examples or a precise characterization of a target pattern does not mean that we know *nothing* upon which to base a search. If that were the case, we wouldn't recognize a target pattern if we found one.

It is possible in many search applications to form reasonable hypotheses about what some target patterns might look like, even though specific examples are not available. In this sense, supervised learning may be likened to a police officer who familiarizes herself with photographs in a blotter. Unsupervised learning is like her partner, who relies on hypothetical descriptions created by a *profiler*. Discovery in the first case is done by matching suspects with a set of known examples, and in the second by matching suspects with a set of hypothesized properties.

10.3 Recommended Data Mining Architectures for Unsupervised Learning

Unsupervised learning architectures have three functional components:

1. Unlabeled feature vectors (training set)
2. An objective function (measures the performance or quality of a model)
3. A learning algorithm that uses vigilance parameters and the output of the objective function to modify the model (incrementally updates the model)

A training set for unsupervised learning is just like a training set for supervised learning, except that the vectors do not have ground truth labels.

An objective function for a system accepts as input the state of the system, and assigns to it a measure of quality. It is a scoring mechanism. Suppose, for example, that the system is a chess game. A simple objective function might count the number of pieces a player has taken from his opponent. A more sophisticated objective function could incorporate measures derived from the configuration of pieces on the board, look-ahead to possible future states, etc.

Learning algorithms range from the mindlessly simple (e.g., Monte Carlo methods), to the tremendously complex (e.g., Simulated Annealing). The purpose of a learning algorithm is to make changes to the model being developed so that its performance (i.e., quality as determined by application of the objective function) attains a level that makes it a usable model.

To determine the type and magnitude of changes to make during learning, training algorithms must have notions of significance that make sense in the problem domain. This information is supplied by one or more vigilance parameters. A *vigilance parameter* is a threshold of some sort that is used to determine when things are sufficiently similar/different, good/bad, right/wrong, etc., for a decision to be made. For example, if a police officer is looking for a tall suspect, does someone who is 5'10" qualify? If he is looking for a tall building, do six stories suffice?

Figure 10.1 reiterates the general learning architecture for supervised learning on the left, and shows the general learning architecture for unsupervised learning on the right. It is the intentional parallelism seen here that allows us to understand unsupervised learning by noting its similarities and differences with supervised learning.

The box at the top of the unsupervised learning loop (evaluate and learn) is the learning algorithm. It uses the output of the objective function (the box at the bottom

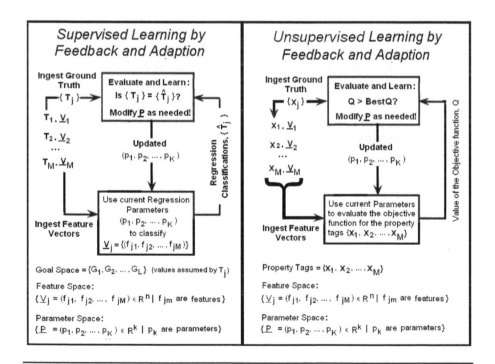

Figure 10.1   Architectures for supervised and unsupervised learning.

of the learning loop) to make an inferences about the current model, and updates it. The model has two parts: the parameters $(p_1, p_2, \ldots p_k)$ of the objective function; and the inferred symbols $x_1, x_2, \ldots x_M$.

There are no ground truth tags in the unsupervised scenario. Instead, there are property tags x_j inferred by the learning algorithm. These can be numbers, names, vectors, URLs, documents, complex structures, pieces of code—instances of whatever it is the unsupervised learning process is attempting to associate with the training vectors.

10.4 Examples and Case Studies for Unsupervised Learning

We now apply the metaphor of Figure 10.1 to implement an unsupervised learning application using what is usually regarded as a supervised learning paradigm (a multilayer perceptron).

For this example, a set of unlabeled feature vectors is provided. It is desired to aggregate these into clusters of vectors that are similar to each other to facilitate categorization for subsequent processing. We formulate the following unsupervised learning process by selecting the three fundamental components of unsupervised learning:

1. *Unlabeled feature vectors (training set)*

   We already have a data set. The standard data preparation methods are applied as needed (e.g., segmentation divides the data into disjoint calibration, training, and validation sets; gaps are repaired; data are normalized, etc.)

2. *An objective function (measures the performance or quality of a model)*

   Because we don't know anything about the problem space from which these data come, there aren't any *a priori* formulae or heuristics to use as a basis for clustering. Therefore, we fall back on the metric properties of Euclidean space, and formulate our own definition for what good clustering might mean in terms of distances in feature space.

   Here are some distance-based properties of good clustering of numeric data:

   - **Property 1**—Clusters that are more tightly packed are better than clusters that are loose.
   - **Property 2**—Vectors are less likely to be assigned to the wrong cluster when the clusters are far apart.
   - **Property 3**—Each vector should be close to its own cluster, and far from the others.

   These must now be turned into an objective function that can be efficiently evaluated. Rather than perform a large number of point-to-point distance computations, we compute the centroid (center of gravity = average) for each cluster by averaging its member vectors coordinate-wise. The centroid of cluster J will be the vector:

$$\mu_J = \frac{1}{L_J} \sum_{k=1}^{L_J} \left(v_{Jk1}, v_{Jk2}, \ldots, v_{JkN} \right)$$

Here μ_J is the centroid of cluster J; it is a vector having N components. L_J is the number of vectors in cluster J; N is the number of features in a feature vector; and v_{Jki} is the ith feature of vector k of cluster J.

Define a metric for each property:

- **Metric 1**—A = Intra-cluster distance: the sum of the distances from each vector in a cluster to its centroid. Smaller is better.
- **Metric 2**—E = Inter-cluster distance: the sum of the distances from each vector to the centroids of clusters of which it is not a member. Larger is better.
- **Metric 3**—C = Centroid distance: the sum of the distances between all the centroids. Larger is better.

These can be rolled up into a single number whose value is increased when any of these metrics gets better. When better means larger, the metric goes into the numerator. When better means smaller, the metric goes into the denominator:

$$D = \frac{CE}{A + 0.1}$$

The 0.1 is an arbitrarily chosen small number that is added in the denominator to avoid division by zero, which happens if all the vectors are at the same location (usually due to some data conditioning error).

This is our designer objective function. It is an abstract measure of clustering quality, so particular values don't mean much. But larger values mean better quality, and that is all that matters here. The various component metrics can be seen below (Figure 10.2).

3. A learning algorithm that uses vigilance parameters and the output of the objective function to modify the model (incrementally updates the model). We decide to use my favorite learning method: LUCK.

Monte Carlo Methods conduct repeated trials of random instantiations of the model being developed. This is an undirected search of the model's parameter space for settings that optimize the objective function. The process is simple:

a. Initialize the model by assigning valid values to its parameters.
b. Ingest the best model parameters seen so far.
c. *Jiggle* the best model parameters by applying a random adjustment to them (e.g., if they are real numbers, add or subtract a tiny value from each one).
d. Apply the objective function to the *jiggled* model.
e. Run the entire training set using the jiggled model, and evaluate the objective function on the resulting clustering. If it is better than the best clustering, the jiggled model becomes the new best model. If not, it is discarded.

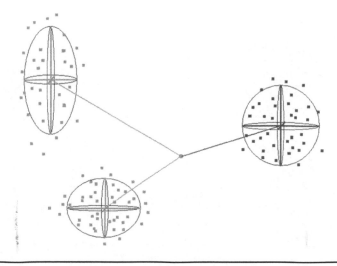

Figure 10.2   Component metrics for clustering quality.

Steps 1–4 are repeated, producing occasional incremental improvements in model quality. Each repetition is one *training epoch*. If the objective function is well-chosen and efficiently computable, it can be repeated many times at a reasonable computational cost. The incremental improvements on an epoch are usually small, but a million small improvements can produce a high quality model.

This unsupervised clustering method was applied to the Fisher iris data, giving the result depicted graphically in Figure 10.3. The vigilance parameter required by this application is the number of clusters to create. The value used for this run was 5.

The model form used was a three-layer neural network; it ingested the feature vectors and assigned them to clusters. During a Monte Carlo run, it was the weights of this neural network that were randomly *jiggled* to vary the model. As these weights varied, the neural network would give higher and lower values for the objective function value, D. Over many epochs, this allowed the neural network to find weight settings that maximized D, resulting in a good clustering.

Ground truth is known for this problem, so it is possible to check the results of the unsupervised clustering (which did NOT use the ground truth). This was done by assigning all vectors in an inferred cluster the actual ground truth of most of its members. This is the so-called the *majority rule*, and is often used in applications. This gives an accuracy score of 85.3% for this run.

Notice that 1,624 epochs were run. During an epoch, all 150 patterns in the Fisher set are processed. Even so, the total execution time including disc I/O was 2.58 seconds. With an implementation this efficient, it is possible to run millions of training epochs per hour, providing fairly good coverage of the parameter space.

It is important to note that there is nothing special about using a neural network here. Any paradigm that has sufficient representational power could be used (e.g., a polynomial of sufficiently high-degree). Principled paradigm selection is a deep subject; however, in applications the choice is usually made empirically.

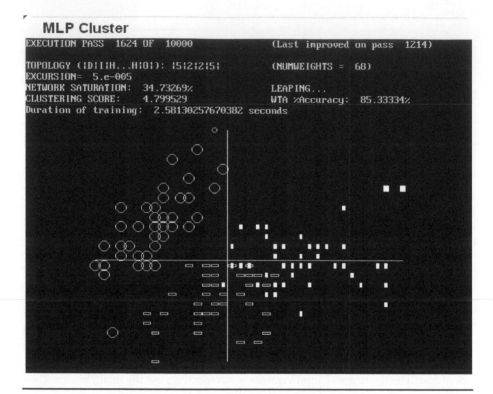

Figure 10.3   Unsupervised clustering applied to Fisher iris data.

For comparison, Figure 10.4 shows the output of a deterministic clustering routine, that is, it has no random element, and always gives the same clustering. It used the same vigilance parameter setting (5 clusters). Its result does not align as well with the actual ground truth, and there is nothing that can be done about this. Because it is deterministic (rather than trained), its result cannot be improved by additional processing.

10.4.1 Case Study: Reducing Cost by Optimizing a System Configuration

This case study describes a project to determine the optimal placement of hundreds of vehicle tracking signposts around a city to facilitate tracking and timing of municipal busses. A signpost is a small, stationary radio installed near the roadway that periodically transmits its "ID number." This transmission is picked up by passing busses and sent back to a tracking center, which knows the location and ID number of all the signposts. In this way, a precise position and time for busses is obtained inexpensively and can be monitored by the tracking station. Optimizing this system is an unsupervised learning problem because it is based not upon labeled examples, but upon domain heuristics that characterize a good model in terms of its properties. Sampling is used to create candidate models, which are then evaluated using an objective function. Many Monte Carlo epochs incrementally produce a good model.

Hundreds of signposts would be required for adequate bus location and schedule tracking, and to support emergency call-in. Each signpost required a site-survey, installation, and servicing, at a cost of thousands of dollars each. Any significant reduction in the number of signposts that did not compromise system requirements would result in substantial savings. A placement strategy had been prepared manually by a group of municipal transportation experts; this configuration was used as the starting point for the data mining modeling effort.

The work for this effort was carried out almost entirely by a custom-built unsupervised learning application. It used a Monte Carlo simulation very similar to that described above. During each epoch, it simulated a full 24-hour day of busses running the city's 65,000 miles of bus routes. Each epoch used different locations for the signposts.

An *ad hoc* objective function was designed that totaled the vehicle speed and location error of the system moment-by-moment. These metrics were chosen because they were the basis for testing goals called for in the system requirement specification.

When the time allotted to simulation epochs was completed (nearly 200 hours of continuous machine time), the best placement scenario for the signposts was output. It reduced the number of signposts required in the model created by the human experts

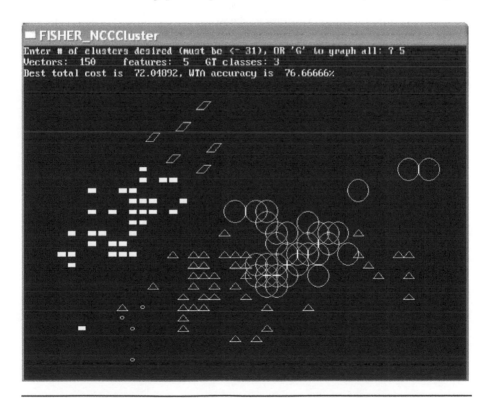

Figure 10.4   Output of deterministic clustering.

by approximately 75%, saving hundreds of thousands of dollars on labor and hardware on this fixed-price municipal program.

The simulation model used for this optimization project was so successful that a graphical user interface was added, and it was turned over to the municipality for use as a route planning tool.

10.4.2 Case Study: Stacking Multiple Pattern Processors for Broad Functionality

This case study describes a prototype constructed to monitor network traffic for suspicious behavior. Suspicious behavior might be the introduction of a known threat (e.g., a virus that has been seen before), or just changes in system operation that indicate that something unusual is going on.

The approach used was to implement a hierarchy of intelligent applications, each designed to perform a very specific task in the detect-assess-react cycle. Since these tasks are of different types, different kinds of machine reasoners were used for each component.

Operationally, the system activates only levels of the hierarchy needed for an adequate response to the perceived threat. The prototype had three subnetworks being monitored; the user could inject a particular attack process that was unknown to the system.

This Cognitive Intrusion Detection (CID) prototype is supposed to detect elevated activity levels on the network, and activate successively more intelligent applications up the hierarchy until the top level actually automatically retrains the bottom level detector to stop this attack process from gaining entry in the future (Figure 10.5).

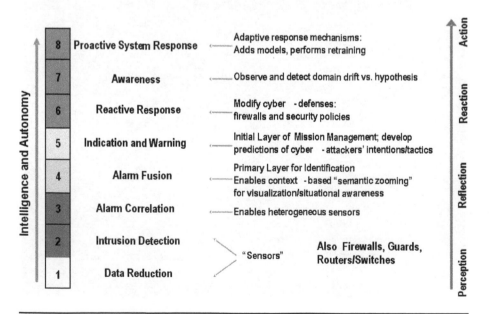

Figure 10.5   Cognitive Intrusion Detection (CID) model.

10.4.3 Multiparadigm Engine for Cognitive Intrusion Detection

A layer-by-layer description of the CID components follows; refer to Figure 10.5.

Layer 1: Data Reduction Layer

It is in this layer that raw packet data are conditioned for ingestion by the system. For example, it is here that packets are rolled up into sessions. The system processes these sessions.

The prototype is merely reading pre-sessionized data from disc. It would be far too complicated to incorporate a sessionizer into a demo, and would not add anything to the demonstration of the 8-layer architecture.

This system is using real session data. The basic data contain no attack sessions: they consists of normal sessions only. The demo does, however, allow the operator to inject real attack sessions into the data stream so that the response of the system can be observed.

The architecture for the prototype assumes a network having three separate subnetworks. Each subnetwork is processed independently, illustrating that the 8-layer architecture can be distributed in a natural way.

Layer 2: Intrusion Detection Layer

It is in this layer that Cognitive Intrusion Detection (CID) engines process the sessions. The prototype has three real, trained nearest-neighbor classifiers (one for each subnetwork). The classifiers were trained separately on slightly different data sets. This illustrates the fact that the 8-layer architecture can have multiple, diverse imbedded CIDs.

Layer 3: Correlation Layer

It is in this layer that the reporting results from all the subnet CIDs are brought together, along with system performance information. For this prototype, the correlator is ingesting synthesized subnetwork packet loading information, and statistics on email traffic for each subnetwork. In practice, any measurable operational phenomena could be processed in layer 3.

The prototype correlator uses a real, fully parametric rule base to implement a fuzzy correlation. This correlation merges disparate pieces of evidence to develop estimates of the likelihood that the system is in various operational modes (e.g., nominal vs. intruded). The rule sets create Conclusion Justification Reports (CJR), which are written to the display for review by the operator.

Layer 4: Fusion Layer

It is in this layer that all the information generated by layers 1–3 are brought together in an intelligent join, which is interpreted by a real, operational Bayesian Belief Network (BBN).

This layer is also responsible for checking support data; to illustrate this, the prototype simulates access of a database of known attack phenomenology. Synthesized results are passed back to the system, and are used in subsequent processing.

The prototype's BBN consists of 11 nodes in 4 levels. These nodes correspond to components of the system state variable, and logically partition this variable into modes that are mutually exclusive within each level. Default prior conditional probabilities are specified at initialization time; these are updated dynamically as the system transitions through various states to yield optimized assessments of system state.

Layer 5: Indications and Warnings

It is in this layer that alerts and status are developed based upon notifications from the layers below.

This layer is only invoked when the layer 4 (fusion) determines there are indications the system might have been compromised (based upon system behavior, whether the CIDs detected an intrusion or not.).

The prototype's decision engine for layer 5 is just a case statement that selects from among several reasonable alert and warning messages, based upon information for the layers below. In practice, it would probably be a knowledge-based expert system (KBES) or a decision tree.

Layer 6: Reactive Response

It is in this layer that the alert and status information from layer 5, along with information form earlier layers is reviewed, and hypotheses are developed about the system state. These hypotheses are expressed in the form of an option list, from which subsequent layers may select courses of action.

The prototype's decision engine for layer 6 is just a case statement that selects from among several reasonable options for action, based upon information for the layers below. In practice, it would probably be a KBES or a decision tree.

Layer 7: Awareness

It is in this layer that the system reasons about the network state, and selects actions from those presented by layer 6, or decides that no action is required. These actions are bound into a system level action plan which is passed to layer 8 for implementation.

The prototype's decision engine for layer 7 is just a case statement that selects from among several reasonable options for action, based upon information for the layers below. In practice, it would probably be a KBES or a decision tree.

Layer 8: Proactive Response

It is in this layer that the system-level action plan developed in layer 7 is carried out. Any action the system is capable of performing can be commanded from this layer. For the prototype, there are three actions that are supported: do nothing, close/watch a port, or retrain a CID.

When layer 4 determines that there has been a network attack by reviewing system behavior and checking a database of known attacks, but the attack session was not detected by the subnet CID, it will retrain the CID. It retrieves the sessionized data from the attack sessions (e.g., by using the database information), constructs a training set, and retrains the failed CID dynamically as the system runs. This prototype actually implements the retraining capability, illustrating the fact that the 8-layer architecture supports self-awareness and online self-correction.

10.5 Tutorial on Neural Networks

Neural Networks (NN) as the basis for a computing paradigm (both supervised and unsupervised) have been around since the work of McCulloch and Pitts (1943), and perhaps longer. The neural approach has had a colorful history, and has been successfully applied to some very hard problems. One of the first generally acknowledged commercial applications was the use of one-layer NNs for time-domain noise cancellation on long-distance phone lines. This is an unsupervised application, because the machine is not trained on examples of noise types; rather, it dynamically adapts its response to previously unseen line noise as it occurs.

10.5.1 The Neural Analogy

The human brain has tremendous processing capability. If this capability has a physiological basis, it might be possible to build artificial analogs of the human brain which exhibit some of its processing characteristics. Of course, it is entirely possible that this function follows form approach will not work; we try it anyway.

The human brain appears to consist of many billions of small processing elements (living neurons) which are organized into cortices, lobes, and hemispheres, and highly-interconnected to form a massively parallel device (Figure 10.6).

Artificial neural networks are constructed to mimic this brain architecture. Artificial neural networks are highly-interconnected networks of simple artificial processing elements called neurons (Figure 10.7) which have been organized (trained) in such a way that their stimulus/response patterns solve domain problems.

So, while the conventional approach to hard problems has led to the development of sophisticated compute-bound single-processor systems with few inputs and outputs,

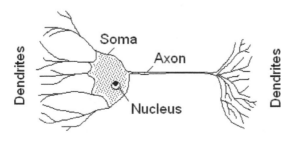

Figure 10.6   A biological neuron.

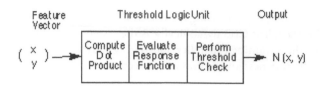

Figure 10.7   Functional block diagram of an artificial neuron.

the neural approach has led to the development of primitive I/O bound multiprocessor systems with many inputs and many outputs.

10.5.2 Artificial Neurons: Their Form and Function

Some (but not all) artificial neurons are direct analogues of biological neurons. The Threshold Logic Unit (TLU) is one such commonly used analogue, and will serve as the basis for the following discussion. The TLU is in many ways archetypal; it appeared early in the history of the field, and most other artificial neuron architectures have formal and functional characteristics very much like those of the TLU. A direct comparison of the TLU with a biological neuron shows clearly the structural and functional similarity of the two.

The TLU (Figure 10.7) emulates the biological neuron in both form and function. Input stimulation (in the form of numeric data rather than ions) arrives at the TLU, where each datum is multiplied by a weighting factor to simulate the various dendritic sensitivities (e.g., their electrical resistances, or gains). Just as an electrical charge obeys the superposition principle in accumulating on the cyton, the TLU sums the weighted inputs, and applies a response function.

If a threshold check determines that the resulting transformed weighted sum is sufficiently high, the TLU fires, forwarding its transformed weighted sum for processing by other neurons. Notice that the simulation of dendrite action in the TLU is performed by the computation of the dot product of the input data with the input weights. It is, therefore, a correlation measurement. For the TLU of Figure 10.7, note that if the response function is $R(t)$, then: $N(x, y) = R(ax + by)$.

In order to perform useful work, both biological and artificial neurons must be arranged in networks so that they can process and forward information. Infinitely many arrangements (topologies) are possible, but layered architectures occur frequently in nature and artificial neural work. In a layered architecture, neurons are organized into successive layers, with layer N receiving its input from layer $N-1$, and forwarding its output to layer $N+1$. In artificial neural networks, layers are usually either one or two dimensional arrays of artificial neurons. The layer which receives raw input data from the world is called the input layer. The layer which dumps its output back out to the world is called the output layer. All other layers have no direct contact with the world, and are called hidden layers (Figure 10.8).

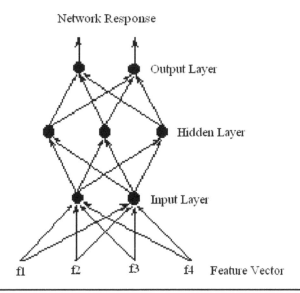

Network Response

Output Layer

Hidden Layer

Input Layer

f1   f2   f3   f4   Feature Vector

Figure 10.8   A multilayer neural network.

10.5.3 Using Neural Networks to Learn Complex Patterns

One of the fundamental application problems in computing today is the development of systems that can carry out the rapid, reliable, automatic recognition and classification of complex patterns.

Artificial neural networks are naturally suited to solving pattern classification problems through machine learning. The TLU of Figure 10.9 has two input weights, a and b, and its response function is the identity function, $R(d) = d$, where $d = ax + by$ is the dot product of the input ordered pair (x, y) with the vector of input weights (a, b). A firing threshold of minus infinity is assumed, so the neuron will always produce an output. This single artificial neuron, viewed as a one-layer neural network, is a linear

R(aX+bY)= response

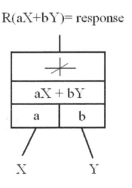

Figure 10.9   A threshold logic unit.

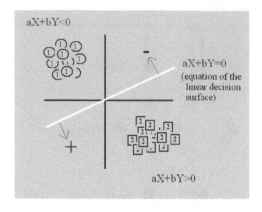

Figure 10.10　A decision line in feature space.

classifier which assigns positive values to points in one half-plane and negative values to points in the other. With properly chosen values of a and b, it would discriminate between the two clusters shown in Figure 10.10. The values of a and b are determined during training, and will depend upon the application.

The 1-neuron network just described can ingest any pair of numeric features and render a linear classification decision. It could, for example, be used to classify computers as good or bad, where x is cost and y performance. For any particular candidate

Topology	Decision Regions	Example
f1 f2	Hyperplane	
f1 f2	Convex Regions	
f1 f2	Arbitrary	

Figure 10.11　Complex networks supporting complex decision regions.

computer, measurements of the two features x and y would be made, the feature vector (x, y) formed, and the neuron allowed to render its decision. This decision will appear at the neuron's output as either a positive or negative number. To consider more than two features, additional input weights must be used, and the dot product becomes longer, say $d = ax + by + cz + ew$ for four features.

A more general problem is the assignment of a phenomenon to one of several classes based upon its feature vector. For example, it might be desirable to classify a seismic event into one of several possible categories, based upon a suite of numeric features obtained through direct measurement. For such a problem, it is natural build a neural network with the same number of output neurons as there are classification categories. After training (to obtain the correct input weights), the neural network can be shown newly measured feature vectors, and the output neuron producing the highest response will correspond to the machine's classification decision. Further, the relative magnitudes of the output responses can sometimes be used to develop a network confidence factor, and catch-22 output neurons can be used to flag I-Don't-Know answers, or classify to subcategory.

Of course, few interesting problems yield to a linear classifier. It has been shown that artificial neural networks with multiple layers can solve arbitrarily complex, but well-posed, classification problems (Figure 10.11).

For problems too hard to attack directly, learning machines provide an implementation strategy that gives results that are as good as the developer's ability to collect examples.

Text mining takes a different approach to unsupervised learning. Text mining technology has two broad components: *syntactic* methods, and *semantic* methods. Syntactic methods are those that base their processing only on the representation of information in text: grammar, vocabulary, and term statistics. The simplest of these are so-called *bag of words* methods, which rely entirely on relative word frequencies, ignoring word order entirely.

Syntactic methods are based upon the assumption that particular words are chosen to say specific things about particular topics, and that by tabulating these correlations and co-occurrences, it is possible to indirectly infer the text's latent information.

Semantic methods are those that base their processing on information content: aspects of *meaning* such as context, word order, document externals, denotative and connotative definitions of terms, and structure of discourse. Semantic methods are much more sophisticated and computationally expensive methods. They might use combinations of grammatical processing to parse a block of text, lexicons to assign meaning to words, and ontologies to recognize and assign meaning to phrases, figures of speech, idioms, and perhaps even similes, metaphors, and other analogies.

Semantic methods generally require the use of a *domain ontology*: a structure that enumerates and characterizes all domain entities, and gives the facts, rules, and processes governing their operations and interactions. An ontology is a comprehensive, high-fidelity domain model. They are difficult and expensive to construct.

Syntactic methods, being statistical in nature, can be used without any understanding of the actual meaning of a document. In fact, when using bag of words methods, it is often not even necessary to understand the language involved as long

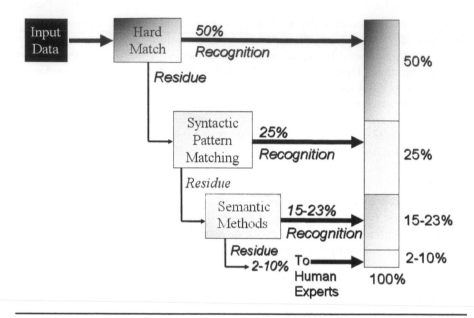

Figure 10.12   Cascaded functionality of a syntactic/semantic application.

as terms can be reliably identified and counted. However, this can be a problem for inflected languages.

When semantic methods are used, it is often in conjunction with, and subsequent to, the application of syntactic processing. This presents an opportunity to understand text using both structure and meaning by building a hybrid syntactic/semantic application. An obvious architecture for such an application would be to cascade the functionality by first applying inexpensive syntactic methods, and invoking the more expensive semantic processes to difficult cases when the former fall short (Figure 10.12).

10.6 Making Syntactic Methods Smarter: The Search Engine Problem

Suppose we have a collection of documents, $\mathbf{D} = \{d_1, d_2, \ldots, d_M\}$. Each document is composed of character strings, which we call terms. Most terms will be words, but some will be numbers or more complex symbols, such as 12/25/2011.

Consider the search engine problem: locating a document or set of documents based upon a list of search terms (in this context, these are often referred to as keywords). Assuming that the search will be using an exact match (usually referred to as a hard match) on the search terms to identify documents of interest, what list of keywords is best?

A bit of thought suggests that this problem is analogous to the clinical screening problem: when screening for a particular disease or disease group in the general population, what set of tests is best? In the clinical context, the measures of accuracy used for such a *disease search* are *sensitivity* and *specificity* (discussed in detail in Chapter 7).

- **Sensitivity**—The proportion of persons with the condition who test positive.
- **Specificity**—The proportion of persons without the condition who test negative.

In the search engine problem, a search having a high sensitivity will be able to identify instances of the desired pattern. It will have a high detection rate. A search having a high specificity will be able to identify (and therefore, reject) instances that do not have the pattern. It will have a low false alarm rate. These are exactly the characteristics desired: a good search result is one that has all of what you want and none of what you do not want.

There are many ways our hard match search engine could be implemented. Here are three simple bag of words strategies:

- **Implementation 1**—A document is returned if, and only if, it contains every term in the keyword list.
- **Implementation 2**—A document is returned if it contains at least N of the terms in the keyword list, where N is a user-adjustable parameter.
- **Implementation 3**—A document is returned if it contains any of the terms in the keyword list.

The stringent match criterion of Implementation 1 will probably give few false alarms, but will also miss many good documents. It is specific, but not sensitive. The loose match criterion of Implementation 3 will probably return most good documents—along with many false alarms. It is sensitive, but not specific.

Implementation 2 is a compromise that falls between these extremes. However, it requires that the user provide a search-specific tuning parameter that they probably cannot estimate accurately. It is a step in the right direction, but a step that the user cannot take.

Additional analysis is required. Thinking again about sensitivity and specificity as they relate to keyword selection, two facts are seen:

- A keyword is *good* for a given document if that document uses it multiple times, because a term that a document uses frequently is likely to be related to what the document is actually about. This will make a search more sensitive to those documents most likely to be relevant.
- A keyword is *good* if it is in documents that are about the topic of interest, but not in documents about unrelated topics. This will enable the search to detect and ignore irrelevant documents, making a search more specific.

These two considerations suggest a way to calibrate search terms by assigning each one a numeric weight that is determined by its effect on sensitivity and specificity. Moreover, these weights can be computed *a priori* by the search engine, and need not be provided by the user.

The perfect keyword would occur many times in the documents I want and nowhere else. That probably won't be the case for most keywords, but we can still create a metric that measures how close a particular keyword comes to this standard of perfection for a particular document.

10.6.1 A Submetric for Sensitivity

Recall that our entire collection of documents is $\mathbf{D} = \{d_1, d_2, \ldots, d_M\}$. We form the set of all terms that occur anywhere in any document; call it $\mathbf{W} = \{w_1, w_2, \ldots, w_L\}$.
Define:

$$T_i(w_j) = \text{number of times term } w_j \text{ occurs in document } i$$

From this, it is possible to compute the total number of times a term occurs, counting multiplicities, in the entire collection $\mathbf{D}$ by adding the occurrences in each document:

$$\text{Total count of occurrences of term } w_i = \sum_{k=1}^{M} T_k(w_i)$$

To measure a keyword's sensitivity to a specific document, we compute the proportion of all occurrences of a term that are in that one document. This is called the *term frequency* for that term and document. The term frequency (*TF*) for term *j* in document *i* is:

$$TF_{ij} = \frac{T_i(w_j)}{\sum_{k=1}^{M} T_k(w_j)}$$

This is the number of times w_j appears in document *i* divided by the number of times w_j appears in all documents, and *M* is the number of documents in the entire collection.

The term frequency is a number between 0 and 1 inclusive. It is zero for documents in which the term does not occur. If there are lots of documents, *TF* will be a very small number for most terms and it will be a larger number for rare terms. If a term occurs in only one document, its *TF* will be 1 for that document, and 0 for all other documents.

10.6.2 A Submetric for Specificity

To incorporate a metric component that will keep precision high, we must measure how common a term is across the entire set of documents. Terms that occur in lots of documents will not be very discriminating for any particular document. This is the reason that certain parts of speech are poor standalone search terms:

Part of Speech	Examples
Adverbs	quickly, as
Articles	a, an, the
Conjunctions	and, but, however
Interjections	hooray, ouch
Prepositions	on, over, beside
Pronouns	she, you, us

We will return to this concept when we discuss stop-words below.

The specificity of a search term for a corpus $\mathbf{D}$ of documents measures whether the occurrence of that term is concentrated in a small percentage of the documents, or found in many of the documents. A natural way to measure this is to compute the proportion of all documents that contain the term.

Define:

$$A\left(w_j, d_i\right) = 1 \text{ if term } w_j \text{ occurs in document } d_i, 0 \text{ if it does not}$$

The total number of documents among the M documents in $\mathbf{D} = \{d_1, d_2, \ldots, d_M\}$ that contain term w_j is then given by:

$$DocCount(w_j) = \sum_{k=1}^{M} A\left(w_j, d_i\right)$$

Then the proportion of all documents that contain the term is given by the document frequency for w_j:

$$DF(w_j) = \frac{DocCount(w_j)}{M}$$

The Document Frequency (DF) is a number between 0 and 1 inclusive. It is 1 if the term occurs in every document and it will be smaller number for terms that occur in few documents. If a term occurs in no documents, its DF will be 0 for all documents.

10.6.3 Combining the Submetrics to Obtain a Single Score

A good search term w_j for a document d_i will have a large TF and a small DF. These can be combined into a single metric by taking a ratio where the *large=good* submetric TF is in the numerator, and the *small=good* submetric DF is in the denominator.

To avoid carrying around a quotient of fractions that is four lines high, it is customary to write this quotient as a product of TF with the reciprocal of DF referred to as the Inverse Document Frequency (*IDF*). A term's *IDF* value is usually quite a bit larger than its *TF* values, so it is customary to take the logarithm of *DF* to control its magnitude so that it doesn't overwhelm *TF*:

$$\log(\text{IDF}) = \log\left(\frac{M}{DocCount\left(w_j\right)}\right)$$

Since there is no need to compute *DF* for terms that do not occur in any document in **D**, *DocCount*(w_j) will always be at least 1.

Combining the sensitivity enhancing *TF* submetric with the specificity enhancing submetric log(IDF), we obtain:

$$\text{TF.IDF} = \left(TF(w_j, d_i)\right)\left(IDF(w_j)\right) = TF\left(w_j, d_i\right)\log\left(\frac{M}{DocCount\left(w_j\right)}\right)$$

The TF.IDF score for a term is a numeric measure of how specific and sensitive that term will be as a keyword for documents on topics associated with the term. The embedded period in the name is a reminder that this is the product of *TF* and *IDF*. (The log is usually taken using to the base 2, but the base doesn't really matter.)

Some important observation can now be made:

1. TF.IDF can be pre-computed for every term in a document by just counting terms and performing a couple of quick calculations. It boils down to computing some term and document histograms and taking log-normalized ratios. This can be done efficiently and quickly even for large, dynamic collections of documents. When documents are added or removed from the corpus, updating the term score is accomplished by adjusting the frequencies for the affected terms.
2. Because this computation is performed by the search engine at the document repository, the user need not provide weights or thresholds for a search. They simply have to choose salient keywords, which will then be TF.IDF, weighted by the search engine.
3. The search engine doesn't necessarily need to look at all the words in a document to determine whether to return it on a search. By sorting the TF.IDF terms scores within a document, the search engine can match on only the best keywords within each document—those with the highest TF.IDF values. These will be the most sensitive and discriminating terms in that document, so in theory, this will give both high sensitivity and high precision.

10.6.4 Putting It All Together: Building a Simple Search Engine

Given what has been done to this point, describing a step-by-step process for building a simple search engine is relatively easy.

It is assumed that a corpus of documents is to be searched using keywords. The goal is to conduct a document retrieval application that will return documents based upon a list of search terms supplied by the user.

Note: Single-word search terms only; no multiword phrases for our simple engine.

Step 1

Prepare three word lists: a spell-check list, a stop-word list, and a synonym list, and use them as follows:

The spell-check list is just a large word list. A good one to start with is the *Orchy Word List*, which is available free online. It contains over 100,000 English words.

To perform a naive spell-check for a term, locate the term in the spell-check list. If it is present, assume it is correctly spelled. If the term is not present, either discard the search term, or replace it with a near-match from the spell-check list.

A *stop-word* is a word that serves only a structural purpose (e.g., a, the), so it will never be helpful in a search. Lists of stop-words can be found on the Internet (Figure 10.13).

Before using the search terms passed by the user, remove any that are in the stop-word list. These contribute nothing to our simple search.

The synonym list will be used to allow the search engine to provide a limited *search by concept* capability. Instead of requiring the user to select exactly the right search term in exactly the right form (e.g., plural/singular, present/past tense), append the synonyms for each search term to the search term list passed by the user.

Synonym lists are available free on the internet (e.g., a public-domain version of Roget's Thesaurus).

1	a
2	able
3	about
4	above
5	according
6	accordingly
7	across
8	actually
9	after
10	afterwards
11	again
12	against
13	ain't
14	all
15	allow

Figure 10.13 The first few entries of a stop-word list.

	A	B	C	D	E
1	**word**	**Doc**	**TF**	**IDF**	**TF.IDF**
2	bilingual	195	0.1411378	4.56087	0.6437111
3	fram	92	0.1187613	2.809603	0.333672
4	nomex	1697	0.1419402	7.60589	1.079582
5	coalescing	1076	6.32E-02	5.995955	0.3791798
6	resurface	893	5.36E-02	6.50678	0.3489578
7	jelepla	761	0.130189	7.60589	0.9902033
8	apartheid	307	7.04E-02	4.56087	0.3212107
9	mcduck	620	5.34E-02	7.60589	0.4064215
10	saurophaga	1852	0.1610622	7.605392	1.224941
11	lough	1882	8.75E-02	4.660953	0.408042
12	jai	712	0.1654027	4.469898	0.7393329
13	entrusted	1712	0.1184784	5.995955	0.7103908
14	repeaters	1281	0.1214953	6.219098	0.7555909
15	deficient	1125	9.31E-02	5.040443	0.469225
16	schmidt	254	5.17E-02	6.50678	0.3361322
17	americans	104	2.70E-02	7.605392	0.2055511
18	transcribed	670	0.1553293	5.120486	0.7953617
19	segregating	836	2.90E-02	6.912245	0.2001229
20	abashidze	782	7.27E-02	7.60589	0.552955
21	sacrificed	1192	0.1490607	5.995955	0.893761
22	pollenizers	104	0.1186048	7.605392	0.9020362
23	padishah	1758	7.04E-02	7.60589	0.5357256
24	estonian	1691	8.87E-02	7.60589	0.6742831
25	intensity	935	0.1315638	3.916513	0.5152712
26	concubine	400	0.1337654	7.605392	1.017338
27	phoebastria	54	0.1150292	7.60589	0.8748993
28	tularemia	1506	0.1612902	6.912245	1.114877
29	valenciana	80	0.1425678	7.605392	1.084284
30	struggle	382	0.1372798	3.116757	0.4278679
31	kalighat	1030	0.139699	7.60589	1.062535
32	sentiment	236	6.01E-02	4.309556	0.2591332
33	parsecs	1766	4.08E-02	5.659482	0.2306857
34	connection	35	0.1294118	2.904913	0.37593

Figure 10.14　Computation of TF.IDF scores.

Note: To really make this search fast, apply spell-check and stop-wording to all the documents in the corpus.

Step 2

For each document, compute the TF.IDF scores for the words it contains (Figure 10.14).

Step 3

Place the N keywords having the highest TF.IDF scores for each document into a keyword table for the documents. It is the terms in this table, rather than the document itself, that will be matched. In Figure 10.15, $N=10$.

If you want to try to assign some kind of meaning to terms, then a lexicon must be created (Figure 10.16).

Document	Term	key1	key2	key3	key4	key5	key6	key7	key8	key9	key10
1	1906 San Franciscc	1906	1908 in literat	1910 in literature	Aftershock	Amadeo Giannini	18-Apr	Arnold Gentr	Bancroft Libran	Carnegie Ins	Correlation
2	1923 Great Kanto e	1923	1960 Akagi		Anarchism	Bombing of Tokyo	Beso Peninsu	Chiba	Enoshima	Firestorm	Geologic fault
3	1970 Ancash earthc	1970 Aija		Ancash Region	Ardes	Avalanche	Belgium	Calle&iacut	Chimbote	Deposit (get	Earthquake
4	1976 Tangshan eart	1556	1556 Shaanxi	1900	1920	1923	1927	1976	2004 Indian Oc	About.com	Aftershock
5	1980 eruption of Mo	1980	1981	2004 volcanic ac	Airport	Alaska	A'alfa	Altitude	Animal	Apple	10-Apr
6	1985 Mexico City e:	1985	20	Alan Garc&iacut	Earthquake	Epicenter	Feult line	Felipe Gonz&	Jaime Lusinchi	José	Mexico City
7	2001 Gujarat Earthc	2001 Ahmedabad	Bhuj	Earthquake	Gujarat	India	Intraplate ear	26-Jan	Mumbai		Plate tectonics
8	2003 UB313	(55665) 2 (55637) 2	2002	(87269) 2000 Oc	2000 Varune	2003	2003 EL61	2003 UB313	2004 XR190	2005	2005 FY9
9	2004 Chuetsu Earth	1995	2004	2005 200 Series S		Chubu region	Earthquake	East Japan F	Great Hanshin	Heisei	Hokuriku region
10	2004 Democratic Ni	2000 Der	2003 invasion	2004 2004 Republi	2004 U.S. presid	2008 Democr	9/11 Commis	Abortion	Abu Ghraib	Acclamation	
11	2004 Indian Ocean	Thailand	Kata Noi Bea	1556 Shaanxi ea	173F	1755 Lisbon eart	1952	1957	1960	1970 Bhola	1 E1 m
12	2005 Kashmir earth	1906 Sar	1935	2001 Gujarat Ea	2004 Indian Ce	2005	2006	ABC News	AFP	Afghanistan	Aftershock
13	2005 Lake Tangany	2005	African Great	Angola	Burundi	Burundian Civil W	5-Dec	Democratic F	Earthquake	East Africa	Epicentre
14	2005 Sumatra earth	1833	1861	1964	2004 Indian Ocea		2005	2005 Sumatr	AUD	2-Apr	Australia
15	Aardvark	1766 Aardvark (dis	Africa	Afrkaans		Afrosoricida	Animal	Ant	Anteater	Armadillo	Australasia
16	Abidjan	1990s	1 E9 m&sup2	2002		Abengourou	Abobisso	Accra	Adiaké	Africa	Agboville
17	Abkhazia	16th cent	1950s	1960s	1980s	1989 1990s	1990s	1991	1992	1994	1996

Figure 10.15   Document keyword table.

	A	B	C	D	E	F	G	H	I	J	K	L	M	N
1	Persian	CULTURE	Cat		Cat	Cat breeds	Cat show	Chinchilla	Domestic	Grooming	Himalayan	Iran	Pedigree	Persian Empire
2	Pelican	ANIMAL		Australia		American White Pelic	Antarctica	Bestiary	Bird	Booby	Brown Peli	Carolus Lin	Pedigree	Chordate
3	Acholi language	CULTURE				Acholi peo	Acholiland	Back vowe	Central vow	Close-mid	Close vowe	Eastern St	Front vowe	Gulu District
4	Proton	NATURAL				Acid	Acid-base	Alpha parti	Antimatter	Antiparticl	Antiparticl	Antiproton	Atom	Atomic nucleus
5	Saint Petersburg	PLACE	1918			1924	1941	1943	1944	1959	1970	1979	1989	1991
6	Clarinet	CULTURE				1690	1812	1839	1910s	1930s	1940s	19th centu	2006	20th century classical music
7	Snake	ANIMAL				Adam and	Adaptive r	Adder	American	Anaconda	Anaconda	Anal spurs	Andhra Pr	Anilidae
8	Arctic Circle	PLACE		Alaska		Antarctic (	Arctic	Arctic Circ	Axial tilt	Canada	Circle of la	Circumpol	Dalton Hig	Degree (angle)
9	Plate tectonics	TECHNOL	1960s			20th centu	Africa	African Pl	Aleutian Is	Alfred We	Alps	Antarctic F	Antarctica	Appalachian Mountains
10	New Zealand	PLACE	.nz			13th centu	15th centu	1616	1642	1643	1769	1840	1841	1845
11	Mouse	ANIMAL				Arthur Den	Biology	Bird-of-pre	Brain	Cancer	Carolus Lin	Cat	Cells	
12	Asparagus	FOOD				Abensberg	Adam Ferr	Amino aci	Aphrodisia	Apicius	Asparagac	Asparagi	Asparagin	Asparagus (disambiguation)
13	Theatre	PLACE			Acting	Actor	Alexander	Antonin Ar	Aristotle	Ballet	Bertolt Bre	Black com	Broadway	California
14	Wombat	ANIMAL	Africa			Australia	Australian	Breastfeed	Cartilage	Chordate	Climate ch	Crepuscul	Cyperaceae	
15	Palace of Westminster	PLACE	1834			1974	2005	Airey Nea	Ancient G	Anglo-Sax	Anston	Arthur Wel	1st Duke of Wellington	
16	Maseru	PLACE				1871	1884	1966	Basotho	Basutolan	Caledon R	Camptown	Candle	Carpet
17	Yuri Gagarin	PERSON	1934			1943	1955	1957	1960	1961	1968	1986	Afterburne	12-Apr
18	Norway	PLACE	.bv			.no	.sj	1066	11th centu	1349	1387	1450	1537	17th century
19	Ancient Egypt	PLACE	1000 BC			10th miller	1160s BC	11th centu	1250s BC	1300	1300 BC	1400 BC	1500 BC	1550s BC
20	Iguanodon	ANIMAL	1822			1878	1882	Alphonse	Briar	BBC	Barremian	Belgium	Bernissart	Brussels
21	Turkish Republic of Northe	PLACE	.nc.tr		1960 Treat	1963	1964	1967	1974	1975	1983	1 E9 m&s	2004	
22	Saint Lucia	PLACE	.lc			1500	1660	1663	1667	1814	1924	1958	1962	1979
23	Nagaland	PLACE			2001	Alichen-M	Andaman	Andhra Pr	Arunachal	Assam	Baptist	Bengali	Bihar	
24	Persian Gulf	PLACE			Agricul	Alcohol	1991	Arab	Arabian P	Arabian S	Arabic lan	Arvand/Sh	Bahrain	
25	Sweet potato	FOOD	1960s			1980	1988	Americas	Annual pla	Archaeolo	Binomial n	Burundi	Caribbean	Carolus Lin	China
26	C...dia	ANIMAL				1987	Africa	Alligator	Alligatorid	Americar	Americar			

Figure 10.16   Lexicon of keyword terms.

10.6.5 The Objective Function for This Search Engine and How to Use It

Document retrieval is done by evaluating an objective function based upon the TF.IDX scores for the search terms, as follows:

1. Spell-check the search terms passed by the user.
2. Remove search terms that are in the stop-word List
3. Append search term synonyms to the search term list if a pseudo-semantic search-by-concept capability is desired.
4. Step through each of the rows in the document keyword table (Figure 10.15). For each document, retrieve the terms from the search term list that are also in the document's keyword table entry. Place the matching terms into what we will call a *match list* for that document.
5. For the terms that are in the match list for a document, sum the TF.IDF scores from the TF.IDF table (Figure 10.14). This gives the *match score* for this document, and completes the computation of the objective function for this document.
6. Return to the user the *N* documents having the highest match scores. Sort them in order of decreasing score so the best choice is at the top of the list.

That's it. You have used text mining to construct an objective function that implements a customized search engine for your set of documents, **D**.

Note: The technique described here can be applied to data mining in any problem domain where fast search upon subpatterns is desired. This includes image search, graph search, and many other domains. This is obvious once you realize that TF.IDF is really just a statistical feature extraction method.

10.7 Summary

Having read this chapter, you now understand supervised and unsupervised mining methods as they relate to each other. You understand data clustering as an unsupervised mining process. You have seen examples of the formulation of objective functions, and a hierarchical architecture for unsupervised processing. You are familiar with the fundamentals of multilayer perceptron neural networks. You have seen how text mining can be used to build sensitive and specific search applications.

Coming up

The final chapter presents a detailed treatment of knowledge-based applications. It includes a discussion of reasoning under uncertainty. It lays out a methodology for conducting structured knowledge-acquisition interviews of domain experts, and capturing their heuristics in executable form. Rule induction and optimization of heuristic systems are also discussed.

Chapter 11

Genre Section 3— Knowledge: Its Acquisition, Representation, and Use

Purpose

The practical purpose of this chapter is to present data mining methods for inferring knowledge from data, and embedding it in decision support applications. The issue of uncertainty in reasoning systems will be addressed, and a proven protocol for conducting knowledge acquisition from domain experts will be presented.

Goals

After you have read this chapter, you will understand the fundamentals of using data mining methods to develop applications for both structural reasoning (e.g., decision trees) and non-structural reasoning (e.g., expert systems). You will be familiar with the practical considerations involved with reasoning under uncertainty. You will know a concrete methodology for conducting structured knowledge-acquisition interviews of domain experts, and capturing their heuristics in executable form. You will be aware of some techniques for rule induction and optimization of heuristic systems.

11.1 Introduction to Knowledge Engineering

Knowledge Engineering is the general term used to refer to the discipline of obtaining human knowledge, and embedding it in software applications. It includes all aspects of the principled, formal manipulation of knowledge, including structured interview methods, knowledge extraction from data, knowledge representation, and the architecture, design, implementation, validation, and maintenance of Knowledge Based Systems (KBS).

Knowledge engineering is best understood as a generally applicable problem solving methodology rather than just another tool in the data mining suite. Virtually all well designed, nontrivial data mining applications will have some embedded knowledge and a knowledge component for making best use of domain data. This embedded knowledge often serves to validate and fuse mining results derived by other means. It is the functionality that stands closest to the human user, and is the ideal means for vetting, preparing and explaining the results of data mining processes to the user.

For most data mining applications that don't interact directly with a user, embedded knowledge is implicit; it is inserted here and there into the application as needed. In this section, we focus on data mining projects that are very knowledge intensive—those for which knowledge is the core of the solution, rather than merely an adjunct to some other paradigm.

11.1.1 The Prototypical Example: Knowledge-Based Expert Systems (KBES)

Conventional software development methodologies often represent a functional design in terms of data and control flows. These methodologies, and the block diagrams they produce, are not natural for representing state-oriented, knowledge-based software for three reasons:

1. Knowledge-based applications behave more like state machines than procedural systems. Rather than execute predetermined sequences of routines to service previously defined use cases, they transition from belief-state to belief-state as facts are received and evidence is accumulated. Control flow in these systems tends to be very simple, and doesn't vary much from problem instance to problem instance. Knowing the control flow of a knowledge-based system tells you little about the system, and doesn't advance the design process much at all. This is why it is possible to build generic expert system shells that can be deployed in disparate problem domains.

   Summarizing this point: Procedural applications derive their power from their structure; this structure implements a (usually complex) sequence of carefully planned steps that mirror the structure of the problem domain. Knowledge-based applications have trivial, domain agnostic structures; they derive their power from their embedded knowledge.

2. Knowledge-based software (as the name suggests) is knowledge intensive rather than data intensive. In conventional procedural applications, data is volatile and in motion (I/O, parameter passing, etc.). Conventional applications operate by moving and transforming data.

Knowledge, however, is usually stable and stationary. Knowledge Based (KB) systems solve problems by undergoing state changes rather than transforming data. The results they produce are decisions, not transformed data. These decisions are representations of the final belief-state of the KB system following its review and adjudication of the facts provided as evidence.

Summarizing this point: Data flows are secondary to the operation of KB applications, and do not depict salient information about their operation.

3. Conventional procedural applications freely mix data and control (branch on data, call with arguments, inline case statements, etc.), while KB applications strictly segregate data and control. This is essential to preserving the simplicity of the inferencing architecture, and to making the embedded knowledge maintainable and extensible.

For these three reasons, and others, the use of data and/or control flows to represent the operation of KB applications produces design documents which are not very informative. Therefore, the design of KB applications and systems should focus on the following components.

1. Characterizing the knowledge to be used
2. Selecting the inferencing mechanism to employ
3. Designing the human machine interface

If the problem being addressed was amenable to crisp, high-precision evaluation using some closed-form expression, a KB approach would not even be used. Knowledge-based methods are used when such *a priori* formulae do not exist; therefore, their output is usually a list of options ranked by confidence rather than a single, firm answer.

In this sense, KB applications are not deterministic (i.e., two well-informed human experts can disagree). This makes complete specification of the problem solution difficult, which introduces schedule risk if a *waterfall* methodology is used. For this reason, a spiral methodology is typically used for the development of KB applications. Here is a notional example appropriate for KB application development:

Spiral Methodology for Knowledge-Based Application Development

1. Collaborate with users/domain experts to characterize the problem.
2. Identify other domain expert(s), a chief expert, and resource materials.
3. Write a Knowledge Acquisition Plan (KAP), schedule spirals, and prototypes.
4. Characterize the legacy environment and determine the method to deploy application.
5. Execute KAP, conduct structured interviews with users and domain experts.
6. Select solution approach:
   • Characterize Human Machine Interface (HMI)
   • Characterize inference engine (forward-chaining, Dempster-Shafer, etc.)
7. Create development environment:

- Create inference engine software
- Create HMI software
- Create knowledge representation mechanism

8. Develop first prototype
9. Expert critique and peer review of prototype
10. Upgrade prototype using new/amended/corrected knowledge.
11. Iterate steps 9 and 10 **until requirements are satisfied or resources are exhausted**

This approach is sometimes referred to as *rapid prototyping*. This methodology proceeds by creating successively more complete versions of the final application as experts and developers interact. The prototyping is considered *rapid* because calendar time between spirals is kept short (~ 30 – 60 days), and the foundational software structure is completed in step 8. Prototype evaluation and extension steps 9 and 10 are focused on knowledge exploitation, and the HMI.

11.1.2 Inference Engines Implement Inferencing Strategies

Reasoning can be conducted in a variety of ways. The reasoning method chosen for a particular problem is called an *inferencing strategy*. The inferencing strategy defines what knowledge and facts will be used, and how they will be used to produce conclusions for the user.

If inferencing is thought of as being a step-by-step process of deriving conclusions using evidence, it is clear that this can be done in two distinct ways: first, we can reason *forward* from facts to conclusions; or second, we can reason *backward* from conclusions to facts. The former is called forward chaining, and the latter, backward chaining. These two approaches appear in many guises, and the methodology actually used is sometimes a matter of semantics (Figure 11.1).

Forward Chaining:

We want to classify Socrates as either mortal, or immortal. We are given two facts: All men are mortal, and Socrates is a man. We apply a transitivity property of sets. If x is a member of A and A is contained in B, then x is a member of B. Using this property, we move from the facts *forward* to the conclusion: Socrates is mortal. Forward chaining is analogous to *direct proof* in mathematics.

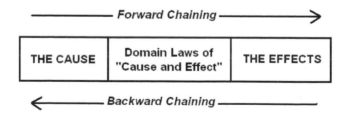

Figure 11.1   Forward and backward chaining inference engines.

Backward Chaining:

We want to decide whether our patient has the measles, or the mumps. We have three facts: body temperature is elevated, red spots are present, and no glands are swollen.

Our domain ontology has a fact table giving symptomology:

- Measles will present with red spots, elevated body temperature, and sensitivity to light.
- Mumps will present with elevated body temperature, difficulty swallowing, and swollen glands.

We begin with the hypothesis that the correct conclusion is mumps. Looking *backward* toward the symptomology that would precede this diagnosis, we see a poor match with our given facts. We then try the hypothesis that the correct conclusion is measles. Looking *backward* toward the symptomology that would precede this diagnosis, we have a good (but not perfect) match with our given facts.

The hypothesized conclusion that allows us to most effectively reason *backward* to our facts is the preferred one: measles. Backward chaining is analogous to *indirect proof* in mathematics (e.g., proof by contradiction).

The inferencing strategy to use is determined by the type of problem. Thinking of facts and conclusions as being placed into a graph, it is usually best to reason in the direction that has the lowest *branching factor*. For example, it is possible to solve a quadratic equation by backward chaining, which amounts to guessing answers until you find one that works. But there are an infinite number of guesses to check, so the backward branching factor is infinite. On the other hand, using the quadratic formula, I can reason from the coefficients in the problem *forward* to the one, unique solution in a few steps.

11.2 Computing with Knowledge

Knowledge-based applications are white box state machines (Chapter 6), because they rely on an understanding of domain internals. In making decisions using knowledge, the application transitions from state to state, where each state is characterized by a set of beliefs. The final set of beliefs is the final state of the application, and is the application's recommended decision.

This is completely different from decision making by a domain-agnostic regression machine like a neural network or support vector machine, which is pure black box input-compute-output calculation. The differences between these reasoning paradigms drive the functional differences between the two approaches.

Some of the advantages of white box, KB computing over black box domain agnostic regression are:

- It allows principled, domain-savvy synthesis of circumstantial evidence.
- It copes well with ambiguous, incomplete, or incorrect input.
- It enables justification of results in terms domain experts use.

- It facilitates good pedagogical helps.
- It solves the problem like a human, so it is comprehensible to domain experts.
- It generally degrades gracefully as difficulty of problem instances increases.
- It can grow in power with experience (either by manual or automatic extension).
- It preserves perishable human expertise.
- It allows efficient incremental upgrade, adjustment, and repurposing.

11.2.1 Graph Methods: Decision Trees, Forward/Backward Chaining, Belief Nets

Graph based methods for reasoning are structural methods: they represent knowledge explicitly as a formal structure (usually a graph, table, or ordered list), and perform reasoning by navigating the structure. Attention here will be restricted to graphs, which have mathematical richness sufficient to encode any computable relation among domain elements (e.g., entities, facts).

There are several formalisms for principled reasoning that are based upon graphs. Graphs are mathematical structures consisting of vertices (also called nodes) that are connected by edges (also called links). In general, the edges do not have a direction associated with them; they just indicate that two vertices are related. A connected graph which has edges with directions and contains no loops (also referred to as a Directed Acyclic Graph, or DAG) is called a tree (Figure 11.2).

Graphs are very general mathematical objects that can be used to represent all kinds of useful, real-world relationships, including correlation, causation, source/sink, priority, implication, and many more. This allows knowledge engineers to use graphs

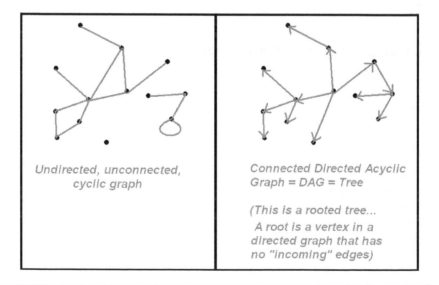

Undirected, unconnected, cyclic graph

Connected Directed Acyclic Graph = DAG = Tree

(This is a rooted tree...
A root is a vertex in a directed graph that has no "incoming" edges)

Figure 11.2   Cyclic and acyclic graphs.

(and the data structures that encode graphs) as a knowledge representation scheme. Because graphs can be stored as data, new knowledge can be incorporated into an application by updating a data structure. Further, knowledge encoded in a graph can be shared among users, saved, and passed along to future generations of users.

This type of knowledge encoding can be made actionable by thinking of domain processes as *sequences of states* that can be modeled and predicted. If domain facts and conclusions are placed into a graph where the edges represent evidentiary relevance within the process (e.g., by cause and effect, or merely correlation), forward and backward chaining can be used to look at paths between them: we *reason over the graph*. The resulting decisions can be quantified by attaching probabilities or levels of confidence to the edges between vertices; these are accumulated as the graph is traversed, and used to compute beliefs or confidence factors once inferencing is complete.

An obvious example is a decision tree describing a multi-stage experiment. Consider the following simple two-stage experiment.

Stage 1:

This stage involves a single toss of an unfair coin. The coin is unfair because the probability of heads is ¾, and the probability of tails is ¼.

Stage 2:

This stage involves selecting a single poker chip from one of two urns. Urn I has 3 red chips, 2 green chips, and 1 blue chip. Urn II has 1 red chip, 3 green chips, and 4 blue chips (Figure 11.3).

- Stage 1 of the experiment: A person tosses an unfair coin one time.
- Stage 2 of the experiment: If the result of the coin toss is heads, the person draws one poker chip from Urn I. If the result of the coin toss is tails, the person draws one poker chip from Urn II.

The outcome of the two-stage experiment is the color of the poker chip drawn. There are clearly three possible outcomes: red, green, or blue. We ask the question: What is the probability that we end up with a red chip? A decision tree can be used to model and predict elements of this experiment.

In this type of analysis, it is customary to use upper case letters to denote events (e.g., H = the toss produced heads), and p to denote probabilities (e.g., $p(H)$ = probability of the event heads = ¾). When it is desired to consider the probability of several events occurring together, these are placed in a comma separated list:

$$p(A, B, C) = \textit{probability that the events A, B, and C all happen.}$$

A decision tree for the two-stage experiment above will begin with a node having two edges emanating from it: one for each of the two possible outcomes for Stage 1. It is often helpful to annotate the edges with the probability that that edge will be the one traversed out of the previous vertex.

Stage 1: toss the unfair coin.

Outcomes: "H" , "T"

p(H) = 3/4, p(T) = 1/4

Stage 2: draw a chip from an urn as follows:

i) if the coin toss was "H", draw from Urn I
ii) if the coin toss was "T", draw from Urn II

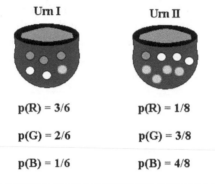

Urn I

p(R) = 3/6

p(G) = 2/6

p(B) = 1/6

Urn II

p(R) = 1/8

p(G) = 3/8

p(B) = 4/8

Figure 11.3   Two-stage coin toss experiment.

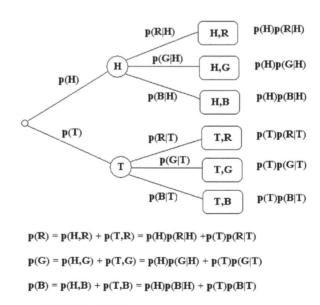

p(R) = p(H,R) + p(T,R) = p(H)p(R|H) +p(T)p(R|T)

p(G) = p(H,G) + p(T,G) = p(H)p(G|H) + p(T)p(G|T)

p(B) = p(H,B) + p(T,B) = p(H)p(B|H) + p(T)p(B|T)

Figure 11.4   Decision tree with expressions.

The vertical bar character (| or pipe) is used to denote a conditional probability: the probability that an event will occur given the fact that some other event has occurred. In the case of our experiment, the conditional probability that a red chip will be drawn, given the fact that the coin toss was heads is:

$$P(R|H) = probability\ of\ red\ given\ heads = 3/6$$

Notice that the conditional probability that a red chip will be drawn, given the fact that the coin toss was tails is:

$$p(R|T) = probability\ of\ red\ given\ tails = 1/8$$

Filling out a two-tiered graph for this two-stage experiment yields Figure 11.4.

The laws of probability show that the probability of taking a particular path through the decision tree is just the product of the probabilities of the edges in the path (the *path product*):

$$p(H,R) = the\ probability\ of\ getting\ a\ red\ chip\ by\ tossing\ heads = p(H)\ p(R|H)$$

$$p(H,G) = the\ probability\ of\ getting\ a\ red\ chip\ by\ tossing\ tails =\quad p(H)\ p(R|T)$$

Obviously, the probability of ending up with a red chip will be the sum of the distinct ways this can occur, as indicated by the expressions in Figure 11.4. This is sometimes referred to as the Decomposition Theorem.

The key observation in all this is that you can compute the probabilities of outcomes for multi-stage experiments if you can compute the probabilities for each stage, which is often straightforward. By substituting the easily computable numeric values for each stage into the decision tree, Figure 11.5 is obtained.

The answer to our question is $p(R) = 13/32$ (probably not what someone would guess!). This is all pretty intuitive. What is not so obvious is that it is possible to reason backwards through a decision tree.

Now consider this question: suppose we ended up with a red chip. What is the probability that the coin toss came up heads or tails? If a general method can be determined for answering *reversed* questions like this, it can be used to interchange the roles of cause and effect in inferencing. Not only will it be possible to determine the likely outcomes from initial conditions, but it will be possible to determine the likely initial conditions that gave rise to an observed outcome.

The method we seek was developed by the Reverend Thomas Bayes in the latter part of the 18th century. Accordingly, it is named Bayes' Rule. It explains how to interchange the order of an outcome and a condition, that is, given all the $p(A|B)$ values, compute the $p(B|A)$ values (Figure 11.6).

Using Bayes' theorem, we can answer our second question: If the final outcome is red, what are the probabilities of heads and tails on the coin toss (Figure 11.7)?

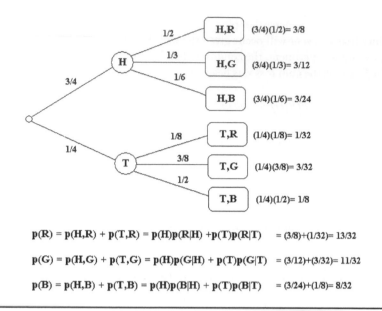

$$p(R) = p(H,R) + p(T,R) = p(H)p(R|H) + p(T)p(R|T) \quad = (3/8)+(1/32)= 13/32$$

$$p(G) = p(H,G) + p(T,G) = p(H)p(G|H) + p(T)p(G|T) \quad = (3/12)+(3/32)= 11/32$$

$$p(B) = p(H,B) + p(T,B) = p(H)p(B|H) + p(T)p(B|T) \quad = (3/24)+(1/8)= 8/32$$

Figure 11.5   Decision tree with substituted values.

Bayes' Rule

$$p(A \mid B) = \frac{p(A,B)}{p(B)} = \frac{p(B \mid A)p(A)}{p(B)}$$

$$p(A_i \mid E) = \frac{p(E \mid A_i)p(A_i)}{p(E)} = \frac{p(E \mid A_i)p(A_i)}{\sum_i p(E \mid A_i)p(A_i)}$$

- Based on definition of conditional probability
- $p(A_i|E)$ is posterior probability given evidence E
- $p(A_i)$ is the prior probability
- $P(E|A_i)$ is the likelihood of the evidence given A_i
- $p(E)$ is the preposterior probability of the evidence

Figure 11.6   Bayes' Rule.

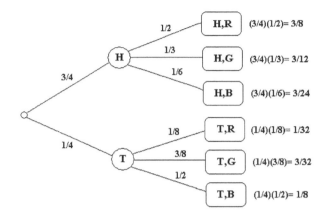

By Bayes' Theorem, we can reason backward:

$p(H|R) = p(R|H)p(H) / p(R) = (3/8) / (13/32) = 12/13$

$p(T|R) = p(R|T)p(T) / p(R) = (1/32) / (13/32) = 1/13$

Figure 11.7   Decision tree applying Bayes' theorem.

This method is widely used in predictive modeling applications. For example, if years of historical data tell us the probability that a certain bond goes down when stock S goes up, Bayes' Rule can reverse this to estimate the probability that stock S goes up when this bond goes down. Much more can be said on this topic in a probability and statistics course.

11.2.2 Bayesian Belief Networks

In any inferencing problem involving uncertainty, it is the joint probability distribution of the facts we want to model: $p(A,B,C, \ldots N)$. Bayesian Belief Networks (BBN) represent what is known about this distribution using a graph. Each node in the graph is a variable, and edges explicitly model probabilistic relationships between the variables. This provides a computational architecture for computing the impact of evidence on beliefs.

BBNs are a graph-based framework for representing and analyzing models involving uncertainty. They are used for intelligent decision aids, data fusion, intelligent diagnostic aids, automated free text understanding, and data mining. They arose from the cross-fertilization of ideas between the artificial intelligence, decision analysis, and statistics communities.

The interest in BBNs has increased dramatically since the mid-1990s, when computationally viable methods became available for implementing them. Other factors were the development of easy to use commercial software, and a growing number of creative applications. The principal difference between a BBN and other knowledge representation and probabilistic analysis tools are:

- BBNs handle uncertainty in mathematically rigorous, yet simple way.
- BBNs can easily be visualized as graphs (Figure 11.8).

The capabilities of BBNs:

- BBNs naturally support reasoning with uncertain and incomplete evidence.
- BBNs can reason both forward and backward.
- BBNs model the domain in terms of cause and effect, which is very intuitive to human experts.
- BBNs force us to think about all the relationships among the facts, and allow us to model these relationships explicitly and objectively.
- BBNs provide a mathematically rigorous way of applying evidence consistently. They are deterministic, non-monotonic, and insensitive to the order of updating.
- BBNs can be generalized to include temporal reasoning.
- BBNs provide an inferencing architecture that reduces computational complexity.

The presence of an edge in a BBN is an explicit statement of a direct causal relationship between the connected nodes. The absence of an edge in a BBN is an explicit statement of the lack of a direct causal relationship between the unconnected nodes. BBNs and decision trees are strongly related, but as implementation formalisms for probabilistic reasoning, BBNs have a number of advantages (refer to Table 11.1):

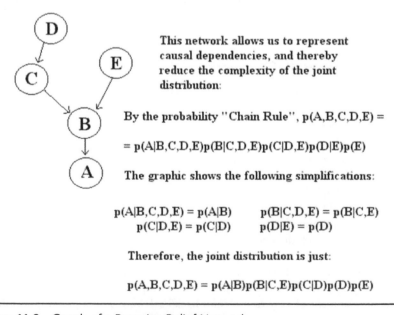

This network allows us to represent causal dependencies, and thereby reduce the complexity of the joint distribution:

By the probability "Chain Rule", $p(A,B,C,D,E) =$

$= p(A|B,C,D,E)p(B|C,D,E)p(C|D,E)p(D|E)p(E)$

The graphic shows the following simplifications:

$p(A|B,C,D,E) = p(A|B)$ $p(B|C,D,E) = p(B|C,E)$
$p(C|D,E) = p(C|D)$ $p(D|E) = p(D)$

Therefore, the joint distribution is just:

$p(A,B,C,D,E) = p(A|B)p(B|C,E)p(C|D)p(D)p(E)$

Figure 11.8   Graph of a Bayesian Belief Network.

Table 11.1 Advantages of Bayesian Belief Networks over decision trees

Decision Trees	Bayesian Belief Networks
• Require that the edges exiting each node are disjoint and exhaustive.	• Do not require that the edges exiting each node be disjoint or exhaustive.
• Require that values are known for all relevant features.	• Do not require that values are known for all relevant features.
• Reason *forward* by computing sums of path products.	• Reason both *forward* and *backward* by using the probability calculus.
• Compute probabilities of outcomes based upon certain knowledge of the evidence.	• Compute beliefs of outcomes based upon uncertain knowledge of the evidence.
• Represent assumptions about independence with the probabilities used.	• Represent assumptions about independence with the network topology.

11.2.3 Non-Graph Methods: Belief Accumulation

Non-graph-based methods for reasoning represent knowledge implicitly as functions. These functions are usually a collection of rules with an adjudicator, a regression function, or clauses with a resolution method. They perform reasoning by function evaluation. A good example is the multi-layer perceptron described in Chapter 10.

Attention here will be restricted to systems that reason by using *heuristics*: terse rules of thumb, usually obtained from human experts, and apply evidence (facts) in discrete units to adjust confidence in one or more plausible solutions. These systems are also referred to as expert systems, rule-based systems, and production systems. They implement the classical "Perry Mason" sort of forensic reasoning that combines all the evidence in a principled way to arrive at a resolution that is consistent and coherent with all the evidence taken together.

Not all truth is created equal. In the real world, every piece of evidence has a pedigree. This pedigree includes, among other things, the credibility (nature and status) of the source, means of transmission, timeliness, precision, topical relevance, method of interpretation, and effectiveness of conformation with other evidence. None of these elements comes with a guarantee of perfect fidelity, so reasoning by evidence accumulation is inherently uncertain in the sense that even valid reasoning can produce *untrue* conclusions. We begin with a couple common definitions for reasoning strategy:

Monotonic reasoning strategies are those assuming that the truth values of facts do not change during the reasoning process. Of course, in actual practice, particularly when reasoning under uncertainty, facts may be revised, updated, or even contradicted as evidence is collected. These changes can require the withdrawal of previous assertions and amendment of subsequently drawn conclusions. Reasoning strategies supporting both the assertion and withdrawal of facts are said to be *non-monotonic*.

Reasoning under *uncertainty* occurs when asserted facts are imprecise, incommensurable (can't be made consistent), incomplete, and/or false. Imprecision is inherent in all measurements, but the more important aspect of uncertainty is the presence of outright misrepresentation of information, whether accidentally through error, or intentionally by action of an adversary. Uncertainty can be thought of in two ways:

- **Uncertainty is unavoidable.** Uncertainty exists in the input, processing, and output of all real-world systems. On the input side, decision support tools use a variety of techniques for capturing uncertainty (e.g., statistics, fuzzy logic). During reasoning, uncertainty is best managed by selecting modeling paradigms that intrinsically handle the type of uncertainty presented by the problem at hand.

  For example, uncertainty arising from the inability to precisely measure problem variables is well-handled by maximizing estimation margins, suggesting the use of Support Vector Machines, while uncertainty arising from the inherent inability to predict human actions is well-handled by formalisms that directly model biased indeterminism such as Bayesian Belief Networks and Knowledge-Based Systems. On the output side, uncertainty is handled by providing metric adjuncts that represent the certainty/support of the result. Examples are interval estimates, likelihoods, and confidence factors.

- **Uncertainty should be modeled.** If multiple models or stages contribute to the output of a decision support sequence, each must estimate its own uncertainty so the conclusion can be properly annotated for the user. Good design of such applications often includes not only measures of confidence, but also Conclusion Justification Reports (CJR) that explain the reasoning of the application.

  For decision support systems to be trusted by human users, they must be able to estimate the quality of their outputs and be able to explain them in the language of the user. When conclusion justification processes are automated, they provide decision support functionality that provides the user with a recommendation, a numeric measure of confidence (in the user's own terms), and the reasoning used to arrive at these conclusions.

11.3 Inferring Knowledge from Data: Machine Learning

Humans continue throughout their lives to expand their cognitive power by assimilating their experiences, in a yet unknown way. In light of this analogy, it makes sense to make the following empirical definition of machine learning:

Machine learning is any process that automatically characterizes experience in a manner that improves the machine's performance. While observation may be regarded as a collection process, the act of organizing experience is a process involving a complex mix of cognitive operations, including hypothesis generation and testing, simulation, planning, and assessment.

Machine learning is the automatic organization of execution history into machine resident structures in such a way that machine performance is improved. Under this definition, machine learning is something a machine does, not something that is done to the machine. Machine learning is distinguished from programming in exactly the same way that human learning is distinguished from hard-wired animal instinct.

While this definition is imperfect, it does capture the fundamental point: learning is a matter of behavior, not composition. Learning must be more than just the accumulation of bulk information; a small expert system with the ability to automatically create new and useful rules should be called a learning machine; a conventional database, of whatever size, probably should not.

Note: Collecting data is no more learning than pasting text is writing.

Machine reasoning is the principled estimation of belief vectors. Machine reasoners use symbols to represent concepts, and consistently organize these symbols within a system according to the rules governing the domain. As a cognitive task, learning builds on itself. This must be done in an order that insures fundamental facts and methods are in place before more advanced extensions are addressed. Learning is assessed empirically: a system can claim to have learned a datum when it can produce it *and* it can claim to have learned a method when it can perform it.

Both humans and machines learn new things by relating them to things they already know. A dictionary provides a good example: it defines unknown words in terms of (hopefully) known words, so they can be understood.

11.3.1 Learning Machines

There are some very good reasons for building machines using adaptive methods. Development of conventional software requires detailed knowledge of the problem domain, while development with learning machines consists more of training than programming. Risk and expense can sometimes be reduced by relying more on real-world examples than the guidance of human experts.

There are a lot of problems for which no closed-form algorithmic solutions are practical, or even known. Learning machines can develop usable solutions for some of these. Machines, which are only programmed, often don't cope well with ambiguity or incomplete information. Learning machines can be more robust.

Machines don't mind dull, repetitive work. They never ask for a raise, retire, or take time off. They can be put anywhere or everywhere. They are not protected by OSHA standards. If machines can be trained to act as smart assistants to overloaded human experts, they multiply the human resource. When a machine focuses the human's attention on the 50% of the problem that is hard (and interesting), and handles the other 50% that is easy (and boring), the human-machine pair is twice the human alone. Also, learning machines that can explain their reasoning can be used as training tools for new personnel. And machines tend to be consistent and unbiased (but not necessarily predictable).

Machines cannot learn from experience unless they have experiences. To make this possible, a learning machine developer will typically program a learning machine shell having (at least) three components: an I/O interface, inferencing mechanism(s), and training algorithm(s). This novice system is much like John Locke's Tabula Rasa—a blank slate upon which experience writes. Having been endowed with these components, the shell can be apprenticed in the problem domain to its master.

To train, the novice learning machine applies its ignorant inferencing mechanism to the feature vectors in the training set, producing an output for each one. Some of these outputs will be correct, and some incorrect. The training algorithm compares these outputs with the correct associations in the training set, and makes adjustments to the parameters used by the inferencing mechanism. The extended repetition of this process allows the learning machine to incrementally improve its performance in terms of scope, accuracy, and confidence.

Of course, there is no free lunch. Learning machines can discover things about the problem domain that their developers didn't know (it has happened to me!), but those things will always be seen in retrospect, to have been implicit in the training set. If they were not, the machine was not learning, it was hallucinating.

How does the learning algorithm know what adjustments to make to the decision parameters to improve system performance? That is the question upon which most researchers in the field spend the bulk of their time.

There are many approaches. Some rely on gradient searches, some rely on recursion, and there are even so-called genetic algorithms that invoke mutation and natural selection to evolve learning machines that can solve a given problem. Each technique has its strengths and weaknesses.

The question becomes, "What does knowledge look like?" Before a learning machine can be built, a scheme for representing domain knowledge must be formulated. This knowledge representation problem is one of the fundamental problems of intelligent system design. As machines learn, they bind domain knowledge into fundamental units of a type corresponding to the learning machine paradigm selected by the developer.

KBS as they exist today were invented by Dr. Edward Feigenbaum of Cornell University in the 1960's, though the use of heuristics has been around as long as the IF statement. KBS captures expert-level human knowledge in executable rules. These rules are strictly segregated from other code, and codify experts' intuitive approach to the domain problem.

11.3.2 Using Modeling Techniques to Infer Knowledge from History

Knowledge can often be inferred from electronic sources by data modeling techniques. This generally takes the form of rule induction: automatically detecting semantic patterns in data and characterizing them in the form of heuristics.

Data modeling engines operate on data to provide two basic types of decision support: they help the system obtain domain understanding; and, they enable appropriate user action. Underlying these operations are various *pure reasoners*. Each *pure reasoner* has an architecture that is driven by the type of reasoning it must perform:

- **Classifiers.** Classifiers ingest a list of attributes, and determine into which of finitely many categories the entity exhibiting these attributes falls. For the integrated learning problem, classifiers would be used to identify the components of a complex plan.

- **Estimators.** Estimators ingest a list of attributes, and assign some numeric value to the entity exhibiting these attributes. The estimation of a probability or a risk score are examples of this type of reasoning. For integrated learning, the assessment of information value and cost is an estimation problem.
- **Semantic mappers.** Semantic mappers ingest text (structured, unstructured, or both), and fill in a data structure that gives meaning to the text. For integrated learning, this capability is needed to understand (segment, parse, interpret, store) the dialogue between human and machine during the observation phase of learning. Semantic mapping generally requires some kind of domain ontology.
- **Planners.** Planners ingest a scenario description, and formulate an efficient sequence of feasible actions that will move the domain to the specified goal state. Next-event prediction (What step should follow this one?) is an example of this type of reasoning.
- **Associators.** Associators sample the entire corpus of domain data, and identify relationships among entities. Automatic clustering of data to identify coherent subpopulations is a simple example. A more sophisticated example is the forensic analysis of travel records to infer the planning components of a trip.

Integration of Pure Reasoners:

Hard problems are often hard because their solution cannot be readily obtained by a single pure reasoner, and the integration of multiple pure reasoners is problematic. A system able to automatically handle a wide range of user questions would integrate certain aspects of each of the five pure reasoners described above. In fact, even pair-wise combinations of pure reasoners can provide benefit (e.g., integrating a classifier with a semantic mapper yields a system that can categorize entities, and justify its reasoning.)

Some Intuitive Formalism:

A bit more rigor will be added in a later section (Mathematizing Human Reasoning), but we are now ready for an intuitive, and formal description of how heuristic reasoning might be implemented.

The user wants to make best use of information. This has several aspects. First, he will want to establish minimum levels of belief that he feels are necessary to trade one proposed action against another. Second, he will want the ability to dynamically adjust the weight given by his tools to each factor that contributes to a decision.

User-directed dynamism is achieved in different ways, depending upon the reasoning scheme being used. In the case of Bayesian Belief Networks (BBN), for example, it can be achieved by making the node probability tables editable.

Let b_j be a numeric value in $[0,1]$ expressing how much a potential solution satisfies constraint j, and let d_j be a numeric value in $[0,1]$ expressing how much a potential solution violates constraint j. A final decision can be made by adjudicating (combining in a principled way) the satisfaction and dissatisfaction scores. The type of adjudication is determined by the expression that combines the beliefs and disbeliefs collected as the rules fire. Such an evidence-combining rule is sometimes called an *aggregation rule*.

- Satisfaction=expression that aggregates all the beliefs, bj
- Dissatisfaction=expression that aggregates all the disbeliefs, dj
- Then, the solution score=Satisfaction–Dissatisfaction.

An overall measure of how well a solution simultaneously satisfies all constraints can be generated by subtracting the dissatisfaction score from the satisfaction score. With proper normalization, this scoring method can be made to yield solution scores that lie within a desired range. Common choices are [–1, +1] and [0%, 100%].

This approach to simulation modeling of a set of hypotheses by aggregating positive and negative contributions of elements of a work plan has many advantages, the principal ones being:

1. It is quantitative, systematic, and extensible.
2. It is computationally efficient.
3. It can be made independent of the order in which factors are considered.
4. It makes explicit the effect of each piece of evidence on the final conclusion.
5. It is closer to the way human experts actually solve problems than to structural methods like decision trees and belief networks.
6. It explicitly addresses the manner in which positive and negative evidence interact.
7. By using our confidence in each piece of evidence to weight the beliefs and disbeliefs during aggregation, we obtain a natural, quantitative way to incorporate the effect of uncertainty into our reasoning.
8. It allows objective and consistent adjudication of many pieces of evidence.
9. Using a smooth aggregation rule allows the solution score to serve as an objective function for mathematically optimizing the set of heuristics.

This last advantage is tremendously important, because it shows that heuristic systems can be made *trainable* by numerical optimization of the solution score. Genetic algorithms, Monte Carlo methods, and Gradient Descent can be used in this way to enable a heuristic system to learn by experience. During a maintenance training session, an updated training set is collected, and the b_j and d_j are adjusted to optimize the solution score in a supervised learning mode (Chapter 9).

Performed as part of periodic maintenance, this reweighting of the heuristics adjusts the system for changes in domain processes. This kind of self-updating ability is an aspect of *future proofing*: making a system robust to changes in the problem domain.

11.3.3 Domain Knowledge the Learner Will Use

Learning is a process requiring the integration of new knowledge with old. Therefore, learning requires a representation scheme and repository for knowledge. The representation must be rich enough to support knowledge from any source and of any type; the repository must be organized for efficiency, extensibility, and, as much as possible, independence from idiosyncrasies of the domain.

Domain knowledge exists in documents, electronic form (databases, data warehouses, etc.), and in the minds of human experts. At a high level, the domain knowledge needed to support machine reasoning must be collected into an ontology consisting of static and dynamic components.

It is not possible here to delve into the details of constructing and using domain ontologies, but it is useful to know something about the types of structures and information that ontologies might contain. To this end, we present a notional table of contents for a domain ontology:

The static component consists of three corpora, and the dynamic component consists of two corpora:

The Components of a Static Domain Ontology

1. Static Linguistic Knowledge:
   - A term taxonomy (hierarchical glossary)
   - Synonym list (terms that can be equated to reduce size of vocabulary)
   - Stopword list (terms used in smooth discourse, but which carry no information)
   - Phrase/structure grammar for the domain
2. Static Spatio-Temporal Rules:
   - Hard temporal constraints (time zones, calendars, etc.)
   - Hard spatial constraints (maps, etc.)
3. Constraint Base:
   - Logistical rules (equipment, site protocols)
   - Resource data bases (data bases, web pages, etc.)
   - Personnel databases (names, contact information, skill sets, experience)

The Components of a Dynamic Domain Ontology

1. Dynamic Linguistic Knowledge:
   - State of Discourse (goals, user and system state vectors, etc.)
   - Segmented recent discourse (topics, concepts, etc.)
2. Dynamic Hypotheses:
   - Hypothesized plan (what the system thinks it is observing)
   - Facts currently known with high confidence
   - Facts hypothesized
   - Facts needed but unknown
   - Planned actions (classifiers to run, simulations to perform, etc.)

11.3.4 Inferring Domain Knowledge from Human Experts

In developing knowledge from human experts during the knowledge acquisition interview, the knowledge engineer must get three things: the expert's *rules* (heuristics, tip-offs, associations), the expert's *methods* (means of reasoning in the domain), and the expert's *confidences* (subjective assessment of the evidentiary value of each element of information).

You can't just ask an expert for these. Rare is the expert possessing a detailed, formal understanding of his/her own thought processes. However, approximations of these can be elicited during a structured knowledge acquisition interview.

Frankly, data mining and automated decision support systems constitute a psychological double threat to the domain expert. Firstly, from their perspective, you are asking them to give you the keys to their kingdom so you can build a system that will make them obsolete. Secondly, you believe that what they do is simple enough that any non-expert off the street (you) can automate it. Of course, neither of these perceptions is accurate; nevertheless, the experts must be won over. They must understand that everyone knows they cannot be replaced. They must be shown unreasonable deference. They will not be indifferent to you: they usually become either powerful advocates or invincible adversaries.

Some general guidelines for interacting with experts:

1. The knowledge engineer must be open, childlike, and empathic.
   - This is essential to avoid appearing to be a threat. You are the student; the domain expert is the master. If you start acting like a peer, they'll stop talking to you.
2. Interviews must be with one expert at a time.
   - Isn't it more efficient to interview multiple domain experts together? NO. It is incredibly wasteful. For, if experts regard themselves as peers, the interview will turn into a one-upmanship barrage of war stories, with the experts interacting more with each other than with you. Or, if an expert is subordinate, they will merely parrot what the highest present authority says; talking to them privately later will not get them to tell you otherwise. In both cases, you have wasted your experts.
3. A Chief Expert must be designated.
   - Different experts will approach the same problem in different ways—sometimes very different. Someone with acknowledged technical authority must be chosen to help you harmonize disparate accounts, or you will end up building a schizophrenic system. (Don't laugh: I've seen it.)
4. Interviews should be 2-on-1: one to direct, one to write.
   - Three people should attend each interview: two interviewers, and one DE. Only one of the interviewers interacts with the DE; the other takes copious notes, and keeps their eyes and ears open. After the interview, the two interviewers can do a debrief, going through the notes and making sure that everything has been correctly documented.
5. Regular contact with frequent follow-up is essential.
   - Don't let the DEs forget that you exist. Find ways to keep them engaged (e.g., suggest that they be invited to design walkthroughs and prototype demonstrations). If you need expert help and your main contacts are not available, you'll need some backups.
6. "Cut Metal" ASAP
   - Get a first prototype out quickly. This shows you are real. It might not be much more than some screen mock-ups hung together by a case statement,

but that's ok. You can get useful feedback on your HMI concept, and ask for additional suggestions. Be sure to explicitly incorporate and comment on how the advice of the domain expert(s) drove your work.

The structured knowledge acquisition interview consists of a sequence of discourses, each designed to elicit a particular kind of knowledge from the expert. For best results, the expert should not be given a pre-briefing explanation of the discourses. Some of the discourse techniques include:

A. Stream of consciousness monologues
B. Visualization (scenario walkthroughs, seeing the solution, etc.)
C. Prioritization
D. Standard scenarios
E. Standard anomalies
F. Single-factor variations
G. Opinionated regurgitation

These are applied according to a sequence typified in Figure 11.9.

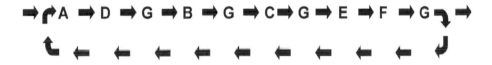

Figure 11.9 Structured knowledge acquisition interview flow.

- **Stream of consciousness monologue.** The domain expert is asked to think silently for 60 seconds about the problem domain. They then express their thoughts in terse phrases (two or three words) as long as they can until they *run out*. These phrases are collected and analyzed after the interview for the presence of key words, jargon, acronyms, which ideas were mentioned first, which are ideas were repeated, what seemingly important ideas were left out, etc. By the way: I've never met an expert who could do this for more than two minutes before "running out"!
- **Visualization.** The domain expert mentally walks through a work day. Set them up by saying, "You just arrived. You have your coffee, and you sit down at your desk. Then what?" They describe step-by–step precisely what they see and do. The interviewer can interrupt and add elements, such as, what types of problems might arise here?
- **Prioritization.** To determine the relative significance of domain elements, and flush out hidden rules, priorities, and assumptions; pose hypothetical dilemmas that force a hard choice. "If you are in situation A, and can only use one tool, which tool will it be?"

- **Standard scenarios.** Ask the domain expert to set up and describe the nominal, day-to-day situations that arise in the domain, and how they are addressed.
- **Standard anomalies.** Once the domain expert has described a nominal day, find out what *unusual* might mean: "Let's assume that everything is normal; what sorts of unusual things or conditions might arise? How are these addressed?"
- **Single-factor variations.** Recount for the domain expert a normal scenario, but toggle some element: "Suppose we are in normal situation A, but condition B is *not* present? Can this happen? Does it happen? What then?"
- **Opinionated regurgitation.** In interviews of this type, domain experts tend to speak in categorical terms. They might generalize, leave out special cases, etc. To identify these, recap the last segment of the interview in hard, black and white terms. The interviewer says, "Ok, every single day always begins with scenario A, and is then always followed by scenario B and never some other scenario." At this point, the domain expert will jump in and say, "Well, sometimes. . .", and lay out the various allowable conditions that cause deviations that are still within the range of normal activity.

These techniques are very effective at flushing out hidden assumptions, rules, constraints, biases, etc., that the domain expert might not think to mention, and the knowledge expert won't know to ask about. They work best if the domain expert is not aware of the underlying method behind your madness.

How Do Interview Questions Turn Into Embedded Knowledge?

Most knowledge derived from domain experts during structured interviews is encapsulated in heuristics represented as structured constructs: case statements, if-then-else structures, etc. This example pretty much tells the tale:

What the Expert Says:

KE: What evidence makes you certain an animal is a primate?
KE: If it's a land animal that'll eat anything . . . but it bears live young and walks upright, etc.
KE: Any obvious physical characteristics?
DE: Yes, no feathers, of course, or wings, or any of that. Well, then, it's got to be a primate.
KE: So, ANY animal which is a land-dwelling, omnivorous, skin-covered, unwinged featherless biped which bears live young is necessarily a primate?
DE: Yes.
KE: Could such an animal, be, say, a fish?
DE: No, it couldn't be anything but a primate.

What the KE Hears:

If $(f1,f2,f3,f4,f5)$ = (land, omni, feathers, wingless biped, born alive)
    Then primate and (not fish, not domestic, not bug, not germ, not bird)

11.3.5 Writing on a Blank Slate

Consider a categorical approach to computational perception after the fashion of Kant in his *Critique of Pure Reason*[10]; one that is plastic in accordance with Locke's *tabula rasa* described in *An Essay Concerning Human Understanding*.[11] He said that the mind is a blank slate (*tabula rasa*) upon which experience writes. Such an approach to system building can be realized mathematically in various ways (BBNs, Dempster-Schafer). This will be discussed below.

Before interaction with expert knowledge or domain data, the learning machine must be endowed with a cognitive form for which a software architecture can be created. Even after the software structure is in place, the machine is merely a collection of empty containers for collecting and interpreting experience.

It is the knowledge engineer's (KE) task to formulate a cognitive form appropriate to the decision support needs of the user, and infer from it a software architecture that will support its operation. This cognitive form includes (from lower level to higher level):

Low:

1. A domain symbolic representational scheme
2. A domain lexicon
3. Instances of domain-appropriate data structures
4. A collection of fact templates (relations on data) as OO-objects with methods
5. A collection of information templates (relations on facts)
6. A collection of knowledge templates (relations on information elements)
7. A catalog of domain user goal patterns
8. A catalog of reasoning patterns
9. A domain inferencing calculus
10. A domain generative grammar
11. A trainable non-monotonic reasoner that can handle uncertainty

High:

Because these elements initially have form but no content: they are a *tabula rasa*. When instantiated (populated with content), they constitute a domain ontology.

How is the content to be derived? There are two ways:

1. Knowledge can be manually placed into the application by direct encoding. This is the approach used by groups developing machines that emulate complex human behaviors (Wolfram Alpha, IBM's Watson, Cyc).
2. Knowledge can be learned by experience. Adaptation that produces useful change requires evaluation of experience in a context supported by domain knowledge. This suggests an effective architecture for computational perception will be hierarchical, knowledge intensive, and built around multiple heterogeneous adaptive reasoners using dynamic information structures.

11.3.6 Mathematizing Human Reasoning

While propositional and predicate logic are powerful reasoning tools, they do not mirror what human experts actually *do*. Either do decision trees, Bayesian analysis, neural networks, or support vector machines.

Pose a problem for a human expert in their domain, and you will find, even given no evidence, that they have an *a priori* collection of beliefs about the correct conclusion. For example, a mechanic arriving at the repair shop on Tuesday morning already holds certain beliefs about the car waiting in Bay 3 before they know anything about it. As the mechanic examines the car, they will update their prior beliefs, accruing *bias* for and against certain explanations for the vehicle's problem. At the end of the initial analysis, there will be some favored (belief=large) conclusions, which will be tested, and thus accrue more belief and disbelief. Without running decision trees, applying Bayes' theorem, or using margin maximizing hyperplanes, they will ultimately adopt the conclusion they most believes is true. It is this *preponderance of the evidence* approach that best describes how human experts actually reason; and it is this approach we seek to model.

Bias-Based Reasoning (BBR) is a mathematical method for automating implementation of a belief-accrual approach to expert problem solving. It enjoys the same advantages human experts derive from this approach; in particular, it supports automated learning, conclusion justification, confidence estimation, and natural means for handling both non-monotonicity and uncertainty.

Dempster-Shafer Reasoning is an earlier attempt to implement belief-accrual reasoning, but suffers some well-known defects (Lotfi paradox, constant updating of parameters, monotonic, no explicit means for uncertainty). BBR overcomes these.

11.3.7 Using Facts in Rules

For simplicity and definiteness, the reasoning problem will be described here as the use of evidence to select one or more possible conclusions from a closed, finite list that has been specified *a priori* (the classifier problem).

Expert reasoning is based upon facts (colloquially, interpretations of the collected data). Facts function as both indicators and contra-indicators for conclusions. Positive facts are those that increase our beliefs in certain conclusions. Negative facts are probably best understood as being exculpatory: they impose constraints upon the space of conclusions, militating against those unlikely to be correct. Facts are salient to the extent that they increase belief in the truth, and/or increase disbelief in untruth.

A rule is an operator that uses facts to update beliefs by applying biases. In software, rules are often represented as structured constructs such as if-then-else, case, or switch statements. We use the if-then-else in what follows.

Rules consist of an antecedent and a multi-part body. The antecedent evaluates a Boolean expression; depending upon the truth-value of the antecedent, different parts of the rule body are executed. The following is a notional example of a rule. It tells us qualitatively how an expert might alter her beliefs about an unknown animal should she determine whether or not it is a land-dwelling omnivore:

If (habitat = land) and (diet = omnivorous)
    Then
                Increase Belief (primates, bugs, birds)
                Increase Disbelief (bacteria, fishes)
        Else
                Increase Disbelief (primates, bugs, birds)
                Increase Belief (bacteria, fishes)
End Rule

If we have an *Increase Belief* function, and a *Decrease Belief* function ("aggregation functions," called AGG below), many such rules can be efficiently implemented in a looping structure:

In a data store:

Tj(Fi)   truth-value of predicate j applied to fact Fi
bias(k,j,1)   belief to accrue in conclusion k when predicate j true
bias(k,j,2)   disbelief to accrue in conclusion k when predicate j is true
bias(k,j,3)   belief to accrue in conclusion k when predicate j false
bias(k,j,4)   disbelief to accrue in conclusion k when predicate j is false

Multiple rule execution in a loop:

If Tj(**F**)=1 Then   if predicate j true for **F**i
    For k=1 to K   for conclusion k:
        Belief (k)=AGG(B(k,i),bias(k,j,1))   true: accrue belief bias(k,j,1)
        Disbelief(k)=AGG(D(k,i),bias(k,j,2))   true: accrue disbelief bias(k,j,2)
    Next k
Else
    For k=1 TO K   for conclusion k:
        Belief(k)=AGG(D(k,i),bias(k,j,3))   false: accrue belief bias(k,j,3)
        Disbelief (k)=AGG(B(k,i),bias(k,j,4))   false: accrue disbelief bias(k,j,4)
    Next k
End If

This creates a vector B of beliefs (b(1), b(2), . . . , b(K)) for each of the conclusions 1, 2, . . . , K, and a vector D of disbeliefs (d(1), d(2), . . . , d(K)) for each of the conclusions 1, 2, . . . , K. These must now be adjudicated for a final decision.

Clearly, the inferential power here is not in the rule structure, but in the knowledge held numerically in the biases. As is typical with heuristic reasoners, BBR allows the complete separation of knowledge from the inferencing process. This means that the structure can be retrained, even repurposed to another problem domain, by modifying only data; the inference engine need not be changed. An additional benefit of this separability is that the engine can be maintained openly apart from sensitive data.

Summarizing—thinking again in terms of the classifier problem:

When a positive belief heuristic fires, it accrues a bias $\beta > 0$ that a certain class is the correct answer; when a negative heuristic fires, it accrues a bias $\delta > 0$ that a certain class is the correct answer. The combined positive and negative biases for an answer constitute that answer's belief.

After applying a set of rules to a collection of facts, beliefs and disbeliefs will have been accrued for each possible conclusion (classification decision). This ordered list of beliefs is a *belief vector*. The final decision is made by examining this vector of beliefs, for example, by selecting the class having the largest belief-disbelief difference (but we will formulate a better adjudication scheme below).

11.3.8 Problems and Properties

There are two major problems to be solved; these are, in a certain sense, inverses of each other:

1. The adjudication problem—reasoning forward from biases to truth:
   What is the proper algorithm for combining accrued positive and negative biases into an aggregate *belief vector* so that a decision can be made?
2. The learning problem—reasoning backwards from truth to biases:
   Given a collection of heuristics and tagged examples, how can the bias values to accrue, β_{kl} and δ_{jl}, be determined?

Conventional parametric methods (e.g., Bayesian inferencing), compute class likelihoods, but generally do not explicitly model negative evidence. Rather, they increase likelihoods for competing answers. They are inherently batch algorithms, performing their analysis after all evidence has been presented. They have the nice characteristic that they are capable of directly modeling the entire joint distribution (though this is rarely practical in actual practice). Their outputs are usually direct estimates of class probabilities.

BBR does not model the entire joint-distribution, but begins with the assumption that all facts are independent. This assumption is generally false for the entire population. We have found that this is effectively handled by segmenting the population data into strata within which independence holds approximately; rules are conditioned to operate within particular strata.

BBR supports both batch and incremental modes. It can roll up its beliefs after all evidence has been collected, or it can use an incremental aggregation rule to adjust its bias with respect to each class as evidence is obtained.

Desirable properties for a BBR:

1. Final conclusions should be independent of the order in which the evidence is considered.

2. The aggregation rule should have compact range, e.g., it must have no gaps, and there must be a maximum and minimum bias possible.

3. A bias of zero should mean that evidence for and against an answer are equal.

11.4 Summary

Having read this chapter, you understand using fundamental data mining methods to infer and embed knowledge in decision support applications. You are familiar with methods for dealing with uncertainty in reasoning applications, and know how to conduct effective knowledge acquisition interviews with domain experts.

References

1. Jolliffe, I. T., *Principal Component Analysis,* Springer Series in Statistics, 2nd ed., Springer, NY, 2002, 487 pp., 28 illus. ISBN 978-0-387-95442-4

2. Cottrell, G. W., Munro, P., and Zipser, D., Image compression by back propagation: An example of extensional programming. In: Sharkey, N. E., ed., *Models of Cognition: A Review of Cognitive Science,* Vol. 1., Ablex, Norwood, NJ, 1989. [Also presented at the Ninth Annual Meeting of the Cognitive Science Society, pp. 461–473.]

3. Pyle, D., *Data Preparation for Data Mining,* Morgan Kaufmann Publishers, Los Altos, CA, 1999. ISBN 1558605290

4. Eubank, R. L., *A Kalman Filter Primer,* CRC Press, Boca Raton, FL, 2006. ISBN 0-8247-2365-1

5. Hancock, M., Near and Long-Term Load Prediction Using Radial Basis Function Networks, Ch. 13. In: *Progress in Neural Processing,* Vol. 5, World Scientific Publishing Co., 1996.

6. Duda, R. O. and Hart, P. E., *Pattern Classification and Scene Analysis,* Wiley-Interscience, NY, 1973.

7. Hecht-Nielsen, R., *Neurocomputing,* Addison-Wesley, 1990, 433 pp.

8. Fisher, R. A. The use of multiple measurements in taxonomic problems, *Ann. Eugenics,* 1936, 7(2), 179–188.

9. Fischer, R. A., *Contributions to Mathematical Statistics,* John Wiley, NY, 1950.

10. Kant, E., *Critique of Pure Reason,* Cambridge University Press, 1999 (Trans. by P. Guyer and A. Wood).

11. Locke, J., *An Essay Concerning Human Understanding,* Prometheus Books, 1995.

Glossary

Adaptive Logic Network (ALN)—A powerful, trainable, piecewise, linear regression function.

basic analysis (e.g., unnormalized roll-ups)—Analysis methods relying on simple aggregation (collecting, counting and sorting) of unprocessed data: low-end OLAP.

best-in-class tools vs. enterprise suites—Enterprise suites are usually easier to use (since they have a single, integrated operational paradigm) but will generally not be optimized in all functions. Using the best-in-class for each separate function provides optimal function-by-function performance, but sacrifices consistency, functional interoperability, and ease of use.

black box—Not having insight into the workings of the system. Only concerned with input and output and the relationship between them.

bulk—Data size, rates, and complexity.

concept—Formally, a relation on a set of attributes. Intuitively, a thing or idea described in terms of its attributes (e.g., a competent person, a high-speed data source, high quality information).

concept representation—As a noun, the formal scheme used to depict the attributes of a concept. As a verb, the process of defining and instantiating such a scheme.

correlation tools—Tools that provide a measure of relation between two variables.

DBMS—Data Base Management System.

data management—The management of the data being mined. This includes data collection, preparation, evaluating data quality and relevance, and data classification.

data mining—The detection, characterization, and exploitation of actionable patterns in data. Data mining has two components: knowledge discovery and predictive modeling.

data mining program management—Management (cost, schedule, performance) of the data mining process. The empirical experimental nature of data mining as a rapid prototyping effort necessitates the use of special management techniques.

data mining as rapid prototyping—Data mining, as an empirical search for hidden latent patterns, cannot be completely planned in advance. Therefore, it is usually conducted under a rapid prototyping (spiral) methodology, allowing goals and methods to be adjusted as discoveries are made.

data mining standards—Data mining is essentially the application of the scientific method to data analysis; it cannot be done haphazardly. Several methodologies are in use, SEMMA and CRISP-DM being predominant in the industry. A markup language for predictive modeling, PMML, is currently under development by a committee of industry practitioners.

data preparation—The process of conditioning data for analysis; includes normalization, registration, error detection and correction, gap filling, coding, quantization, and formatting.

data quality—General term referring to the readiness of data for processing. Data is of higher quality when it is representative of the domain, contains few gaps and outliers, and offers easy access to relevant actionable information.

data representation—Data types, formats, and schemas.

decision trees—Separate out data into sets of rules which are likely to have a different effect on a target variable.

demographic and behavioral data—Data about entities that exhibit behaviors, such as persons, companies, governments, etc. Demographic data describes what an entity is (its attributes), while behavioral data describes what an entity does (actions, motivations, history).

distributed data and information—Data required for analysis is often not available from a single source: it is distributed. Once data has been collected, this problem is encountered again with information: information is often only found when many data items are brought together in the proper combination.

enterprise intelligence tool suite—An integrated or interoperable collection of information analysis tools designed to be used according to a consistent methodology to solve enterprise problems.

features—Symbolic representation of attributes of a member of a population (weight in points, revenue in dollars, gender as M/F, etc.).

feature set operations—Operations performed on feature data, such as normalization, rounding, coding, etc.

high-end custom applications (general non-model based regression)—The use of advanced adaptive regression methods for predictive modeling (e.g., neural networks, radial basis functions, support vector machines). These so-called black box methods are used when the data or the domain are not well understood, or are extremely complex.

HMI (Human Machine Interface)—Refers to the means by which a computing system and its users interact.

infrastructure—The environment the data mining system will reside on. This will include system architecture, supported languages, and HMI.

knowledge base—An organized collection of heuristics relevant to a particular problem domain.

Knowledge-Based Expert System (KBES)—A predictive model that applies codified expert-level human knowledge in a particular problem domain according to an appropriate inference methodology. KBES are typically built for forensic applications (diagnostics, planning, classification, etc.). KBES are architecturally primitive and strictly segregate heuristics (their knowledge base) from the inference engine.

Knowledge Discovery (KD)—The first component of data mining. Systematically using manual and automated tools to detect and characterize actionable patterns in data.

metadata—Information about data. This includes such facts as the number and type of data stored, where it is located, how it is organized and so on.

meta-schemes—Frameworks for integrating inferencing applications. The notion is similar to the software notion of "design patterns."

model management—The method of managing models and results when using the models.

model test and evaluation—To test and evaluation the models used to consider the best single or best combination of models in addressing the problems at hand and satisfying the objective.

Neural Network (NN)—Mathematical transform whose values are computed through the cooperation of many simple transforms. Usually a synonym for multi-layer perception.

Online Analytical Processing (OLAP)—Conventional data aggregation and representation for the support of (mostly manual) data mining by an analyst: retrieve, segment, slice, dice, drilldown, count, display, and report.

operational issues—Considerations that must be made when a sophisticated application is ported from the development environment, where conditions are carefully controlled, to the operational environment, where they are not controlled. Problems in this area often arise because of false assumptions made about the operational environment during development.

predictive modeling—The second component of data mining: using the results of knowledge discovery to construct applications (models) that solve business problems, predictive models are generally classifiers (detect fraud, categorize customers, etc.) or predictors (estimate future revenue, predict churn, etc.).

query and reporting—An OLAP function by which data satisfying a set of user-specified constraints are accessed and formatted for presentation.

Radical Basis Function (RBF)—A very powerful kernel-based classification paradigm.

relevance/independence of features—Features are relevant when they contain information useful in addressing enterprise problems. Features are independent when the information they contain is not present in other features.

rule—A relationship between facts expressed as a structured construct (e.g. IF-THEN-ELSE statement). The rule is the fundamental unit of domain knowledge in a KBES.

rule induction—Creating rules directly from data without human assistance.

specification suite—Establishing requirements and expectations.

statistical tools (e.g., Excel)—Analysis tools based upon sampling and statistical inferencing techniques (e.g., high-end OLAP).

supervised learning—A training process that uses known ground-truth for each training vector to evaluate and improve the learning machine.

Support Vectors Modeling (SVM)—A powerful predictive modeling technique that creates classifiers for modeling class boundaries.

tools for cognitive engine parameter selection—Automated tools for guiding the selection of training and operational settings for cognitive engines, such as learning rates, momentum factors, termination conditions, annealing schedules, etc.

tools/methods for application profiling (user, data)—Tools for assisting the developer of cognitive engines in analyzing the problem domain and domain experts in order to quickly and accurately focus data mining efforts. No automated tools exist, but manual processes do.

tools and methods for model scoring and evaluation—Tools for assessing the relative performance of cognitive engines. Includes such things as lift curves, confusion matrices, ambiguity measures, visualization, statistical measures, etc.

tools for predictive modeling paradigm selection—Automated tools for assisting the developer of cognitive engines in selecting the proper analysis and modeling paradigms (e.g., neural net vs. rule-based system).

unsupervised learning—A training process that detects and characterizes previously unspecified patterns in data.

visualization—Depiction of data in visual form so that quality and relationships may be observed by a human analyst.

white box—Have insight into the workings of the data mining system and how the outcome is produced.

Index